Here's What We'll Say

Here's What We'll Say

Growing Up, Coming Out,
and the U.S. Air Force

REICHEN LEHMKUHL

CARROLL & GRAF PUBLISHERS
NEW YORK

HERE'S WHAT WE'LL SAY
Growing Up, Coming Out, and the U.S. Air Force

Carroll & Graf Publishers
An Imprint of Avalon Publishing Group, Inc.
245 West 17th Street, 11th Floor
New York, NY 10011

AVALON
publishing group incorporated

Copyright © 2006 by Reichen Lehmkuhl

First Carroll & Graf edition 2006

All photos courtesy of the author.

This memoir is a product of the author's recollections and is thus rendered as a subjective accounting of events that occurred in his/her life.

Library of Congress Cataloging-in-Publication Data is available.

ISBN-13: 978-0-78671-782-8
ISBN-10: 0-7867-1782-3

9 8 7 6 5 4 3 2 1

Interior Design by Maria E. Torres
Printed in the United States of America
Distributed by Publishers Group West

This book is dedicated to my grandmother, Betty Stagg Turner, who flew for her country as a pilot in World War II with the WASPs— the Women's Air Service Pilots— and who not only gave me the gift of flight, but the rare and precious human privilege of knowing how to fly.

CONTENTS

AUTHOR'S NOTE

This story portrays events that have decided and continue to decide the fate of thousands of people who have served or who are still serving in the U.S. Department of Defense. To protect these people by keeping their identities private and safe from investigation, names and situational details have been carefully changed. In addition—and only to protect certain individuals—some of the events in the final chapter of this book that are portrayed as having happened to me actually happened to others. I integrated their stories into my own to ensure that their stories were told.

Although I wanted to write a book that was completely true to life and true to the way that everything actually occurred, I felt that it was in the best interests of a majority of people and organizations to change those details that threatened the security of those individuals being discussed.

Because some details of this book had to be changed, this story, although based on true events, is not a conventional memoir, as the details chronicled sometimes are not a literal account of events. You as the reader can, however, be confident that you will finish this book with a real sense of the current environment and actual atrocities committed in the United States' service academies and their corresponding services.

The U.S. Armed Forces' Don't Ask, Don't Tell policy did not stop the terror. Over ten thousand U.S. servicemembers have been, at the very least, discharged simply for being gay since its implementation. And the policy continues to encourage the humiliation, abuse, and murder of gay people in the U.S. Armed Forces.

Diving deep into the environment and goings-on at one of our nation's taxpayer-funded service academies, I show what happens to innocent cadets caught in a vortex of laws fueled by hatred, ignorance, and bigotry.

It is my hope that, after finishing this book, you are outraged by what happens within the base gates of our U.S. Air Force Academy. If you are a taxpayer, I urge you to find the courage to join the fight against one of the last legal human rights abuse scandals that our nation continues to support with our tax dollars. If you believe in equal rights for all U.S. military personnel and citizens, I urge you to join the same fight.

Thousands of men and women who have served, fought, and even died for the principles of our people and our nation have been denied the recognition and honor they deserve for the simple reason that the U.S. Armed Forces considers homosexuals unfit to serve. The U.S. Armed Forces continues to fail miserably at providing rational or proven evidence for this philosophy and its treatment of our servicemen and servicewomen.

It is important to me that you know that I am *not* writing this book in opposition to the U.S. Armed Forces, the U.S. Air Force, or its beloved U.S. Air Force Academy. On the contrary, I have written this book out of the great respect I have for these institutions. There is room for all of the branches of the U.S. Armed Forces to improve, and to augment their abilities to complete our military missions. It should be our goal to make all of our military institutions better places by educating our military members, as well as our citizens, about the current unacceptable and destructive system of human rights abuse that prevails within them.

Reichen Lehmkuhl
United States Air Force Academy
Class of 1996

PROLOGUE

"Now it's going to look different because you're flying left seat. I would say to turn final . . . *now.*" For the first time in my life, I was sitting in the pilot's seat. My palms were sweating and my knuckles were white as my instructor led me through what was to be a windy landing. "Good boy! Now put in ten more degrees of flaps. Either give it more power or push her nose down. Good job."

Just when I felt relaxed, like I had control of the airplane, I hit a pocket of wind shear and the plane dropped about fifty feet in a second. "Give it power, we're too low! That's it. Now she's gaining airspeed, so pull up." I pulled up gently but nothing was happening. "Do *not* let this airplane fly you. *You* fly this airplane. Tell it what to do." I pulled up harder and the plane started to ascend. "Good. Now the runway lights are telling us that we're on the right track to land this old bird."

I knew what to do from there. I had done it a hundred times, even though I was only thirteen years old. I crabbed the plane with almost full rudder to keep us on course, despite the crosswind. "And easy, easy, easy—now *flare!*" my instructor said sternly. I gently pulled up and the wheels greased the runway in the smoothest landing I could remember. "Brake hard and steady, and let's get off the runway at the first turnoff so the tower knows what you can do. Good, very nice. Now make your radio call."

"Lunken ground this is november-eight-kilo-delta, request to taxi?" I asked, nervous as always on the radio. They gave me permission and, in minutes, I had parked the plane. My instructor looked at me with more pride in her eyes than I had ever seen. "Grandma, thank you so much."

"You're welcome, sweetie. You're picking it up just like I did. You might very well be the most natural pilot I've ever seen fly." My grandma smiled and started unbuckling her seat belt. "Next time we go up, we're going to start some aerobatic maneuvers. I want you to be fearless up there. Once you're fearless, you can concentrate on what matters: flying an airplane through the worst of conditions—and surviving." A warm feeling came over me, and I couldn't wait for the next flight with my instructor. My copilot. My grandma. This must have been a dream.

Fearless was a great word to describe my grandmother. She graduated pilot training in the U.S. Army Air Corps during World War II. Many women were helping the war effort by working in factories and supporting the men, but my grandma cut through social and sexist discrimination tirelessly and followed her dream to help the war effort the way *she* wanted to—by flying. During the war, with the other WASPs—Women Air Force Service Pilots—she flew missions in training aircraft before she was allowed to fly the heavier planes of the war, such as the B-29s and the P-51 Mustangs. She was my idol and my inspiration. Her there-I-was stories fascinated me, filling me with confidence that pumped adrenaline straight into my soul. She even told me the stories I wasn't supposed to hear. "Don't tell your mother that I told you this, but . . . " would always be the start of a juicy tale. One of my favorites was about all the girls in pilot training driving off the airstrip to an out-of-the-way field in Texas and having a party—complete with Coca-Cola bottles filled with bourbon.

Although my grandmother died in 2003, she is not gone. The stories she passed on to me will be passed on to my kids some day, like a legacy.

We all have a first memory that stays with us forever—that first moment we can recall. All memories before that have been erased from our minds. Why that first memory doesn't also fade away remains a mystery. And that moment holds more importance than we give it credit for. For most of my life, that memory was from when I was nine years old: lying in the back of a rusted-out 1970s Dodge Dart, owned by my mother and driven by her new boyfriend, Allen; they were taking me on a trip that would change my life forever. We were driving from Cincinnati, Ohio, to Attleboro, Massachusetts to start a new life.

As I've matured, memories of events that occurred before that trip have surfaced. I am amazed that I had repressed so much, and since those repressed memories found their way into my consciousness, I have been determined to continue searching for more lost moments in order to better understand why I am the person that I have become. More important, I continue to discover from where I've derived the strength to deal with the challenges that I've met, accepted, and conquered. This book recalls those memories in the best, most accurate way possible. For readers, it will reveal the happiness and horrors that I've witnessed in my home life, my military life, and my "new" life, as I like to call it. I am thirty-two years old. My name is Reichen Lehmkuhl. I was born to a policeman and a nurse in Cincinnati. Sometime between then and now, I managed to graduate from the U.S. Air Force Academy, serve in my nation's military, and come out of the closet on national television. Life, love, passion, sex, fear, and death. This is my story.

chapter one

A BRAVE NEW FATHERLESS CHILD

When I was six years old and my only brother Bobby was eleven, our dad left a note for our mom saying that he had left us for good. I remember waking up, climbing down from my bunk bed, and hearing my mom crying in the kitchen. I went to her and she showed me the note. I could not read at the time; my brother simply said, "Dad left." I stood there in shock and confusion.

Sometimes, when I watch a healthy, happy kid with his parents, I think about how devastating it would be if his mother showed him such a note. The child's trauma and disbelief would have to be life changing. I'm sickened at this thought and cannot really bear to think about it. I wonder about what sort of trauma that child would experience when, as his mom is crying, he is told the truth—that his dad has left for good.

The real trauma didn't hit me until about a week later. My dad showed up in front of our house in a car that I didn't recognize. I was playing in the front yard and he got out of the car and walked over to me, intending to pick me up. I remember being so scared and confused by his return that I ran away from him, back into the house. I told my mom that Dad was home. She went out to talk to him.

Being only six years old, I rationalized why he had left us. I remember thinking that my dad must have gone someplace better.

Since he wasn't at home with us, I imagined him living at a country club, playing tennis and lying out in the sun all day long. I thought our home must therefore have been a very undesirable place for him. That, in turn, meant that my mom, brother, and I were all undesirable, too.

When I saw my mom and dad talking on the sidewalk, I began to cry because I thought my dad was trying to talk my mom into leaving us for a better place also. I ran up to them and cried, holding on to my mom's leg in confusion.

At the end of their conversation, my mom told me that she was going to pack a bag for me and that I could go with my dad for a couple of days. I was terrified and refused to go. I cried and screamed, saying that I didn't want to leave the house. There were several scary unknowns for me, including not knowing if I would ever come back. If my dad had left for good, then maybe that meant he would try to keep me for good as well. I remember my dad saying to my mom, "What did you tell him about me?" as he shook his head and left in his strange new car, a look of disgust on his face.

My dad had always encouraged me to play sports, and he was often very hard on me if I did something wrong on the playing field, shaking his head and look down in disappointment. I dreaded this reaction whenever I had the ball stolen from me on the soccer field, or if I struck out in T-ball. I would react to his disappointment by crying, and he would tell me not to be such a "big girl." I came to associate crying with acting like a girl. His intensity was so obvious, other parents would approach me at the end of games and tell me not to listen to my father whenever he yelled at me. I think my dad may even have told the coaches to be hard on me.

When I was about five years old, my T-ball coach was throwing the ball to me during a practice session. I was catching only about half of them. He told me he was going to start throwing the balls faster. He threw one so fast that I missed it, of course—and it hit me square in the forehead. This hurt really badly; it was probably the worst pain I had ever felt. I dropped my glove and started crying. Rather than checking to see if I was OK, the coach just walked away from me in disappointment. I stopped crying and stood there by myself, feeling worthless. I had a welt on my head for days. From then on, I avoided, was afraid of, and even hated sports. I didn't like people who liked sports, and never wanted to be around anyone who talked about sports. To this day, when someone asks me about some game on TV, I laugh and tell them just how much I care about any game, anywhere, in any professional sport—which is to say, not at all.

When my dad got in the car and left us that first week after he walked out on our family, I felt, once again, as if I had disappointed him by crying and for acting "like a girl." I was ashamed of myself.

The worst part of that day was that my brother Bobby did get into the car. The situation must not have been as confusing for him. He was able to go with my dad without feeling afraid to leave the house. I don't know *exactly* how my parents should have handled that day. I do know that the way they handled it left me traumatized. If there is any moment in my life that caused me to lose confidence around men, it was that one. For a long time afterward, I avoided looking into the eyes of any man when he talked to me. I was ashamed of who I was. I was quiet around boys and men in the hopes that they would not challenge me to do anything I didn't want to do. I was afraid to say or do anything that would disappoint someone.

My mother was helpless to change the situation or the feelings I was experiencing. She appeared to be devastated as my dad and brother drove away. She went back into the house in tears, and I stood by myself in the front yard, crying. The two main male figures in my life had left me. If my dad had possessed more maturity, he might have stayed with me until I calmed down, or even taken me with him against my will, explaining that he loved me. Instead, I was left feeling I wasn't worth the time it would have taken him to do either. I felt worthless. My only protection was a mother too upset by her own life to even face me. I felt alone in the world.

During the ensuing nights, I would walk into my mother's room, where she would be sobbing. She would ask me to hold her and I would lie down in the bed behind her and hold her as best I could: my five-year-old arms weren't long enough to do the job. "Is that OK?" I would ask, and she would nod quietly as her crying stopped.

It felt somewhat good to know that I was responsible for her being able to rest.

A few months later, my brother decided to move out and live with my dad. I was afraid of my dad and I didn't trust him. I had no desire to leave our one-thousand-square-foot house on Haskell Drive. I felt like I was one and the same with the house. We were both worthless to all the male figures in my life.

My attachment to the house grew more extreme. I became afraid to leave it at all. My mother was working full time as a registered nurse at the local Eastern Star Nursing Home, so I was left alone to watch television all day. She had no idea what I watched while she was at work. I saw scary movies and a lot of nudity on various cable channels. I watched as much of each as I could find.

When school started, I was petrified. My mother had enrolled me at St. Ann Catholic School in Hamilton, Ohio, near Cincinnati. I had no confidence and was extremely shy. I was made fun of constantly by kids on the playground.

The first day of first grade was horrible. We had a substitute teacher; I didn't even know the meaning of the word *substitute*. I simply went with the flow and hoped for the best. To make it worse, God played a trick on me that day by making our substitute teacher's name Mrs. Dick. *Dick* was a word that I knew the exact meaning of because my brother and his friends had told me, and called me a dick so often that I'd never forget. Knowing the meaning of this word landed me in trouble. When the substitute introduced herself as Mrs. Dick, I started to giggle, looking at other kids—who then started laughing and putting their hands over their mouths. Suddenly, I was pulled out of my chair by the back of my shirt and forced to stand in a corner for more than four hours. I became the laughingstock of the class for weeks.

The nuns at St. Ann certainly didn't help my confidence. They held fast to the notion that physical punishment maintained discipline. I became afraid to open my mouth at all. I saw a nun actually tie one of my classmate's wrists and ankles to his chair with his own shoelaces after she had warned him not to play with them. I saw another classmate get smacked in the head several times with a ruler that he had dropped on the floor in an attempt to playfully disrupt class. I saw a student trapped in a corner by a bookcase slid into place by a nun while everyone else left to catch the buses after the bell rang.

When I came home from school, I would never go out to play with the other kids when invited to play soccer or baseball in the neighborhood. My fear of messing up in those games was so strong that I would just stay in my house. Occasionally, I would ride my bike or do other things by myself.

Most often, I would come home from school and lock myself in my bedroom to play alone for hours. I had control over solitary activities, so they appealed to me. I set up an entire make-believe house in my room, with a sink, dishwasher, garage, and piano. I made my stuffed animals my family. I was so adamant about pretending that my small room was a real house that I designated a corner by the door as the bathroom. Instead of leaving my room, I would actually urinate on the carpet in the corner of my bedroom. Suffering from early onset of severe social anxiety, I would do anything at all not to leave the world I had created for myself.

Meanwhile, my mother struggled to handle the pressure from her recent separation from my father. I have a terrible memory of being in the basement of our house with her while she was going through boxes, figuring out what to throw away and what to keep. I was supposed to be helping her, but no matter what I did, she would yell at me for it. I became frightened of her. But even though I was apparently doing everything wrong, she wouldn't let me leave the basement. She kept yelling at me for looking at her like I was afraid of her. "Don't look at me like that!" she screamed at me over and over again. "If you look at me like that again, I'll smack you!" I'm sure that additional stressful situations in my childhood, such as that one, contributed to the self-imposed exile in my bedroom.

I remember my mother taking me to counseling a few times. She was concerned about my behavior and my poor marks in school. The counselor told her that I would always be shy, socially inept, and learning deficient.

As the second-grade year passed, I became slightly better adjusted to the world around me. I made a friend named Christopher, who lived directly behind us. He and I had big backyards with a fence dividing the two, and we would meet at that fence to decide what games to play. Superhero games were our first choice, and Batman was our favorite. We would use beach towels from his house, and have his mother safety-pin them around our necks as capes.

I contacted Christopher years later, when I was twenty-two years old and a senior at the Air Force Academy. I had tracked him down by his last name and ended up on the phone with his grandparents. They gave me his number when I explained to them who I was. I called him, and he was very happy to hear from me. He told me that he had a wife and a baby and worked on the assembly line at a local manufacturer in Cincinnati.

Soon after we talked on the phone, I sat down and I wrote Christopher a letter, telling him that I had realized I was gay and that I hoped we could keep in touch. Unfortunately, I never heard from Christopher again.

Toward the middle of the second grade, I talked to my dad over the phone on a few occasions. Then I even left the house with him for one or two days at a time, but I was always very afraid to be with him. My visits with him were especially difficult because he hadn't settled down. One time when he took me for the weekend, he lived in an apartment in God Knows Where, outside of Cincinnati. The next time I went with him, he lived in an old house in Delhi (pronounced DELL-high), Ohio, that had lots of farmland. That place provided some excitement because he would let me drive an old tractor that was kept in an old barn on the property.

I quickly became obsessed with tractors because of the one in Delhi and one owned by my Grandpa Turner, my mother's father, whom I would visit occasionally. When given the chance, I was happy to be left alone in a garage or a barn, sitting on the tractor and pretending to drive it. My Grandpa Turner told me that no one needed a license to drive a tractor, and that anyone could drive one in his or her own yard. It fascinated me that even I could drive this machine with a steering wheel, as if it were my car. From that point forward, I treasured any chance anyone gave me to drive or even sit atop one of those big machines. Sometimes, I would go to sleep dreaming about my family buying me a tractor for Christmas so that I could drive it up and down my neighborhood street, the envy of all the other kids.

The scariest of my visits with my dad were when he took me to his new house in Mount Washington, where he lived with his new wife, Mary Ann. She had three other kids in the house, and I remember my brother living there for a little while. I never really came to know that family. I would always stay very quiet around them, and they didn't really pay much attention to me. They would just look at me, saying nothing. That freaked me out.

Later, my dad divorced Mary Ann and got his new girlfriend, Kim, who was a hairdresser. I was seven years old when they got together, and despite new surroundings, things got better for me. Again, he picked me up from home and took me to a new apartment where he lived with Kim and her daughter from a previous marriage. Kim was very nice to me, and Stacie, her five-year-old daughter, was a fun new playmate. Kim's brother, Mike, was a candy salesman, so they would always have different kinds of gum and jawbreakers for us.

At Christmastime, when I turned eight years old, I spent the holidays in Columbus, with my Grandma and Grandpa Turner, my mother's parents. Their shiny blue tractor was parked in their garage and I could sit on it for hours, pretending to drive. My grandparents' house was always a safe haven for me. I felt comfortable and welcome. There was order in their home. They kept it clean and, since my Grandpa had a pretty good job in insurance, their house was large and in a good neighborhood. They had two dogs, named Sherry and Shay. They were Irish setters and I used to ride them around the house whenever I was away from prying eyes. Grandma and Grandpa Turner had seven children, so there were always lots of aunts and uncles who gave me lots of attention at family gatherings.

My Grandma Turner had been a pilot in World War II, and I was the only person in the house who seemed to want to hear her stories. She would show me photo albums full of black-and-white pictures of a world that looked nothing like the world I knew. In the pictures, she was in uniform or wearing heavy aviation equipment and flight suits, and she was usually standing with other women who were dressed the same. I loved the huge airplanes that my grandmother was always standing in front of. I would sit there in awe as she explained to me that she flew this or that airplane. "I want to do that," I would tell her. "I want to be a pilot in the war, too." I saw the excitement in her eyes when I would tell her this.

"Well, luckily, there is no war right now, but you can still fly planes," she explained to me.

"Can we fly now?" I always asked. Sometimes my mother would drop me off with my grandparents for long weekends, or even for a whole week. When I stayed with them, my grandmother would sometimes take me to the local airport. I loved how everyone knew her there and how strangers would approach me to tell me what a good pilot she was. They would ask me if I was going to fly, too.

"Yes!" I would scream out to whoever would listen. My grandmother's friends would usually take us up on a flight. If they didn't take us up in the air, they would at least let the two of us sit in the plane. My grandmother would answer the endless questions I would ask about the plane and the controls in the cockpit. I loved how she knew every answer and how to work everything. My love and longing for flying started there.

My grandmother introduced me to many things I would not normally get to see. When I was turning eight, I opened a present on Christmas morning that changed my life for the better—a beautiful new guitar. I even remember its brand name: Global. In addition, I was given a self-teaching guide with instructions for playing a few songs. It was the perfect gift for a child who preferred to be alone. Starting that day, I would sit in closed-off rooms with my guitar, teaching myself how to play. Soon, I was playing all the chords except F, since my fingers weren't big enough to create a bar chord.

Just about a month after receiving the guitar, I began writing and composing my own songs. My mother was so excited that she took me to a guitar coach at the local music shop in Cincinnati. I sat down with him and my guitar to play a few songs I had written. Shameless, I sang along with the chords I played. After performing for him, the overwhelmed instructor admitted that I needed a much higher level of instructor than the music shop could provide. He recommended a man in town named Jose who was a professional classical guitarist. My mom put me into lessons with him, and there I learned to play notes along with chords, which opened up a whole new door for me. As time went on, I wrote more complicated songs that included solo segments and duets.

I loved bringing my guitar to school with me. I had a big black case for it, and the other kids on the school bus would ask me about it. I would immediately pull the guitar out, right there on the bus, and start playing for them. This was my first chance to feel that other kids admired me for something. But because I was still often made fun of by other kids on the playground, I would use the guitar as an excuse to stay inside during recess, asking the nuns if I could practice indoors because my guitar couldn't be out in the sun.

Soon, after the nuns saw how well I could play, St. Ann's offered me the chance to play in the church band. Everyone else in the band was at least twenty-five years old, and then there was me, an eight-year-old. One of my proudest moments was playing in the church band on a Wednesday morning for school Mass, and seeing my mom in the audience, smiling at me in her white nurse's uniform. She had taken some time off from work to see me play. I played extra carefully that day, for her and for everyone.

Despite my shyness, I found it necessary to have a girlfriend in school. My brother and his friends always asked me who my girlfriend was and I had to have an answer for them or they would make fun of me. My girlfriend in the first and second grades was a not-so-shy girl named Barbara Newton. I explained to her, all by myself, what a boyfriend was, and then let her know that I would be her boyfriend from there on out. I explained to her that, as my girlfriend, she was not allowed to be any one else's girlfriend or I would get very mad; that we could kiss each other now because of our new status; and that we would call it "going out with each other," since that was what my brother called it. Our relationship consisted of holding hands quickly and then letting go as we passed each other in line from math to spelling classes twice a day. Barbara was a good girlfriend and as loyal as a first- and second-grade girlfriend could be. She used to tell me that she loved me and that we would be married some day.

I spent the summer after second grade playing my guitar, writing songs, swimming in the neighborhood pool, getting along better with the other kids, and sleeping over at Christopher's house. I was getting pretty used to things and becoming better able to deal with my world. I even asked my mother if I could join a soccer league. She signed me up and I began practices. Perhaps I was trying to fit in with the other kids, or trying to prove I wasn't the quiet pussy everyone thought I was. I had fun, for the most part, but when I heard other parents yelling at their kids, I would get very upset on the field and yell at them to "shut up and come out on the field yourself and try it." This landed me in some trouble with the coach, which made me think he didn't like me anymore. I convinced myself, over time, that he wanted me off the team and I started dreading going to soccer practice.

That summer, I went to my dad's and Kim's apartment for a weekend and I ended up in a terrible situation that hammered my confidence despite my slow but continuing adjustment to the world. I had already dismissed my dad as a parental figure. Although I knew he was my father and that I should love him as such, he was really no more than a friend to visit, a friend whose loyalty I had come to question. On this particular visit, my dad sat down with me and Stacie, Kim's daughter, and started showing me pictures of their recent trip to Disney World in Orlando. Epcot Center had just been built, and they were telling me how much fun it had been and about all the new things that visitors could do there. I had never been to Epcot and I felt extremely crushed that he hadn't take me with him. That weekend, I became introspective and quiet and wouldn't talk to anyone. I had become aware of the fact that this new little girl that my dad was taking care of was getting more attention than I was.

The reality and awareness that I could be replaced has never left my head, even to this day. Being abandoned by someone who loves me, or being replaced by another person, remains a daily fear in my life and in many of my relationships.

chapter two

BOBBY THREW MY BIKE IN THE POOL

As an eight-year-old, I became acutely aware of my mother's loneliness. She went out on a few dates and, by being as nosey as I could be, I found out where, when, and with whom. My brother, when he was staying with us and not my dad, would openly critique my mother's boyfriends with descriptions such as "that fat loser" and "that pussy." We had good reason to be wary of our mother's suitors—she was absolutely beautiful, an object of desire to seemingly every man who crossed her path. Doctors, dentists, the bag boy in the grocery store, and even policemen who pulled her over would try to flirt with her.

One night, our mom came home and said that she had met a really promising guy. She had gone to a bar called the Wanda Lisa at the behest of her friends and had met this man there. He was the nephew of the owner of the bar, his name was Allen, and he was in Cincinnati visiting for only a few days. Mom told us that she would be having Allen over for dinner the next night and asked us to be on our best behavior.

The following day, my brother and I were at the neighborhood pool down the street. He and his friends had been picking on me really hard that day. They had pirated my bike and were riding it around the pool, threatening to throw it in if I told on them. When I could take it no longer, I ran back home to tell my mom exactly what Bobby said he was going to do. Completely out of breath, I ran up the last three stairs to our front porch where my mother was sitting next to a dark, handsome man. "Mom, Bobby threw my bike in the pool!" I yelled.

Those were the first words that Allen ever heard come out of my mouth. At that moment, Allen introduced himself to me and said, "Let's go get your bike from your brother." I was stunned that he was going to help me. I walked him to the end of the street, where the pool was. No brother. No brother's friends. Just my bike, standing up by its kickstand, clean and dry. Allen looked at me and said, "I thought you said your brother threw your bike in the pool."

"I thought he did," I replied. The first life lesson that Allen Tetreault would teach me happened right there. "Well, there's a big difference between *thinking* someone did something and knowing for sure that they did." Together, we walked back to the house, where my mom had almost finished cooking dinner.

I immediately turned on the television, where *Friday the 13th, Part 2* was being shown on cable for something like the twentieth time. I had come to love movies, especially horror movies and adult-themed movies, such as *The Four Seasons* with Alan Alda, a bizarre favorite for an eight-year-old. Always trying to be the man around the house, I used these movies, along with *General Hospital*, as my sources for the proper ways to react to situations and people. I blame all of this television watching for my sometimes dramatic personality, and my obsession with the reactions people have to unusual situations.

Instead of eating dinner with my mom and Allen at the table that night, I ate in front of the TV, watching Jason Voorhees chase unknowing campers around with an axe. I remember Allen saying to my mom, "Isn't this an R-rated movie?" Little did I know that this offhand question would lead to a complete ban on all of my favorite TV programs.

Just a few months after her first date with Allen, my mom announced that she wanted to move to Massachusetts with him and asked us to come with her. I sensed that her decision to move was heavily based on our willingness to leave Cincinnati. I had just started the third grade at St. Ann Catholic School, but I was ready to go with Mom.

I know people who have stayed in their hometowns for their entire lives and claim that they are happy and just don't have the desire to leave. But there was something in me at eight years old that just couldn't wait to leave. Maybe it was the thought of leaving behind all the kids that had made fun of me for so long. Or maybe it was the thought of moving and running away to a new place that excited me.

I worked this situation for all I could with the other kids in the neighborhood. I made up big stories about moving to Massachusetts— that we would live in a mansion and my mom wouldn't have to work anymore. I told them all how much cooler all the kids were in Massachusetts and how they thought of Cincinnati kids as backward-ass losers. The latter was actually true, as I found out after the move, but I was simply making it up as I went along.

In November of 1982, after Mom had sold our house and as we prepared to leave, she let me make one last phone call from the house. I called my girlfriend, Barbara Newton, and said good-bye. On that same day, I told my soccer coach, in person, that I would be leaving the team, which was, secretly, a relief for me. Finally, I said good-bye to my best play-buddy, Christopher, who lived behind us.

I was placed on the backseat of our Dodge Dart, and Allen drove the whole way. As we traveled, I pointed out every tractor that I saw; tractors on truck beds, tractors in fields, and tractors in front yards, whether they were moving or not, were all game for my oohs and aahs. Somehow, the Dodge Dart made it through the mountain passes in Pennsylvania, where we encountered a few really bad snow storms. We traveled past New York City, through Connecticut and Rhode Island, and finally stopped in Attleboro, Massachusetts. Allen had previously arranged for an apartment to be set up there for us.

All of this seemed to be a perfect situation for our family. I could tell that my mother was finally showing signs of happiness and I felt, for the first time in years, that an adult male figure had taken an interest in my well-being. Since I was so young, my mother and Allen didn't tell me that Allen had just left an unhappy marriage when he met my mother. He was at a difficult, transitional point in his life. Friends of my mother and many members of our family had warned my mother and Allen not to move so quickly into a new relationship, especially one that involved taking me out of school and to a new state. My mother and Allen didn't listen to anyone; they continued on with their new plans to be married and spend the rest of their lives together.

Our life in Attleboro was short-lived but very educational. I was enrolled in Finberg Elementary School, my first experience in a public school system. I remember being fascinated by how different everyone looked. My classmates were of various races and ethnicities. St. Ann's had been 99 percent white and German, and almost all of us had light hair and light eyes. Feeling the need to have a girlfriend in my new environment, I picked a girl I thought would be a good match for me. Her name was Gloria and she was Portuguese. I sent a picture of Gloria and me on the playground together back to my relatives in Cincinnati, and I remember phone calls from them asking if Gloria was black. I told them that she was not black but Portuguese, and just had very dark skin. The reason my family even asked me this is because the Cincinnati I was born into was, by my standards today, very racist. When a black person entered a white neighborhood, everyone would talk about it as if an alien had infiltrated their homes. A school's worth was measured by how effectively it excluded blacks. I even learned from my own family that this type of discrimination was acceptable. My Grandma Lehmkuhl, whom I adored and who adored me, had told me several times about Bible verses that proved blacks were God's cursed people, justifying a segregated American society. This is what she had been taught and, therefore, would teach her children and grandchildren. My experience with a nonwhite girlfriend in Massachusetts brought me to question those racist sentiments at an early age.

After I finished third grade at Finberg Elementary, my mother and Allen bought a house in Norton, Massachusetts. It was a mobile home, my mother said. I questioned her many times, trying to figure out what she meant.

"Does it have a steering wheel?" I asked. She explained that a mobile home was a house built in a factory and wheeled to a location, where its wheels are removed and it is placed permanently on cinder blocks. This fascinated me. She explained to me that this was a common way for people to live in the Northeast and that, even though many people made fun of mobile home parks in other parts of the country, such as Cincinnati, that "up here" it was OK. I asked her where our mobile home was located and she said that it was right on a lake at the very back end of a mobile home park. We would have our own cove for boating and views of the sunrise over the lake every morning from our bay-windowed dining room.

I have to give kudos to my mom for always looking on the bright side of things. Looking back, I don't know what they were thinking by buying this mobile home on a lake in Norton, Massachusetts. But, for the first summer we were there, my brother and I had a good time. Allen bought us a johnboat with a trolling motor so that we could get around the lake. The battery for the motor would often die and we would end up paddling back to shore. We spent a good couple of months learning that lake. We toured its islands, fished its good spots, and my brother and his new friends stole a dock or two from other parts of the lake and added them on to our own dock. We even swam in the lake that summer.

It wasn't until the school year started with my first day of fourth grade at the J. C. Solmonese Elementary School in Norton that I realized my mother hadn't been completely honest with me about the status of mobile home park residents. When my classmates asked me where I lived, I proudly told them that we had moved into the mobile home park on Mansfield Avenue. "You mean the trailer park by that nasty, polluted Norton Reservoir?" the other kids would ask. It didn't take me long to realize that trailer-park status equaled white-trash status. For the two years of fourth and fifth grades in Norton, I had only two friends. One was Glenn Fields. The other was a lonely, cross-eyed kid named Chris Tack. Chris and I talked extensively about the smart-kid stuff we were interested in, such as science and politics. Chris's parents must have been Democrats because in 1984, at the time when Reagan was about to be reelected, he would tell me how Walter Mondale was going to be our next best president. Other kids at the school hated Chris for his fondness for Walter Mondale because all of their parents were voting for Ronald Reagan.

Norton, Massachusetts, was a primarily blue-collar, workingman's town, and it seemed like everyone was conservative and a Republican. The children carried this attitude into the school system. Anything that was different was gay or weird, something to pick on or hate. Being the new boy from the trailer park, I had a tough time fitting in. Even though Norton was a worker's town, its residents and their children were strongly suspicious and ashamed of those living in the trailer park. It was as if the "white trash" of the town needed an even lower form of "white trash" to regard as lower class.

I have only a few memories that stand out from my time at the J. C. Solmonese Elementary School. Once, Chris Tack and I decided to put gum in the hair of a boy named Danny—the fat kid. Why we did this could be traced back to being disliked and picked on. We probably felt the need to pick on someone else, to feel the sheer power of the experience—like the town's working class looking down on its even less fortunate trailer park residents.

Poor Danny. I can't imagine having the two biggest dorks in school walking up to me with freshly chewed bubble gum and putting it in my hair. The worst part was that he was so embarrassed he just ran away from school that day and found his way home. This sent the teachers into a panic. The police found Danny walking home. When asked what had happened to him, Danny said that two boys had put gum in his hair, but he wouldn't tell them who had done it. He was probably so afraid of having anyone dislike him even more that he didn't tell on us. The only feeling Chris Tack and I took away from this experience was sheer guilt. We couldn't look Danny in the eye from that day on.

Another time, Chris Tack and I entered the three-legged race together on field day. We were pitted against about twenty other teams, including Tommy Assburg and his friend Kory. During the race, Chris and I fell and skidded sideways, accidentally knocking down Tommy and Kory, who were sure that they were going to win the race before it had even started. When we stood up, Kory punched my teammate Chris right in the stomach and knocked him down. Tommy punched me in the stomach even harder and knocked me down. With our feet tied together by a handkerchief in the middle of the race track, we lay there humiliated and feeling as low as ever.

My only positive memory of J. C. Solmonese Elementary was performing the lead in the school Christmas play, *The North Pole Goes Rock 'n' Roll*. I played Santa Claus. This gained me a limited amount of popularity, but for the most part, I was regarded as "The Freak from the Trailer Park." Any kind of social engagement at school was a nightmare. Recess, lunch, and assemblies were all scary occasions at which I would be ostracized and alone rather than socializing with friends, as my other classmates were doing. None of the kids would allow me to stand in their groups or sit next to them. Up to this point, school had always been a pretty humiliating and scary experience. I had tried everything to be friends with my classmates and nothing worked. I pretended to be nice to people that I hated and I pretended to hate people that I wanted to be just like. By the end of fifth grade, I gave up trying to be friends with anyone. The only way from there on out was to be myself.

chapter three

GRADE SCHOOL

By age eleven, I had attended three different elementary schools and hadn't fit in at any of them. I had wanted other kids to like me so much that I became unusually sensitive to what other people thought of me.

The sixth grade landed me in Norton Middle School. I was looking forward to a new beginning. Kids from J. C. Solmonese and kids from the elementary school on the other side of town were brought together into one class. I figured that I had a chance to make new friends. But cliques in the new school formed fast. I managed to befriend a guy named Darren Cox who sat next to me in homeroom. He was a cool guy and we got along very well. He would often sleep over at my house and didn't care that I lived in the trailer park.

The girls in my middle school were pretty cutthroat. I fell in love with one named Kathy DuPont. I often hid what was going on at school from my mother and Allen, but I told them that I had asked Kathy out. What I didn't tell them is that she had laughed at me and said no.

One night, at a parent–teachers conference, my mother ended up sitting next to Kathy DuPont's mother. My mother mentioned that Kathy and I were an item. It only took until the next day for a note from Kathy to end up in my locker. It said I was horrible for telling my parents that we were together. She went on to tell me that I was ugly, disgusting, and to top it all off, a total geek. If it were at all possible to make someone gay, and if there were any situation in my childhood that could have made me gay, this crushing blow from Kathy would have been the one. This was not a mere crush. I was in love with this girl and everything about her.

In the seventh grade, most of my fellow students started to hit puberty except, of course, for me. I wouldn't hit even the early stages of puberty until my freshman year in high school. Darren ditched me, deciding that I was no longer cool enough for his new group of friends, who were all developing into men. Seventh grade was another pretty depressing year in the friends department. To make things even more pathetic, a total asshole in my class named Justin Gibson found every opportunity to pick on me in front of others. I must have been more effeminate than most of the other guys because it was Justin's favorite pastime to say my name in a very girly voice as he passed me in the hall. Justin was postpubescent in the seventh grade and smoked cigarettes in the bathroom. My only ammunition was that he was in the special-education program, while I was in Group 1—the twenty-five smartest, highest-ranked kids in the class. I never, however, used this ammunition, because I was too afraid that he would beat me up.

It was during this year of school that I became very aware of my lack of confidence around guys my own age, and I found that no guys wanted to have anything to do with me. All of this solidified my childhood male-abandonment complex. Feeling unworthy of any man's companionship left a large void in my soul. And my school years are important to understanding my life at the Air Force Academy.

Something wonderful did happen in my eighth-grade year. A classmate named Josh Kidman approached me along with some of his friends on the playground and said, "You look like a cool guy and we're going to hang out with you." Being the shy, prepubescent, skinny, feminine, scared rabbit that I was, I didn't know what to make of this. After all, Josh was a tall, good-looking blond kid. He was from the wealthiest side of town and lived, from what I'd heard, in one of the most beautiful houses in Norton. I was from the trailer park. I wondered if this was a cruel joke as I'd seen played on unsuspecting geeks in movies. But it wasn't. Josh and I started to talk every day. We found out that we had some things in common. We both like to snow ski, water-ski, and read all about cars. We also found out that we were both interested in learning about the adult things in life, such as alcohol and cigarettes.

Soon enough, Josh and I were sleeping over at each other's houses and watching scary movies. Josh's parents didn't know about the rule that kept me from watching R-rated movies, so I was free to see whatever I wanted when I was in their home. I even watched my first porno there. On most occasions when we slept at Josh's, we would get our hands on some sort of alcohol. It was no fun to drink at my family's house because my parents would always say, "If you want to drink here, go ahead, because we would rather have you experiment here than to do it out somewhere you could get hurt." But we didn't want to drink my parents' alcohol because it wouldn't have been rebellious enough. We would get beer by having someone's older siblings buy it for us. My brother had moved back in with my dad in Cincinnati at this point, so I had no older sibling to buy it for me.

My parents had just bought a ski cabin in Maine. Though I had begged them to buy a real house in Norton, to take us out of the trailer park and save me from countless hours of humiliation in school, they decided to keep the trailer and buy the second house in Maine, where we only went on weekends. Josh and I would go to Maine with my parents on the weekends and bring alcohol with us in our suitcases. When my mom and Allen went to bed, Josh and I would stay outside and drink our smuggled goods, talking about everything imaginable and bonding like good friends do. Josh was my best friend and probably the only real friend I had had in my whole life up to that point.

I became keenly aware that the clothes I wore to school afforded me certain levels of attention. I begged my mother to buy me the most up-to-date name brands and styles. She grudgingly took me shopping whenever I could talk her into it, and like clockwork, people reacted more positively to me. I wonder if it was really the clothes or just the confidence I gained from the clothes that attracted my new friends. Either way, I was happy.

Thanks to Josh's friendship, I lowered my guard around boys and men. I became slightly more confident in the eighth grade and even attracted another friend, Gary Riddle. One day, Gary walked up to me in the school hallway and said, "How do you get your pants to roll up that way? It looks so cool." Stunned that another tall, blond kid was talking to me, I respectfully and submissively told him how I did it. Gary was an interesting kid. He was fairly spoiled by his divorced parents, who seemed to compete for his affection by buying him what he wanted. He lived in an amazing house in one of Norton's newer neighborhoods, and I envied him for that.

Despite being spoiled, Gary was full of character. He didn't put up with anyone getting picked on. He must have known that I often got picked on; maybe that's why he chose to befriend me. Some nights, Josh, Gary, and I would all hang out together. They would sleep at my house, and I at theirs. They didn't care that I lived in a trailer. We got along amazingly. These two guys became my life and were true friends of mine through my senior year of high school. Unbelievably, Kathy DuPont and her friends started talking to me again in eighth grade and we became part of the same clique. Before I knew it, I was part of the "in" crowd. It had all happened within one year.

My eighth-grade experience wasn't completely without adversity. There had to be the one asshole that would torture me in public settings. That particular year it was Geoff DeVille. This guy should have been in the eleventh grade, but had been held back more than once. He must have felt very humiliated by this, because he was a very angry person. A girl named Jessica McDonald, who was in his homeroom, had been an acquaintance of mine since the fourth grade and used to tell me about all the things Geoff would say about me in class. Geoff was a very good-looking Italian guy. He had a strapping, developed body and a deep voice, and he would punch dents in lockers in the hallway to impress people. When he would see me, he always had to make a comment. "There's Lehmkuhl. . . . Hey, Lehmkuhl, does everyone know that I caught you jerking off in the bathroom?" I was so scared by this guy that I would never say anything back. I hadn't ever masturbated and didn't start until the ninth grade—apparently, the ninth grade is a late time to start. But I was among hundreds of boys who were denying that they would ever masturbate when the subject ever came up; stupidly, I believed them and actually denied myself the pleasure. A guy telling everyone that I was jerking off was humiliating.

I need to find some personal closure on Justin Gibson and Geoff DeVille, my respective seventh- and eighth-grade bullies. My theory is that both of these guys must have been gay and probably still are now. Because they were both attractive—even gorgeous—they were most likely often approached by both male and female admirers with fond looks and compliments. This constant attention must have made them sensitive to who was attracted to them, causing them to face their own feelings of attraction toward the same and opposite sexes more intensely than an average-looking person might. Their feelings of attraction were already developing toward women—and men. This early attraction to men made them feel angry and insecure, which translated into a need to harass someone they sensed was also gay and whom they could pick on fearlessly. On top of this, I believe they were both very threatened by how much of themselves they saw in me. They must have felt the need to point out my sensitivity and crush it in a public way to make them feel better about their own latent homosexuality. Even if, today, they're both married with seven kids each, regardless of their present lifestyles, I believe that they're both probably gay, always were, and always will be.

chapter four

HIGH SCHOOL LIFE BEGINS

Freshman year of high school rolled around and I found myself in the middle of the most insecure, scared, obnoxious, catty group of people I had ever met. On the advice of my parents, I joined the golf team right away. I had taken up golf in middle school and had become quite good at it. During my first days of high school, I stayed late for golf practice. The golf team would all get into a van for a ride to the Norton Country Club. These van rides were always interesting because the captain of the team found it funny to moon every person he could at intersections. Unsuspecting people standing on street corners would get an eyeful of this guy's hairy ass, and the expression on each and every one of their faces was priceless.

My fears and humiliation over living in a trailer park increased dramatically that year. My way to counteract this was to be as snobby and arrogant as possible. I tortured my mom for all the latest styles and labels to ensure that I was always the best-dressed person in school. I longed to hang out with the kids who wore those clothes, and that meant hanging around with the wealthiest kids. It took me all four years of high school to realize that hanging around with wealthy kids didn't make my life any richer or better; it only made me more miserable about not being able to keep up.

One of these friends was a girl named Susan DelAno. I had heard, through some others in school, that she had a crush on me, despite her being a senior and my prepubescence. One day she took me out for lunch in her 1988 black Mercedes E300 sedan. I'll never forget that car. Riding in it was such a big deal to me. I loved the attention that it demanded and the way that people would look at us in it, as if we were rich beyond imagination. After weeks of my begging for the chance, Susan eventually let me drive the car, without a license. We drove on the open roads and had a blast. I learned the basics of driving a car over about a year's time in this beautiful Mercedes. At the end of this school year, Susan asked me, a freshman, to the prom. Despite everyone making fun of Susan for robbing the cradle, we had a really fun night. Susan and I were strictly friends because I never returned her passes at me. I never wanted anything to happen between us. This began my evident lack of interest in girls in general.

I made many friends with the girls in the senior class during my freshman year. I used to rave about Susan's Mercedes, and another girl asked me if I would like to drive *her* Mercedes. Lisa Mims had a 1971 blue Mercedes 280SE sedan. Driving these girls' cars made me obsessed with Mercedes, and cars in general. I wished I had their cars, and I studied up on them as if this would help me attain them. Soon I knew how much every expensive car would cost and what features each one had.

I had a job my freshman year, too: my first job ever. I worked for the food service at the local college in Norton, Massachusetts—Wheaton College. Josh's cousin worked there, too, and told me how easy it was. She would tell stories of sitting around at the cash register, or serving food to the students in the cafeteria-style food line. When I went there to apply, the manager told me they only had one position left—in the dish room. I wouldn't really be washing dishes, but I'd be running plates into a large machine and then putting them on racks when they came out. I figured this would be pretty easy. They hired me at the new 1988 minimum wage of $3.65 per hour. I look back and think to myself how smart I would have been to figure out any other way to make money. I spent four to five hours there per night, and come home with less than $20. After taxes, I would bring home less than $100 per week.

This was no easy work. I stood between an opening in the wall to the dining room, which was cut too low for me to see anyone's face on the other side, and the actual dishwasher behind me. Students would come by and throw their plates and utensils at me. They could see my torso and my arms, and knew that a human being was standing there, but they didn't care. I would have to pick up their dishes, scrape the waste into a trashcan, and then put those dishes and silverware into a conveyer belt–type dishwasher. Someone would stand on the other end of the dishwasher to take the plates out. That job was actually worse than the job of loading the dishes: the plates would come out so hot that the gloves they gave us to wear were barely able to keep someone's fingers from burning. If the dish was still dirty, that person had to walk to the front of the dishwasher to reload it. When this happened, the dishes would pile up on the receiving end and get jammed in the underside of the dishwasher. Then the dishwasher would have to be shut off and opened, which would piss off whoever was collecting the dishes from the window.

Since then, I pledged never to work near food again. And today, when I see a window like that, and I have to put my tray of dirty dishes through it, I always bend down to look at the people who are in there say thank you. I hand them my dirty dishes, I smile with a grateful heart, and I mean it.

That job ended in a crazy way. I was blessed to get fired, but the way I was fired will never make sense to me. We were one week into having a new manager at the cafeteria. The new manager was a woman who always had a disgusted look on her face when she came into the dish room, which was rarely. She was obviously afraid of something in there. Maybe it was the awful smell, or the loud noise the dishwasher made— a sound so loud that it made my ears ring for two hours after work. I remember those terrible nights, being home after work, cleaning food off my wet sneakers, not being able to hear much because my ears were ringing.

The day of my termination, the new manager came to get me at the end of my shift and brought me near her office. She didn't let me in her office, probably because I was absolutely filthy. As I stood against a wall next to her office door, she said, "I heard you and Jodie were making out in the stockroom. This is inappropriate behavior."

"What?" I asked. "I don't have time to go into any stockroom. I don't know where the stockroom is and I don't have any desire to kiss Jody."

"So you think this is a joke?" she asked.

"No, I think it's ridiculous. Who told you this?" I asked.

"You know what? I don't think we need you here anymore. I don't like your attitude," she said, very sure of herself.

"You're firing me?"

"I'll write you your last check. That includes tonight." And that was it. I had just been fired for the first time in my life. I was fired for kissing a girl whom I didn't kiss, nor would I have *ever* kissed her. The girl she was referring to was, in my opinion, especially ugly. The only girls I ever looked at were ones that Josh and Gary would talk me into seeing, and the *last* thing on my mind, while working, was kissing a girl in the stockroom.

Besides, it was at this job where I started looking at guys more than ever. When I would walk on the Wheaton campus to get to or from work, I would see the college-age guys coming back from the gym. I would notice their hairy legs and worked-out bodies. I would think to myself, *Damn, that looks really good. I want to look like that.* I would have a battle in my mind, realizing I was attracted to these guys and rationalizing my attraction by thinking, *No, you're just looking at them to see what you want to look like.* What I really desired was actually the ability to touch, know, and be intimate with these guys who turned me on.

In the middle of my freshman year, Susan asked me if I wanted to work in the Tax Assessors Office for the town of Norton. Susan's mother was an elected selectman for the town and Susan had heard that the assessor's office was looking for a clerk. I went to interview for the job and realized right away how much better this was going to be than washing dishes. I would be typing memos, filing property profiles, and manning the reception desk.

There were three ladies working in this office, including the manager, Lily Butts. I learned from her that someone can manage an entire office yet have no idea what is going on. The other two were over-weight, one of them quite severely. All three were in their fifties. They would sit at their desks all day and smoke cigarettes. I was the only one who did any work. I found out that these ladies had been in their positions for over ten years. They just sat there and ate and smoked cigarettes all day long. The office would be so smoky from their chain smoking that the air in the office would literally look blue. I remember it being so unbearable sometimes that I would have to walk out of the office to be able to breathe and get rid of my headache.

This was right around the time that I discovered masturbation. I was fifteen years old. The discovery itself was pretty straightforward. I was in my room after school, doing my math homework at my desk. I became aroused for no reason, as many fifteen-year-olds do, about ten times a day. I started touching myself, grabbed on, and couldn't stop until it was *time* to stop.

Having discovered this made my breaks from the Tax Assessor's Office that much more enjoyable. I would go into a strategically placed private bathroom and take care of myself. Sadly, those moments were the most exciting at my job. I was eventually let go because the town cut the budget for a clerk in that office. Just after I was let go, the severely overweight woman had a heart attack. Luckily for her she survived it. I heard she quit smoking after all that.

During my sophomore year, I started dating seriously. I went out with a girl named Tina. She played field hockey for my high school and, although good-looking, was probably the most masculine girl I knew. I was strangely attracted to her and we dated for a few months. While I was still afraid of having sex, I was a good boyfriend. I held her hand and kissed her in the school hallways, and we were considered a cute couple.

Paradise for me and Tina ended when I met two new friends who would change the course of my high school life. Diane Baker and Jack Kuhler were inseparable. They were attractive and were considered smart because they were in all the top-level classes. No one commented about Jack's very effeminate demeanor because he was so intense about it. He yelled a lot and created scenes everywhere and drew more laughs than ridicule throughout the school. One day Diane and Jack asked me to hang out with them after school. They were juniors, so they had their driver's licenses, which made them very cool to me. The three of us went to Jack's house after school; it didn't take me long to realize that these two were obsessed with the subject of sex. I was amazed by these two people, who I had thought were only concerned with good grades and a little school-sponsored fun here and there. They were sex freaks! They started asking me about sex with my girlfriend Tina and I told them that we had never had sex. Then they went on to make fun of her, telling me that I could do so much better and that she had had sex with almost every guy on the football team.

It was right around this time that Tina decided that she and I needed to start having sex. I was petrified of doing it. My new friends had filled my head with enough negative thoughts about her that it made it easy for me to quickly break off our relationship.

Jack and I had something in common. We both hated gym class. We despised everything about it. I was not athletic at all, a carryover from my childhood and my lack of interest in sports. Jack was also inept on the field and on the basketball court. We would talk about creative ways to get out of class. One great way was to stand in the locker room for roll call at the beginning of class and then slip away to the bathroom. Once everyone left the locker room for the field or the basketball court, we would get dressed and head to study hall to finish our homework for the day.

I remember feeling guilty about skipping gym class, and going to the gym teacher, Mr. Gaffey, to repent. I told him that I wanted to get better at sports and asked him to work with me so that I could be more competitive when I got onto the field with the other kids. His response was, "I can't help you. You're out of shape. You need to get in shape and help yourself." After mustering the courage to talk to a big, bad gym teacher about my poor athletic performance, I wasn't exactly motivated by Mr. Gaffey's words. Looking back, I can't believe what a complete asshole this guy was. He only liked the kids who did well in his class: the others could go screw themselves. In fact, our whole school was this way. Athletes and cheerleaders were popular and, for the most part, did and said whatever they wanted.

I decided to rebel against the popular athletes in my school, who always seemed to get away with murder. My mind was made up. Since the athletes in our school ridiculed the negative attributes of nonathletic students, I would do the same thing back to them. The athletes would make fun of fat kids, short kids, feminine kids, kids who dressed differently, and anyone else who didn't fit their mold. Jack, Diane, and I realized that all of the athletes in our school had something in common. Most of them had some sort of acne on their face, and a couple of the more popular ones already had receding hairlines. Diane, Jack, and I all had close-to-perfect skin and nice hair. This was our foundation for an attack that our school had never before seen.

The plan we devised was immature and, in its own way, hurtful. But at the time, it seemed the only way we had to fight back. Even though our plan accomplished what we wanted it to, we all felt terrible about it afterward.

We went to work on Diane's computer. This was in 1990, and Diane had one of the new Macintoshes, which could generate very creative flyers. We found yearbook pictures of all the really judgmental boys in our school, including their nonathletic girlfriends. We cut out the photos of our primary victims and taped them onto a flyer that announced the start of a new group at Norton High School: Athletes for Acne.

The flyer read, "Are you tired of being a boring, straight-A student involved in eight different clubs at school while performing eight hours of community service a week, all so you can get into college? Well, stop that! Come and join us at Athletes for Acne. It's easy! All you have to do is join one of our teams and you can be as cool as we are! Yeah, you'll be a loser later in life, but at least you'll feel cool now. And by the way, be prepared to have LOTS of acne show up on your face. It's part of being WHO WE ARE! Remember, being a LOSER later is OK as long as you're in the pizza-faced, cool group now!"

Since we virtually lived in the school building because of all of our extracurricular activities, we not only had the freedom to roam the halls, but the trust of the administration to take care of the school. And we took care of our school on this particular night. I was staying late for a play rehearsal and Diane and Jack were staying late for a student chapter of Greenpeace they had started. We roamed the halls separately, with tape in our pockets. We put up our signs next to previously posted signs so they wouldn't be noticed right away.

The next day, all hell broke loose. The targets of the posters were publicly humiliated, just as they had publicly humiliated so many other kids for so many years. The prank brought attention to the embarrassing imperfections of the ultrapopular group. It was the equalizing incident of the school year.

Because they were obligated to, the administration of the high school went on its own rampage to find out who had done this. They issued a statement for all homeroom teachers to read the next morning. Student humiliation of any kind was not to be tolerated at our school. Unfortunately, the administration hadn't noticed the humiliation going on before this incident, but this was a wake-up call. They were smart enough to realize that a full-fledged war was developing and that our prank had been provoked.

As usual with my group of friends, we didn't get caught. We were very tight-lipped about our plans and smart enough to know that we would not be able to mention what we had done to anyone, even if it meant giving up bragging rights. We had the satisfaction of knowing what we had accomplished. After that day, the kids who had been picked on constantly were fed up. They didn't like the fact that the administration protected the bullies who had created such a tense environment in our school. They put the new policy of zero-tolerance for humiliation to the test. Complaints to the administration from the more geeky students and their parents began to flow like Clearasil out of a freshly squeezed tube.

* * *

Just after Christmas break, I was in the school cafeteria when a good-looking guy walked up to tell me that a girl in the junior class had a huge crush on me. Her name was Heather. He told me that she would meet me after school that day out by the track. At the end of the day, I walked out to the track to find a beautiful girl standing there. She was a natural blonde, too, not a bleached blonde. She said hello and was as sweet as she could be. Instantly, I had a new girlfriend. I loved everything about her. She was sweet, gorgeous, had big blonde hair, and dressed cool. She was a girl who would make other guys jealous of me.

Our relationship went on for months. We were alone a lot. She would come on to me often and I ended up on a couch in the basement of her parents' house on a nightly basis. I never got aroused by her the way like a straight guy normally would have. I made all kinds of excuses to myself for my lack of interest in her. One was that feelings for a girl would have to grow and that once I was truly in love with her, I would become sexually aroused by her. Another was that she just wasn't the kind of girl I was attracted to. I remember battling with these thoughts in my head and asking God at night, when I said my prayers, to let me be attracted to someone as cool as Heather. That never happened. Heather and I went to her junior prom together. Shortly thereafter, I ended our relationship. I was embarrassed that I didn't want to have sex with her on prom night. She was very upset but told me that she didn't have to have sex with me, and that we could wait as long as I wanted. I just wanted to get myself away from the situation, so I left the relationship with her thinking that I wasn't attracted to her personally, not girls in general. From what I heard, this crushed Heather. Our respective cliques didn't allow us to talk to each other very often afterward.

The summer between my sophomore and junior years of high school I turned sixteen and a half, a magic number in Massachusetts because that is the age when someone can get a driver's license. My mother and Allen surprised me one day with a car that they had bought for me. They paid $900 for a 1973 Mercedes 280. It was a very cool, old four-door sedan. It had been yellow in its glory days, but by 1990, the car was a pale tan. I loved the idea of owning an old Benz, but I quickly learned what it was like to have an older car that would break down. In a few months, I had replaced the entire exhaust ($450), the windshield ($250), the starter ($300), the transmission ($500), and the shocks and struts ($300). My parents paid initially, but then I had to spend my hard-earned money to pay them back. "If you want to have a car, then you have to pay for the repairs," they would say. The $900 car soon drove me into debt with my parents. I remained in debt this particular summer because I did not take a job. I spent my days with Josh and Gary, my two good friends. They were also given cars that summer—new ones. Josh's parents bought him a Mazda RX7 and Gary's parents bought him an Eagle Talon. I had the crappiest car of the group, but I was used to that when hanging out with either of them. I never had the money I would have needed to compete with them.

It seriously fascinated me that Josh and Gary were so nonchalant about their money. Neither of them had ever had a real job. Their parents would give them an allowance as long as they were well behaved and did certain chores around the house. I remember their allowance being disproportionately large compared to the tasks that they were required to do. For instance, Gary would have to clean the litter box and take his mother's car to the car wash. For this he would make $200 a week. I, on the other hand, made a more modest allowance of $20 per week. I had to take out the trash and vacuum the carpet. Living in the close quarters of a mobile home made doing chores inside it very difficult for me. In high school, I grew seven or eight inches all at once, and I remember feeling too big for our home. I hit my head on things, never felt that doorways and the hallway were big enough for me, and was claustrophobic when I had to vacuum twice a week. I hated doing it until I left that trailer for good.

chapter five

DRIFTING FROM HOME

During my junior year of high school I bonded further with Josh, Gary, Diane, and Jack. With no girlfriend, I was with one of the four of them almost every night. I stayed after school often and, since I had a car, would end up at one of their houses for the evening. I hardly saw my parents at all except for a trip we took to Europe.

Every year, my high school would arrange a trip overseas for students in the French and Advanced Placement European History programs. I was in both. Our school secured a deal for $1,000 per student for nine days in Europe. My mother and Allen decided that they would take the trip and be two of our necessary four chaperones.

We left in the spring; it was my first time out of the country. The trip had been planned by a touring company. Because we didn't have a group large enough to fill an entire tour bus, the company combined us with a group from North Carolina. The kids from Hendersonville High School were a stark contrast to my self-righteous, highly opinionated classmates from the Boston area. It was the first time some of us had met kids from the South. Their accents were foreign to us and I was amazed that people actually talked the way they did.

Our itinerary included Germany, France, the United Kingdom, and Switzerland. We spent a great deal of time traveling on a tour bus.

While most of my classmates set themselves apart from the North Carolina kids, Josh and I made it a point to sit in the back of the bus with the more gregarious Southern students. Two of them, in particular, would end up changing my life forever.

The first was Rik Burke. A tall, strapping football player, Rik was a year older than I was. He had been accepted to the U.S. Military Academy at West Point. Based on my lifelong interest in flying and my obsession with my grandmother's service in World War II, many people in my family were urging me to look into the U.S. Air Force Academy. On one of our drives through Europe, Rik taught me about the application process for the three service academies. He told me that his grades guaranteed him valedictorian status at his school. He was also the captain of his high school football team. He told me that applications to the academies required a nomination by a senator, congressman, or the vice president of the United States. The challenges were daunting, but Rik's confidence and excitement were contagious. He inspired me to apply to the U.S. Air Force Academy.

Listening to our conversation was a blonde eighteen-year-old girl by the name of Anne Lane. Toward the end of the time that Rik and I spent talking about the academies, Anne said, "Look how excited you are right now. You *have* to apply to this school." And it was Anne Lane who would make sure that I did. Anne and I laughed and talked for hours and, one night, when we were in a Swiss pub toward the end of the trip, we bonded more seriously over a couple of beers. I remember the waitress asking us, in a very thick accent, if we wanted light or dark beer. While the others played it safe and ordered light beer, Anne and I must have drunk about five or six huge mugs of dark beer together. For the rest of the trip through Europe, she and I were inseparable. I loved making her laugh and smile and I loved how classy she was—unlike any girl I had met up to that point. She was well mannered and had a well-spoken confidence about her.

When it was time to go back to the States, Anne and I said a long good-bye. I had made a new friend and knew that I would have dated her if she lived closer. Anne felt the same way. I returned home, to my trailer park lifestyle, and within a few days, I called Anne on the number she had given me when we parted. To my surprise, a woman answered with an even thicker Southern accent than Anne's. "Is Anne there?" I asked.

"Miss Anne is out right now but I'll let her know you called. Can I take a message?"

"Who is this that I'm speaking to?" I asked.

"Why, this is her maid, sir." With this explanation I gulped. Never in my life had I met anyone who had a maid. I was intimidated and excited at the same time.

A few hours later, Anne called me back. "Do you miss me?" I asked right away.

"Yes, I do," she said. "I told my friends on the day we left, 'I will see that boy again.'" Knowing that Anne had talked about me so directly and passionately filled my heart with a need to see her as soon as possible.

"We need to plan a trip to see each other," I explained. Within a couple of weeks, Anne's parents and mine had been in touch with each other and bought me a ticket to fly to North Carolina to accompany Anne to her debutante ball, something I had never heard of. My mother explained that this was a Southern tradition of the well-to-do, at which girls were "revealed" to society as women. The court of a debutante ball had to invite certain girls to be part of the ball. Anne was invited by the Rhododendron Court to be a debutante in 1991, and I escorted Miss Lane to the ball.

This trip was the first of many I would take to see Anne. She was also an incredible letter writer. She wrote me letters and cards of encouragement through my process of applying to the Air Force Academy, which was a project that took a great deal of my time that year and on through my senior year.

Anne couldn't make it to Massachusetts on the weekend of my junior prom. I ended up going with Katrina Valley, a girl whom I had dated on and off that year. She was a sophomore and was very bold. She would tell me that she had a crush on me and what she liked about me, and would often make flirty comments to me in front of others, but I did not have any intimate feelings for her, as beautiful as she was.

I didn't have intimate feelings for any girl, I realize now. I loved Anne as a friend, and the thought of her being my girlfriend or my wife was very appealing, but I didn't have a passion to hold or touch any girl. All of that was mimicry. Other guys fawned over their girlfriends, and I did the same.

Looking back, I realize that I was taking the least stressful approach to my conflicted sexuality, concentrating on a girl who did not live near me. Having an out-of-town girlfriend was a very convenient way to avoid the advances of the girls at school. I didn't have to face my inability to be intimate with any female. When I did see Anne, we would mess around, but we would always stop when I said, "We should wait." What we were waiting for must have made no sense to Anne. What we were *really* waiting for was for me to feel sexually attracted to Anne. It never happened.

As time passed during my senior year, I became more and more aware of my affection for my male friends. I don't recall thinking of them in a sexual way, but I would do anything for them. It was a curious attraction, one that even applied to guys I didn't know. Like most guys, I am extremely visual when it comes to desires. Throughout my high school years, I had to watch myself and try my best not to turn my head toward every guy who walked by. I knew I wanted to look at them. I just didn't know why.

I continued to date Anne, from afar, throughout my senior year. I went to North Carolina a couple of times to see her and we talked about being together forever, and living together after I graduated from the Air Force Academy. I thought to myself that surely by then, I would want to be intimate with my girlfriend.

In the fall of my senior year I landed a job as a ski instructor at a local resort in Franklin, Massachusetts, called Klein Innsbruck. My brother Bobby had forced me onto skis when I was twelve years old. He had been an instructor then and had built up my confidence in skiing early on. Because I had become such a good skier so easily, I determined that my inaptitude in sports must have been limited to team sports, which intimidated me. I was, after all, athletic when it came to individual sports, such as tennis, golf, running, and skiing.

Realizing this helped to build my confidence. By this time, I had enjoyed years of good, strong skiing in all kinds of terrain, so I was, for the most part, an expert skier. The mountain was lit for night skiing, and I taught there mostly at night after school. It was at Klein Innsbruck that I met Ben Silverman, who eventually became the first person I was ever truly in love with.

chapter six

BEN SILVERMAN

Klein Innsbruck Ski Area had hired me only after I passed its ski school director's tests, interviews, and instructor's certification program. My first day of work was a bright Sunday. At the morning meeting with the ski school director I noticed a tall, dark-haired, blue-eyed guy.

My mind reverted to the self-hating thoughts I had had all my life—echoes of kids taunting me about my big ears, skinny body, and high voice. *He's probably a hell of a skier, too,* I thought, *and he's going to show me up on the slopes and ridicule me all season long.* Immediately, this handsome ski instructor became my competition, someone whose respect I would probably never have unless I earned it. The only things we had in common were our matching red, white, and blue ski-school jackets, with *Ski Instructor* emblazoned on the back.

Just after the director's meeting ended, Mr. Perfect walked by me and whispered, "Loser!" I immediately felt a rush of adrenaline. As he walked out of the lodge, I followed him.

Out on the deck, I tapped him on the back and asked, "Did you just call me a loser?"

"What?" he asked, with a look of confusion on his face.

"You just walked by me and whispered 'loser' under your breath!" I was getting angry. He looked at me and grinned. Then he took a step back, sizing me up.

"I don't know you, but you need to *relax*," he said. "I was talking about Jack, the ski school director. I can't fucking stand him." I stood there, stunned. I felt like an idiot.

"Oh, shit. I'm sorry," I blurted out, but in a masculine way. I think I even lowered my voice a little. I tried to look somewhat cool, keeping my pride. "Uh, why do you hate him?" I asked.

"Because he can't ski," he said. "He thinks he can ski, but he can't. The shit he tells us to teach is all wrong. I'm Ben, by the way. Ben Silverman." I immediately knew that I loved looking at him. I loved talking to him. I wanted to talk like him. I wanted to look like him. At eighteen years old, he stood six feet five inches and had a size fifteen shoe or, in this case, ski boot. "You want to take a run?" he asked. I agreed, and onto the chair lift we went. Even if I had never skied before in my life, I was going to be an expert on this run down the trail with Ben.

Just as the chairlift took off, Ben started pulling his gloves and mask out of his pockets. He asked me to hold his ski poles while he put them on. I remember staring at his huge hands. I wondered if he had seen my hands and what he thought about the fact that I was so much smaller and skinnier than he was. I was about six feet tall at this time, weighed about one hundred fifty pounds, and my ears still stuck way out. I looked like a toothpick. Ben's massive size and energy were making me melt. I didn't know what was happening to me, but I knew I didn't want to leave Ben's side from that moment on.

We got to the top and Ben took off, leaving me to chase after him. He did a perfect side snowplow on his huge skis, and stopped. I caught up to him and did my most impressive side plow and sprayed him from head to toe with snow. "Ass!" he said, and we both laughed. With that we took off again down the hill. I kept up with Ben and even found that my form was better than his. I seemed to have more control of my skis than he did. We had a great run and then got back on the chairlift. This time, Ben suggested that we do the run on one ski. If Ben had suggested that we go down the hill doing a handstand on our skis while holding our poles between our ass cheeks, I probably would have done that, too, just because he wanted to.

Eventually, the ski school students arrived, and Ben and I had to give lessons. I was pumped up with excitement and adrenaline all day because I had met a new friend whom I really enjoyed being around.

Ben lived in Mendon, about five towns away from Norton; the resort town of Franklin was in the middle. Despite the distance, he and I continued to build a strong friendship. I got more than I ever expected. In fact, looking back, I ended up with my first boyfriend, whether or not either of us knew it. Sitting in school all day, I could not wait to get to the mountain to see Ben at work. I would call him before I left my house to make sure he was coming.

As I spent more time with Ben, I began to alienate my friends in Norton. Ben was giving me all the friendship, attention, and closeness that I was looking for.

Ben lived with his dad in an amazing house. Two of the most common topics of conversation between them were how evil Ben's mother was (she had divorced Ben's dad) and how important body-building was. While they never persuaded me to badmouth the ex–Mrs. Silverman, they did talk me into joining their gym. Ben would call me names like "bone rack," making fun of my size, but I would give him a run for his money during wrestling matches, which happened at least twice a day. I loved wrestling him. He would hurt me sometimes by slamming me or hitting me, but I would do it back, giving him charley horse and bruises, too. I enjoyed every minute of it. The best was when we would wrestle in front of the television in his living room. He would get me pinned in a position and then we would start watching something interesting on the screen while he held me that way. I would relax and just feel his whole huge body wrapped around me. It would take everything I had not to close my eyes and just fall asleep, pressed against him.

We went to the gym together every day. Ben literally taught me how to work out. I was an avid runner, but he told me to stop for a while until I built up some mass. I started eating more, drinking protein shakes, and gaining muscle. My whole body changed, and I had more energy than I knew what to do with. Soon, I was addicted to every-thing about Ben.

My parents were addicted to him, too. He would come to stay at our place and didn't care that we lived in a trailer. My mother would make dinner, and almost every night that I was actually home for dinner, so was Ben. They treated him like a son and would even let him take one of their cars if his broke down. Ben had a white Toyota 4Runner. I loved riding in that car with him. He would take me off-roading on weekends and make the car do things that I could never have imagined. I know we came close to death a couple of times on those wooded trails, but I didn't care. I was just happy to be with him.

One day, Ben pulled out his twelve-gauge shotgun from his base-ment and asked me if I wanted to learn how to shoot. We went off-roading way back into the woods and he took the first shot. I had no idea what was going to happen. I put the gun up to my shoulder and pulled the trigger. I learned my lesson that day—to keep the gun right up against my shoulder instead of leaving a space between my shoulder and the butt. The gun kicked back and left a bruise the size of a base-ball on my shoulder for a good month.

Just as all seemingly perfect situations have a drawback somewhere, so did my relationship with Ben. He had a girlfriend. Her name was Patty. In the same way that I saw less of my Norton friends when Ben and I started to hang out, Ben saw less of Patty. When Ben canceled plans with me because of her, I would get really upset. When he didn't come to work at the mountain because he had had a fight with Patty and had to take her to dinner to make up, I would get depressed. From the few times I met her, I could tell that Patty was perfect in every way, at least in the eyes of a straight guy. She was tall, with dark hair, bright-green eyes, big boobs, knock-'em-out-of-the-park legs, and a killer tan. I couldn't stand her because she took Ben's attention away from me.

I first met Patty at Ben's birthday party. We made small talk and she made a couple of half-joking comments about my stealing her boy from her. Ben laughed it off with, "Yeah, he's my other girlfriend, except he's a guy." For me, however, there was no joking about it.

The second and last time I spent any time with Patty was the day that I realized I was actually jealous of her. It was a sunny Saturday afternoon. Ben had invited me over to play pool and drink beer. When I arrived, I saw what I was sure was Patty's car in the driveway. I sighed to myself and debated turning around and leaving. After a few minutes, I decided to go in and found Ben and Patty grilling hamburgers on the back deck.

"Hi!" Patty said.

"What's up, bone rack?" Ben said.

"Not much," I replied with little enthusiasm.

"Something wrong? Patty said. "You look sad. You can talk to Ben about it because I can't stay long." I didn't even answer. I just shook my head and went into the living room and turned on the TV. I sat there and listened while Ben and Patty flirted with each other outside. I felt like a third wheel—completely left out.

All of the sudden, I heard Ben say, "All right, let's go!" The two of them ran through the living room and up to Ben's bedroom. I heard the door shut. They were going to have sex. My body filled with feelings that I had never, up to that day, experienced. I was completely jealous of Patty. After all, I spent more time with Ben than she did. I respected him more than she did. I was a better friend than she was. But why was I jealous that they were having sex? As I sat there and realized that I wanted to be in that bedroom, I started consciously telling myself that I was not gay.

I just have this unnatural feeling for Ben, but I'm not gay, I said to myself.

When they were done having sex, Patty came down with her pocketbook over her shoulder and said good-bye to me, smiling and fixing her freshly fucked hair. How she didn't know that I actually had the feelings for Ben that she had joked about was beyond me. I only wished that Ben felt the same way toward me that I did toward him.

As the school year went on, I continued to cross new lines of intimacy with Ben. When he drove somewhere with me in the passenger seat, I would reach over and play with his ear. Sometimes he stopped me but other times he didn't. I would tell him how much I liked being with him and he would look over at me and smile, without saying anything back. Toward the spring, Ben and I were still teaching together and we both knew it was the end of the season. We were so much in our own world at the mountain that no one could touch us. We did what we wanted. We taught the way we wanted and shrugged off our bosses' warnings when we did something wrong. We would get into wrestling matches in front of our students, in the snow, with our skis on. We had a blast.

On our last day at Klein Innsbruck, Ben ended up in a heated argument with one of the resort's owners about how Ben and I thought we owned the resort. As the tension increased, Ben told the owners that he *and* I were out of there for good. He quit for both of us. "No one is going to talk to me that way, and they're definitely not going to talk to *you* that way," he said.

We went to his house that night to drink beer and play pool. As usual when we got drunk, we ended up having a conversation with our chests nearly touching and our faces right up against each other's. I could have kissed him right then, but I was too afraid of what would happen.

A few weeks later, Ben told me he had found us another job washing Mack trucks. I'm talking about waking up at 5:30 in the morning on weekends and cleaning eighteen-wheelers. This was perfect, because I would have an excuse to sleep in Ben's bed and hold on to him all night, especially if we put down a couple of beers before we passed out. We drove a large van with a steam-cleaning machine built into it to a huge parking lot containing rows of Mack trucks. We ran huge brooms with soapy water running through them up and down the sides of the trucks and trailers. Then we sprayed them all off with powerful spray guns that could slice your hands if you forgot to wear gloves. My hands took a beating from the job, but my body became more muscular over a short period of time. At the end of a day of Mack-truck washing, I was covered in oil. I would get home and my mom would laugh at how dirty I was. I don't know how many pairs of jeans and shoes I ruined doing that job. I did it all to be around Ben.

I continued visiting Anne in North Carolina when I could get there. We talked on the phone almost every day and she learned about Ben and my relationship with him through my daily stories. She wanted to meet him, so on one of my visits to North Carolina, I took Ben with me. Anne's parents had Ben and me sleep on a guest bed on the lower floor away from the rest of the bedrooms of the house. In a crazy display of my dual identity, each evening I tucked Anne into her bed and kissed her goodnight. Then I went downstairs, got into bed with Ben, and held on to him until the morning, in my own girlfriend's house. I continued to deny that I was gay. From all this I learned the power of deception. Today, when someone who I know is gay tells me he is straight, I realize he actually *believes* he is straight. Nothing will bring him out of the closet other than his own self-realization, even if he is having sex with another man every night of the week.

chapter seven

HOME BITTER HOME

While I may have deceived myself about my sexuality throughout my younger days, I always stood firm about my hatred for trailer life. Here is a glimpse of my life inside and around that damn trailer, as well as of my visits to see my father's family in Cincinnati, where much of my adult personality was forged.

I hated where we lived. I'll never forget the address: 157 Mansfield Avenue, Trailer 17, Norton, Massachusetts. Mom and Allen bought this place on the Norton Reservoir because they thought it would be neat to have a house on a lake. And some of it was neat. When the lake froze over in the winter, the trailer park kids played hockey. In the summers, we would take out our rickety johnboat to fish for bass. But while my brother and Allen would reel in three-pound bass time and time again, I only caught bluegills. In all the years we lived on that lake, I never caught a single bass.

It wasn't a real lake by any stretch of the imagination, anyway. It was filthy and shallow. We couldn't swim or water-ski—two things that I consider requirements for a body of water to be called a lake. I eventually realized that the Norton Reservoir was horribly polluted and that we shouldn't have been fishing there in the first place. I became aware of the lake's disgusting smell and the sludge that surrounded it on hot summer days. Toward the end of my stay in Trailer 17, the lake completely grossed me out.

Despite my hating where we lived, my mother and Allen always made great efforts to ensure my happiness. They found it important to do things together as a family. We traveled on car trips to neat places as often as we could. They had good friends who would come over for dinner and I would look forward to seeing them whenever I could. My mother did her best to buy me the things I needed for school, and even things I didn't need but that made me feel better. Allen paid the bills religiously, working hard every weekday of his life. They provided our vacation house in Maine and bought new boats for us to use every couple of years. Although I was bothered by the trailer and some of the situations I experienced within it, I was by no means a deprived child. I could not, however, get past my frustration over living in a trailer.

As difficult as it was for me to adjust to a new father and the differences in his personality from that of my blood father, today I admit that Allen was the best thing that could have happened to me or my family. I truly believe that any and all success I have had in my life is rooted in the trust, confidence, faith, manners, and courage that Allen taught me. I had a steady father-figure in my home who worked hard to provide us with everything we really needed to be happy.

My brother Bobby moved into the trailer with us in 1983. I started the fourth grade that fall, and he started his sophomore year of high school. I was excited to have him back living with us, but that didn't last long. He and I fought a lot. It was Cincinnati all over again. He would pick fights with me and often call me a faggot. I would fight back, but it was of no use—he was so much older and bigger.

At the end of that school year, Bobby announced that he was moving back to Cincinnati to be with our dad. My dad had bought a new house where Bobby would have his own room. In Trailer 17, he shared a seven-by-seven room with me because Allen had given the third bedroom to his daughter, Michelle.

Because my brother and I argued so much, I admit that I was glad to see him leave our home. I had no idea, at the time, how awful it was that my own brother was being taken away from me again. I was too attached to my mom and Allen to leave, and I surely didn't trust my dad enough to move in with him.

I would spend two to four weeks every summer at my dad's house, and all of the little differences between there and home were a huge deal to me. My stepmother, Kim, would get angry at me because I was hungry all the time and because I would often spend time in the kitchen looking for food and making what she considered a "big mess." I asked my brother several times why she was so crazy about keeping a clean kitchen and he told me that he just avoided the kitchen altogether. She was used to feeding her little girl, my step-sister Stacie, who was two years younger than I, not a growing boy. Because of Kim's reaction to my insatiable appetite, I dreaded going to Cincinnati in the summers. I knew I would be hungry the whole time. That always kept me from truly loving or trusting her for many years. Since that time, Kim and I have developed a more real and loving relationship. Our time together has been limited, but I enjoy being around her whenever I go home to Cincinnati.

My only reprieve from being hungry during the summer was the time that I was able to spend with my mother's side of the family—Grandma Turner, the pilot, and my mother's brothers and sisters, who also lived in Cincinnati. The Turners liked to have big summer cookouts and gatherings, and because my grandmother had seven kids, she and my grandfather would usually host these events. I made it a point to bond with my grandma each summer, even if it was just for a couple of days. My favorite thing to do with her was to go to a local airport and look at planes or, even better, to fly them when we had the chance. Besides filling me up with lots of good food, my Grandma Turner kept my interest and passion for aviation alive and strong.

In 1985, my dad and Kim told me that they were going to have a baby. My half sister Kaley was born on February 23, 1986, when I was twelve years old. My dad, Kim, Bobby, Stacie, and Kaley were now all living together as one family in Cincinnati. Michelle, Allen's daughter from his previous marriage, moved out of the trailer to live with her mother. The odd man out, I was again living as an only child in Norton, Massachusetts.

Living in the trailer park was a crazy experience, and life inside Trailer 17 was particularly nuts. Allen was strict and my mother let him have the run of the house. Household chores were a must, and had to be done on time and correctly. The vacuuming had to be done on Tuesdays and Thursdays. Trash had to be taken out on Fridays. I could not begin eating a meal until everyone was sitting down and served. I had to ask, "May I please be excused from the table?" before getting up. To Allen's credit, he practiced what he preached, so I was never confused by the hypocritical parenting philosophy of *Do as I say, not as a I do*. Allen paid me an allowance every week. When report card time rolled around, he would give me $20 for every A and $10 for every B. Cs got nothing, so gym class was a wash.

Life went from manageable to not so manageable when I was in the fifth grade. I came home from school one day and my mom told me that she had hurt her back at work that morning. She was a head nurse at an home for the elderly in Attleboro. She had been lifting a patient who had fallen and ended up falling herself. My mother, whom I knew as lively, active, and strong, would never be the same again.

A few weeks went by and my mother still could not return to work. She ended up going to a doctor, who said she had a slipped disk and recommended surgery. After the operation, mom was in the hospital for a month because they had to go back in and remove more of the disk. Then, a nerve to her leg, which had been pinched by the scar tissue from the surgeries, started to give her unbearable pain. She went back into surgery to have her vertebrae fused. This put her in a body cast for three months.

During all this time, I came home from school and did my homework as fast as I could, before Allen got home, so he could take me to see my mother in the hospital. I went every night, eating hospital food for dinner for the better part of two years. There was always something new wrong when we went to visit her—another complication or another surgery that they were planning. The talk of more procedures would confuse and drain me.

I loved my mother dearly but whenever she came home from the hospital, it was a nightmare for me. She could barely move. She was in dire pain and her medications were ruining the inside of her body. And man, was she bitchy. Everything had to be done for her. She could no longer make it out of bed to a bathroom so she had to use a bedpan. She could no longer do any housework whatsoever. She lay in bed and often cried about how her life was so depressing. She would cry about her pain. Then she would take more medication to fight her depression.

Finally, a neurosurgeon decided that he was going to use some new pacemaker technology on my mother. He inserted a pacemaker into my mother's abdomen and connected an electrical wire from the pace-maker to the nerve in her leg that hurt so much. She went through the surgery and it actually worked. The drawback was that she has a metal box inside of her that set off airport security alarms. To this day, she carries a note with her from the doctor for all airport security check-points. She's not allowed to have an MRI, either—its magnetism would rip the metal box right out of her body.

The surgeries continued through my junior year in high school. My mother could never again stand or sit for long periods of time. This meant that we couldn't go out for dinner and she couldn't take long car rides. She always had to be lying down. I helped her the best I could as a kid. When she went through the time in the body cast, I emptied and cleaned her bedpan for her. I helped her dye her hair, and bathe, and cook. I found myself taking on tons of responsibility, but I also avoided coming home. This was the time when I started making a life and friends outside of my home life. I didn't like my mother's talk of pain and I-can't-do-this and I-can't-do-that, no matter how true it was. It drove me insane.

As the years passed, I had more and more trouble listening to my mother complain of pain. For a very long time, it was all she talked about. She would talk about it at get-togethers, on the phone to other friends and family members, and to *my* friends when they asked how she was doing. I would have to leave the room. I feel bad about it, but even today as an adult, I avoid, as much as possible, any talk about her pain. She went through knee replacement surgery ten years after I moved away from home and, still, I found myself not able to hear her talk about the pain, the surgery, or the recovery. Any mention of it would make me have to change the subject.

Today, because of the scars left over from a childhood with a chronically ill mother, when one of my friends is hurt or sick or in the hospital, it takes every ounce of compassion in me to even ask how they're feeling. I deny that people are in pain or that they even need any sort of medical care at all. I urge people not to take any prescription medications or visit their doctor. "Can't you handle this on your own?" I ask them. "You don't want a doctor to screw up your body when you could just heal on your own." I know that this type of thinking is irrational. I, myself, have had to visit the doctor over the years on several occasions. I've learned that there really are pills that can cure some ailments. I've learned to have some sort of compassion for people around me who are sick, but it's still difficult.

By the end of my high school years, before leaving the trailer for good, I really despised coming home. I loved my parents still, but I wished that we would win the lottery and be in a normal house. I wished my mother weren't lying down on the couch every time I came home. I knew I needed something to take me away so that I could forget about that place forever.

Some people say that homosexuality is a genetic trait, that it's scientific. Some say that homosexuality is learned or developed over the years of childhood. Some say it's a mixture of both nature and nurture. I have often wondered if all that I went through as a kid, including failure in "manly" things like sports, the abandonment I experienced by male figures in my life, and my ailing mother, were all things that actually nudged me toward being gay. Maybe those experiences, in some way, left me in need of male energy to the extent that I would have to be fully intimate with another male to be happy. Maybe my brain simply wired itself this way, during all of these scary experiences of my youth. This theory breaks down, however, when I remember that, even as a very young child, I was ultracurious about and attracted to boys and men. Maybe I was genetically predisposed to being gay, and then my life experiences pushed me over the line, against the wishes of society, to actually act.

I know one thing for sure. If I could actually be straight, I would be. As I moved on in life, I fought my homosexual thoughts and feelings as hard as I could. That just didn't work. Once a person is wired to be gay, that sexuality is there to stay. After all, my belief in God includes a belief that everything is planned out throughout our lives and that our lives are unfolding before us. We simply need to let that happen. I believe God made me a homosexual guy.

Somehow, everything I went through in adolescence led me to the place that would make me the man I am today—the military. How a kid like me ended up doing what I did still amazes me every day.

chapter eight

GETTING INTO THE AIR FORCE ACADEMY

I would love to say that I had overwhelming confidence about getting into the Air Force Academy, but I can't. In fact, I went through all of the arduous motions of applying, but only because people like Anne and my parents continued to push me toward the goal.

Getting into the U.S. Air Force Academy is not merely gaining admission to a school. Getting accepted means that one is actually appointed to a government position. Like many such positions, a higher authority in government has to approve it. Of course, one must possess all of the right attributes to win admission to a top-tier school, but in addition, an applicant to the academy must obtain a letter of nomination from a congressman, senator, or the vice president.

Gaining a congressional nomination begins at the start of one's junior year of high school and is a very political process. Every senator has the ability to offer two nominations for each of the three service academies under the Department of Defense. Every congressman has the ability to offer a limited number of nominations, depending on the population of that congressman's district. Because I lived in Massachusetts, my two senators were Ted Kennedy and John Kerry. My congressman was the Honorable Barney Frank.

Any student who wants to attend the academy will send an application for a nomination to all three of his public officials, and so did I. The application included a form letter that had to be written perfectly and on the letterhead of the applicant's current high school. There were parts of the letter that had to be in my own words to impress the nomination board, mostly about why I wanted to go to the Air Force Academy. I wrote about my grandmother and her time in World War II. I had to send my high school transcripts, reflecting work completed up to that point. That was nerve-racking because I hadn't tried too hard in gym class and I had a couple of Ds in that department. I also had to send a picture of myself. At the time, there was a big push to recruit and offer opportunities to ethnic minorities, so I imagine the picture was for the purpose of verifying that someone was, indeed, a minority. (Years later, as an officer, I worked with ROTC admissions, and realized how much of an advantage minorities actually have in the ROTC and academy admission processes.)

I sent my applications to my two senators and my congressman. Just a few months later, I received a package in the mail, unrelated to academy admissions, looking for students to attend the National Young Leaders Conference in Washington, D.C. It was to be a week-long trip to the U.S. Capitol, where students would be divided into two groups and create a mock congressional debate about a current issue. In addition, the students would get the chance to meet their representatives and senators. It looked like something I wanted to do, but I had never traveled away from home without my parents, as this was before my trips south to see Anne. And there was a thousand-dollar price tag for the weeklong seminar. I showed the package to my mother. She looked through it and quickly said, "You need to go to this." I was very surprised.

"You'll pay for it?" I asked.

"Yes. You don't worry about that. This is a great opportunity for you and a great time to meet Kerry, Frank, and Kennedy." In the literature that they had sent, it was explicitly stated that meeting our representatives and senators was not guaranteed, but that every effort would be made by the organization to make it happen. This was a big financial risk my mother was taking but I promised her that if it were humanly possible, I would meet at least one of my legislators on this trip. We sent in a check with the application, and in the spring of my junior year of high school, I headed to Washington.

I flew there by myself and was herded into a group of other arriving kids at Reagan National Airport. We were put on a large bus and driven to our hotel. For the first time, I met kids from Louisiana, California, Utah, and some from other countries. For many of us, this was our first real taste of freedom away from home. We ended up having parties in each other's rooms at night. We didn't have access to any alcohol or drugs, but we would hang out and act crazy with each other.

What my parents didn't know was that many of us ended up in trouble with the conference chaperones for being in rooms of attendees of the opposite sex. I was caught in some girl's room with a bunch of other guys. It was completely innocent and, looking back at it now, I'm surprised they made such a big deal about it. They took about ten of us into a hotel room and started making calls to our parents to send us back home for bad behavior. One of the chaperones looked like a woman I could reason with, so I started in on her. "You know, I'm here to meet my legislators because I'm trying to get into the Air Force Academy." I continued, "If I don't get to meet them, my parents will come down on me pretty hard."

She looked up at me with a surprised look on her face. "Are your parents in the military?" she asked with fear in her eyes.

"Yeah, they are," I quickly answered.

"Oh," she said, "I know what you're dealing with. My dad was military. OK, listen, you just sit here and I'm going to think about this."

"Please," I said, "I'm *so* sorry. I will not do this again. I will stay in my room and do everything you all ask. Just, please don't call my parents." I said it with a look of dread in my eyes. She walked out of the room and, seconds later, she peeked back in the door and waved her finger for me to follow her. I went out into the hallway.

"Listen," she said, "I'm letting you go and you're lucky this time but if I see you do anything else wrong, you'll be sorry and you and I both know that. Now go!" I walked quickly down the hallway and went back to my room. Not ten minutes after I was back, some kids were knocking on my door to hang out.

"Get out of here, you guys! I just got in *so* much trouble because of you!" They managed to talk me into hanging out in my room within a few days, but I mostly kept my nose clean at the conference.

I ended up staying in touch with most of those kids for a good seven years after that conference. In fact, I'm still in touch with one girl in South Dakota named Amber. We still repeat the same jokes that we laughed at together at the conference.

We performed a few days' worth of a mock debate; the issue at hand was gun control. I had no idea what this meant and didn't really pay attention to anything surrounding the debates. I had my mind set on meeting my senators and representative. That day finally came and different assistants and aides were brought in to meet us on the front steps of the Capitol. There were only two other attendees there from Massachusetts and neither of them was applying to any of the academies, so I would, at least, stand out when I mentioned that I had applied to the Air Force Academy.

The first person who walked up to me was an aide from Barney Frank's office. She said she would escort me to Senator Kennedy's office when Mr. Frank and I were finished meeting. She took me into Representative Frank's office after a rather long wait in the reception area, and there he was, sitting in his chair with his feet up on the desk. He was eating something, relaxing during a lunch break. He saw me enter and took his feet down but did not stop eating. "How are you doing?" he asked in a friendly voice as he smiled as if to also say, *Who is this little kid in my office and what could he possibly have to say to me?* "Sit down, please," he said. I sat down on this large leather couch facing his desk. The room seemed huge, like I was a mile away from him.

"Sir, I'm really glad to meet you," I said in an obviously rehearsed way, "and I wanted to talk to you about the Air Force Academy. You see, I am applying for an appointment as a cadet and I need a congressional . . . "

"Yeah, I know how it works," he interrupted. Being a pretty sensitive kid, I felt like I was wasting his time so I just went right to the point. "You're one of the congressmen that I sent my nomination application to. I'd like for you to consider me for the Air Force Academy. I can answer any question that you may have right now to help you make your decision in my favor." I couldn't believe how well it came out of my mouth. And he had a question right away.

"Why do you want to go?" he asked. I answered him with every nugget of information I knew about the academy and how it fit my life. I told him that I lived in a trailer park and that I just wanted out of all that and to leave home for good. I told him about my grandmother.

Without much emotion he said, "Well, I don't think there will be any problem with my staff seeing you as a viable candidate for my nomination." I sat there, stunned.

I wanted to ask, *What do you mean?* but I just kept my mouth shut and took his words at face value. He was being slightly ambiguous and would probably continue to be. "Thank you, Mr. Frank, sir," I said.

"You're welcome. Do you have any other questions for me?"

"Yes," I said. I knew that my congressman, sitting in front of me, had just been through an entire scandal during which he was outed as a homosexual. This was 1990 and the country was twice as conservative on the issue of homosexuality as it is today. "How are you doing?" I asked. He looked at me for a beat and I could see, in his eyes, that he knew that I knew about his recent scandal.

"I'm doing OK. Sometimes you just have to do your work and believe in yourself, and press on with your goals, and everything will be OK."

"I agree," I said and smiled. He smiled back at me.

"Go out into the lobby and give my secretary all of your information," he said.

"Thank you so much, sir." I got up and went out into the lobby of his offices and shut his big wooden door behind me. I walked up to the secretary and explained to her that Mr. Frank wanted all of my contact information. I wrote it all on a white, letter-size piece of paper, and on the top, in huge letters, I wrote, "AIR FORCE ACADEMY NOMINATION."

Today, I truly believe that one's personal intentions can actually produce a positive energy field and influence the opinions of others toward oneself. I believe that my positive thinking, and even the way I wrote what I wrote on the top of that piece of paper, had something to do with my getting a congressional nomination to the academy. Maybe that paper was floating around the office for a while and they just associated "Air Force Academy nomination" with my name, and when they went to give out the actual nomination, I was a shoe-in. Maybe I just turned in a good application. But maybe I transferred some positive energy during that meeting.

The aide in Mr. Frank's office then took me over to Senator Kennedy's office. I arrived and the secretary at the desk said, "Oh, we've been waiting for you. The senator has left for lunch, but he said he was eating at the local café here in the building. This is your photographer, Tom." I introduced myself to the photographer and he led me out of the office toward where Senator Kennedy was eating. I was so nervous. Not only was I meeting my senator, I was meeting a real Kennedy—and I was interrupting his lunch. I asked the photographer why he was there and his answer made me even more nervous.

"The senator is actually excited to meet you and wanted to make sure you got some press out of it. We'll forward the pictures to your local newspaper in your hometown." I was so excited, I couldn't even breathe. They were making me feel so important. There I was, walking to a meeting with Ted Kennedy, dressed in a suit and tie. I could get used to this life.

Suddenly, I found myself walking toward Senator Kennedy's table. He was sitting there by himself, eating a sandwich in an open courtyard cafe. He was lit by the sun and squinted to look up at me. "Mr. Lehmkuhl, is it?"

"Hello, Senator!" I said with excitement and a smile on my face. The moment took me over. I didn't know what else to say. He looked at me like he was my grandpa.

Excitedly he said, "Well, sit down here with me and let's have some lunch." There was a waiter standing by who asked me what I wanted. I looked at Senator Kennedy. "Order whatever you want, c'mon," he said, knowing that I was scared to death. I ordered and the photographer began to snap pictures of us sitting at lunch. Then he had us stand up and took a few more.

My lunch with Senator Kennedy was very similar to the meeting I had had with Representative Frank just minutes before. He asked me the same questions but he seemed much more aloof about the whole nomination process than Frank did. When I explained to him about how I had submitted an application for a nomination, he said, "Well, that's great. Good for you!" as if I hadn't actually submitted it to *him*. It was a little frustrating. We ate lunch for a while and then, to my great surprise, he asked me a question. "So I'm curious about what you know about me. From the standpoint of your generation, how are things going?"

I figured that he was asking me about the job he was doing in office. There were always Republicans talking about the scandals of the Kennedy family and their evil liberal politics and, being from a small town, I would hear that often. People would talk about how the senator's face was always red and would therefore accuse him of drinking. "Senator," I said, "if you could just keep your private life out of the papers and away from people, I think you would be able to concentrate more on what matters." He looked up from his food and stared at the sixteen-year-old SOB across from him.

"Well. I guess I have to thank you for your candor." And that was it. We didn't say much more and both got up from the table. I shook his hand and away he went to work. At that moment, I wondered if I had just ruined my chances of being nominated by Senator Kennedy.

I didn't have the chance to meet Senator Kerry. We were told that he was busy and unable to meet with the attendees of the National Young Leaders Conference. I figured that meeting two out of three wasn't bad. My mission was accomplished. I called my mother, my father, and Anne that day to tell them what I had done.

I made my way home to Massachusetts and continued with the school year. Nominations would not be awarded until the start of my senior year. I'll never forget the day that my nomination came in. Gary, one of my two best friends, was going through the same process. He ended up with a nomination from Senator Kerry. My official nomination letter came in the mail from Representative Barney Frank. Looking back, it is so very ironic that an openly gay congressman provided me with my ticket to the Air Force Academy. But what is downright disgraceful is that an openly gay congressman can decide who has the chance to go to our nation's service academies, but an openly gay person is still not allowed to serve in the military.

A nomination wasn't the only task I had to complete just to have the privilege to apply to the academy. I also had to pass a physical fitness test. My mother helped me to schedule my test, which was to be held at a local high school in my area. The night before the test was a stressful one for me. I started having doubts. I was afraid of not passing. I was afraid the other candidates at the test would be faster and stronger than I was. The events were pull-ups, sit-ups, push-ups, a long jump, and a six-hundred-meter dash. Points were awarded for various levels of success in each event. There was a total of fifteen minutes for all of the events. I ended up passing, while some of the other guys actually failed the test.

Yet I was still not finished with all of the requirements I needed to apply to the academy. I had to be interviewed by an LO, or liaison officer. LOs are reserve officers who go to candidates' houses, interview them separately from their parents, and then make a decision about whether a candidate is right for the academy. LOs also determine if a candidate is merely applying to the academy to please his or her parents or is actually motivated to go. My nerves were acting up before the interview because I was embarrassed that we lived in a trailer. I told my mother that the shot-in-the-foot that would prevent my acceptance into the academy was our low-class status. I sulked and brooded over this for days. I asked my mother to call to see if we could do the interview elsewhere, which she did, but the academy insisted that the LO come to the candidate's home.

On the night of the LO interview, I was on edge. About an hour before he was to arrive, my mother put me on the phone with my grandmother, the pilot. If there was anyone who would motivate me to succeed through this interview, it was my grandma. I had looked up to her my whole life for all things aviation, so a conversation with her on this night was more than appropriate. "Listen to me. Stop being upset about this LO coming to the house. He doesn't care where you live," she said.

"But Grandma," I said, "the Air Force Academy is a place of class and distinction. This guy is going to see us and walk out of here laughing."

"Now stop it," she said. "The service—and I know this from experience—the service is a place that takes people from *all* walks of life. So many people have made the start of a new life in the military."

"But that's enlisted people, Grandma. This is the academy," I said.

"It doesn't matter," she said. "There will be all kinds of people at the academy. There will be kids from neighborhoods that aren't safe to walk in at night and there will be kids who are sons of congressmen. You need to focus on how you will do at the academy and forget about where you live. If you forget about it, so will the LO. Got it?" I knew she was right. She knew what she was talking about and she made sense to me. I got off the phone and felt calmness wash over me.

There was a knock at the door. It was my LO, dressed in a blue air force officer's uniform, authoritative and intimidating. I invited him in and introduced him to my mother and Allen. Mom and Allen said they would be at our next-door neighbor's to give us some privacy. The LO conducted the interview and it went very well. All of the fears that I had had were put to rest. I even asked him what he thought about my living in a trailer park. His answer was to ask me what *I* thought about it. I told him that I wasn't happy about it but that it didn't affect how I would excel in life. I did, however, tell him that the academy would be a great way for me to ensure I wouldn't live in a trailer park again.

After our interview, I called my parents back to the house and the LO spoke with them. To give them privacy, I left for the night to sleep at Gary's house. Gary had already had his LO interview so we compared notes about what was said and what happened. We were both pretty confident about our chances of getting into the academy. After all, we had both passed the physical fitness test, we both had nominations from our elected officials, we both did well in our interviews with our LOs, and we both had strong grades and extracurricular activities.

We completed our applications, with transcripts, essays, letters of recommendation, congressional nomination letters, physical fitness pass forms, and our LO letters saying that we were positive candidates for the academy. Now all there was to do was wait.

chapter nine

SAYING GOOD-BYE

On a sunny spring day during my senior year of high school, I walked home from school and into a trailer filled with balloons that said "Congratulations!" on them. Running toward me through the balloons was my mother. She gave me the biggest hug I had ever received from her. "Oh, Rick, baby! You did it. You got in!"

"To the academy?" I asked.

"Yes! To the academy!" she screamed. She was ecstatic. "I couldn't wait for you to get home to open the letter so I opened it myself. I hope that was OK." She could barely catch her breath.

"Yes, that's OK, Mom." I started crying and so did she. The weight of the world had lifted off my teenage shoulders. I fell on the floor in relief. I could hardly believe it. "Does Allen know?" I asked.

"Yes! I couldn't wait to tell him," my mother screamed. I thought of all the people I had to tell. First, I called my grandma. She cried for me in pure excitement and told me about the bright future that was ahead of me in the air force. I called my dad, who almost had a heart attack when I told him. He was so happy that he could barely speak. I called Anne.

"Yep, I knew you could do it. I had no doubt in my mind that you would get in. I am so excited. I love you," she said.

"I love you, too!" I yelled.

My life could not have been any better. I had an appointment to the Air Force Academy.

I called Ben Silverman. "Way to go, bone rack!" he yelled. "We're getting drunk together."

I called my friend Gary to find out if he had received any news. He told me that he got a letter saying that the academy could not offer him a slot this year. That baffled me. Gary had better grades than I did and he played baseball, basketball, and soccer. The only thing I had over Gary were more extracurricular activities, such as Greenpeace, school plays, and Amnesty International. From that point on in the school year, I didn't see much of Gary, other than when we passed each other in the hall. His not getting a nomination to the academy had caused some awkwardness between us.

I spent the remainder of my school year getting in shape. I worked out with Ben at the gym in Mendon and I ran almost every day. In the Air Force Academy acceptance package, there was ample information about how physically stressful basic cadet training was going to be. The Air Force Academy in Colorado Springs sits 7,258 feet above sea level. It takes a person's lungs two weeks to acclimate to the higher altitude and process oxygen efficiently throughout the body. People who push too hard before being in shape can develop a condition known as altitude sickness. Getting myself ready for basic cadet training was something that I absolutely had to do.

I started getting acceptance letters from other places that I had applied to as safety schools. I was offered admission to Worcester Polytechnic and the University of Massachusetts. I was often tempted to just give up my academy slot and attend one of these civilian schools instead. I was in for a challenge. With a 20 percent attrition rate between basic training and graduation day staring me in the face, the academy would be no easy place. At times, I was jealous of the other kids who were going to nonmilitary schools. I thought about how I would be in a uniform under constant surveillance all year while they would be partying and drinking and easing into their freshman years. I would be heading for eight first-semester classes.

But then I'd think about moving out of the trailer, and all of my fears went away. I was moving west, where, unlike much of the East Coast, there were still wide-open spaces. I would fantasize about Colorado and the freedom from the limitations of home. I thought about how great it was that I would never have to do another household chore for my mother and Allen. I would be on my own.

With the exception of my schoolwork, I became aloof, already with my head in the Colorado clouds. I kept my grades up to prevent the academy from withdrawing its admissions offer. With the exception of Ben and Anne, I really alienated my friends. I tried to visit Anne more in North Carolina and spent every day after school with Ben in Mendon, working out at his gym or hanging out at his house. After asking my friend Ellen to go with me, I even decided not to go to my senior prom about two weeks before the event. Ellen was devastated. I still do not believe that she has forgiven me for that. I was pissing people off left and right.

The last time I saw Anne before going off to the academy was when she came to Maine to spend a week with us at our summer home there. My report date to the academy was June 28, 1992, less than a month after my high school graduation. Anne and I had a fun week in Maine, but then we had to say good-bye. It should have been an emotional affair, but I was so focused on my upcoming basic cadet training that I didn't feel much when I said good-bye to her. "I'll see you on parents' weekend, right?" I asked. She assured me that she would be there.

The toughest good-bye happened the night before I left for the academy. I had to say good-bye to Ben Silverman. I didn't know how hard it would actually be, but I was dreading it. On the way to his house to say good-bye, I had already started crying. When I got there, I went inside, and we sat at his dining room table. "This is it, huh?" he said in a very sullen voice. He could barely look at me. At that moment I could actually tell how much he was going to miss me, too. I lost my composure for a second and tears poured out of my eyes.

I turned around, away from him, and said, "Maybe we should just say good-bye outside and I'll just go." He didn't move. I turned back to him. "Ben, man, I don't know how I'm going to do this!" I let it all out and started crying. He got up and walked over to me and put his big arms around me.

"Shh," he said. "This is what you wanted. You're going to live your dream. I'm behind you all the way." I cried harder. He continued, "I'm going to write you letters. I've never written anyone a letter in my life, but I'm going to write you." Nothing he said made it better. It was as if the more he tried to console me, the more I realized he loved me, and the more hurt I was to be leaving him. "Come on. Let's go outside and get you out of here."

"OK," I said. We walked outside to his driveway and stopped next to my car. "OK," I said again, trying to hold my tears back. Ben looked at me and I could see tears in his eyes. I lost control again and went toward him and we both hugged each other as tightly as we could. We both cried. He was not as loud as I was. I was screaming out in pain. He reacted to my crying by saying sweet things to me like, "Oh, man," and "Oh, God, I know it's hard," and "I hate this, too."

Just then, Ben's brother pulled up the driveway in his car. Ben's brother was older than Ben and, although he did not live at the house, he was there often. Ben made fun of his brother all the time for being overweight and dumb. They seemed to hate each other. Here Ben was, in his own driveway, hugging me, his best friend, both of us crying, with his brother pulling into the driveway to witness the entire scene. This was something Ben's brother could make fun of for as long as Ben was alive. I figured Ben would release me when he realized his brother was pulling up the driveway, but he didn't. He didn't care. He kept on hugging me and crying with me.

As Ben's brother got out of the car, he said, "Ben?"

"Get the fuck away from here before I break your face!" Ben yelled back at his brother, still hugging me and crying. His brother quickly left the driveway and went into the house. We cried for about an hour together on that driveway. As the sun went down and the temperature started to drop, I got into my car and drove away. I went into another crying fit on my way home and almost lost my voice from crying so hard.

"I love him, I love him, I love him so much! Why God? Why are you doing this to me? Why am I going through this? What is happening? I love him so much!" I cried this out—and even screamed it—a hundred times. By the time I got home, I was so tired that I went to sleep immediately. I can't say I slept like a baby, but I slept hard enough, and my body rested.

* * *

My parents woke me up the next morning; my mother had my bag packed and ready for me to take to the airport. All I was allowed to bring with me was a toothbrush, a change of underwear, a watch, the clothes I was wearing, and an eight-by-ten picture frame. I remember being very quiet that morning. My mother and Allen were kind of quiet, too. You could tell that they wanted to ease me onto the plane and prevent me from saying, "I don't want to go to the academy any-more. . . . It's too much pressure." But by then, this wasn't an option for me. I just wanted to leave home and follow the path I had chosen.

They drove me to Logan Airport that morning of May 27, 1992. They took me to the United Airlines terminal and dropped me off at curbside. I preferred it this way. I wanted to finally be on my own. I cried as I said good-bye to them. Memories of everything that they had done for me flashed through my head. Knowing that I was saying good-bye to my old life, forever, had already made me nostalgic. "We're so proud of you—yes we are," was the last thing I heard them say before I turned away and went into the airport.

I boarded my flight from Boston to Denver and saw a plane full of guys who looked like they were also headed to the academy, but then I thought I was just being paranoid. It wasn't until I arrived in Denver and walked to my connecting gate for the flight from Denver to Col-orado Springs that I found myself on a flight completely booked with incoming cadets. I felt immediately intimidated. *Did I look as athletic as they did? Could I compete with them?* They all seemed smarter, more athletic, and better-looking than me. The last leg of the plane ride was silent. I could feel the fear in each and every person on that plane. At that moment, something happened to me. This was the beginning of my becoming a cadet—a cadet like every other cadet. It was almost as if my instincts to blend in with the pack kicked in right away: no one else was talking on the plane, so I would do the same, and be one of them.

We arrived in Colorado Springs. According to our orders, we were to board buses labeled "Air Force Academy." Before I boarded one, I took a good look. It was a brand-new silver bus with very bold, well-kept writing on the side. The bus would take us to the Radisson Inn just outside the south gate of the academy. This was the day that all of the newly arriving cadets were brought from all over the country and kept in selected hotels nearby. When we arrived, I walked around the hotel. It was a zombie convention. No one was saying a word, even though there were about seven hundred of us there. This would be my last taste of civilian life. I would be catching an 8 A.M. bus for the U. S. Air Force Academy, one of the largest U.S. air force bases in the world. After all the planning and research, and simply trying to get accepted to the academy, I was still not prepared for what I would endure that next day.

I placed my small backpack on the floor next to my bed and threw away the underwear I was wearing since I had another pair that I had packed for my first day. I set my alarm clock, ordered a wake-up call, and went to bed.

chapter ten

IMPROCESSING DAY

My alarm went off, and before I had time to fully wake up, I was in the shower. I kept thinking, *This is the last time I will shower, brush my teeth, and get dressed as a civilian.* I had thought long and hard about the outfit I packed for my arrival at the U.S. Air Force Academy. I didn't want to wear anything that would look too dressed down since, after all, I was going to one of the most elite institutions in the world. I didn't want anything too dressed up because I might be singled out for being overzealous. For the brief time that I would get to wear these clothes, before they were stripped off me by the academy, I wanted to fit in and not stand out.

Brown khaki shorts, a green three-button polo shirt by Ralph Lauren, white tube socks pushed down to the ankles, and the Nike sneakers I had used to train for the physical challenges of the academy. With this outfit, and my small backpack thrown over my shoulder, I left my room and walked downstairs to have my last civilian breakfast in the hotel dining room. I had heard rumors that meals would be stressful at the academy, with the upperclassmen screaming at the basic cadets during each one, so I ate as much as I could that morning. Luckily, they had a serve-yourself breakfast bar, so I loaded up on scrambled eggs, waffles, cereal, biscuits and gravy, and lots of orange juice. I saw other arriving cadets in the dining room but they weren't eating as much as I was. I saw one guy with a bagel and a cup of coffee, as if he were going to a regular day of work after reading the morning paper. In stressful situations, I tend to analyze what everyone else is doing in order to figure out if I'm doing the right thing or if I'm completely overreacting. As I scanned the dining room, I noticed no one was saying a word. It was the same silence I had experienced on the flight from Denver to Colorado Springs.

I finished eating and took my last civilian pee. Then my heart started to pound. I headed to the front doors of the hotel. There was one of the huge buses with "United States Air Force Academy" written on the side. I was finally ready to put my life into the hands of this thing that I had worked so hard to be a part of. I looked at the bus and saw one guy board. Then another guy walked out of the hotel door, passed me, and boarded the bus. I just stood there, staring. There was a man dressed in a very well-fitting uniform stationed next to the door of the bus. Looking straight ahead, he did not even acknowledge when someone would pass him to board.

Without thinking about it, my body just moved. I started walking toward the bus. I stared at the uniformed guy as I approached. He didn't seem to notice me. I was waiting for him to stop me or to ask me if I was OK or if I knew that I was in the right place. But we all knew who we were and what we had to do. I walked past him and boarded the bus. There was another uniformed man in the front seat. He was a black guy with perfectly shined silver-rimmed glasses. He had white gloves on his hands and a scowl on his face. Instinctively trying to blend in, I went to the middle of the bus and took a seat. Across the aisle sat a guy who looked miserable. He had his head in his hands. I looked behind me and saw another guy with his head against the window and his eyes closed. Further back was someone who looked like he had been struck by lightning. He was stiff as a board, with wide eyes, and I could see that his jaw was tightly clenched. I sank down in my seat and looked at the seat in front of me. I had the feeling that I should be more frightened than I already was.

I had read as much as I could about what to expect at the academy, but nothing prepared me for that first day. Day one at the Air Force Academy is day one of basic cadet training—BCT. This would be no easy orientation day. The second I arrived, I would be starting BCT. Because of the pronunciation of this acronym, BCT had the nickname Beast. Beast was divided up into two stages, First Beast and Second Beast. I knew that First Beast would be conducted at the actual academy and that we would be staying in the dorms. This would last about three weeks. Then we would be taken out to the woods to a mysterious place called Jack's Valley, where we would live in tent cities we set up. During Second Beast, we would be subjected to the more physically demanding training lessons.

When the bus was about half full, the door suddenly shut. The two uniformed men were now seated at the front of the bus. As I peered over my seat, I could see the other guys peering over their seats also, to see what the two men up front were doing. They were sitting straight-backed, facing forward, motionless and silent. The bus pulled out of the hotel parking lot and continued up Academy Boulevard, onto Interstate 25 North toward the north gate of the academy. The ride up the highway took about five minutes, and soon we were exiting. We circled the long freeway off-ramp and headed toward a guard gate with flashing red lights along its roofline. There was a guard standing outside. The bus stopped and the driver spoke to the guard. They laughed and saluted. On my right, there was a sign that said, "Welcome to YOUR United States Air Force Academy." The bus started to move.

The second we passed that welcome sign, the two uniformed members at the front of the bus stood up and snapped around toward us, coming to life like carnivorous snakes who had been waiting for the right moment to attack their prey. We had crossed into Air Force Academy territory and we were now their property. I became aware of loud screaming and yelling before I could even understand what they were saying to us.

"Welcome to the United States Air Force Academy! Get onto the front one-third of your seats and do it now! Cage your eyes! If you do not know what it means to cage your eyes then one of us will be showing you! Do not look to the right or the left or down! Look straight ahead unless a cadre member tells you to look elsewhere! Drop your bags! There should be nothing in your hands! Your hands should be on your knees unless you are holding *this* book in front of you!" I looked up at the book that one of the cadre members was holding. It was a thin, blue book about four by five inches and about thirty pages long. The cadre member looked at me. "*Basic!* Did I tell you that you could look at me?" I shook my head. "Basic, can I get a 'No, sir'?"

"No, sir."

"WHAT? I can't hear you!"

"No, sir!" I said, more loudly.

"Sound *off!*"

"No, *sir!*" I said again.

"When I say 'sound off,' I mean to yell it out with all of your might! Now, did I tell you to look at me?"

"NO, SIR!" I yelled as hard as I could.

"Now that's what I'm talking about! You are all basic cadets! That means that you are only allowed to say one of seven things! Your seven basic responses are: yes sir, no sir, sir may I ask a question, sir may I make a statement, sir I do not understand, sir I do not know, and no excuse sir! Is that clear?"

"Yes, sir!" all the guys on the bus roared in unison.

"Basic!" The black cadre member yelled to someone at the front of the bus. "What are the seven basic responses?" Luckily this cadre member didn't ask me because I had already forgotten them. Whoever this kid was, he was either smarter than me or had been paying more attention than I had. Or maybe he had memorized these responses beforehand.

He rattled them off. "Yes sir, no sir, sir may I ask a question, sir may I make a statement, sir I do not understand, sir I do not know, no excuse sir."

"Good. Why do you think I asked you this?"

The poor guinea pig continued. "Because . . . "

"*Why?*" the cadre member yelled loudly.

The basic tried again, "Because . . . "

This time the cadre member got right in the basic's face. "WHY?" he screamed. "The response to any 'why' question is 'No excuse, sir' from here on out! If we say 'how come,' then you can give us a real answer as long as you start it with a 'sir'! Never, ever address any cadre member without slapping a 'sir' or a 'ma'am' onto whatever you're saying! Is that clear?"

"Yes, sir!" the bus roared.

"So, basic? WHY did I ask you that?" the cadre member continued to yell.

"NO EXCUSE, SIR!" the basic yelled back, finally understanding what he was supposed to do. My heart and all of the hearts of the other basics were pumping harder than ever. We hadn't even reached the drop-off point of the academy. We were still on the bus and were already being held to rules that didn't make sense. I started saying the seven basic cadet responses over and over in my head so that I wouldn't forget them. The two cadre members walked down the aisle, one handing out small blue books to each new basic cadet.

"These are your basic cadet knowledge books. You must learn everything in this book right now. Unless you are walking or being talked to, you should have this book in front of your face, reading and learning everything that is inside it. You will hold the booklet with your right hand. Get the books up in front of your faces." Blue books flashed up in front of everyone's faces. I put my book in front of my face. I had it opened, randomly, to a page that had the phonetic alphabet on it. Each letter of the alphabet had a word associated with it. I heard the brakes of the bus squeak, and we came to a stop.

"Let's go!" one of the cadre members yelled. "Grab your bag and get off this bus. Cage your eyes. If you stop moving as you are filing off the bus, you will have your knowledge in front of your face, studying it." We looked like idiots, bumping into each other in the aisle on the bus, half of us bringing our blue books back up to our faces and half of us putting them back down the second we started moving. The entire time we walked off the bus, basics were getting yelled at for not caging their eyes.

When my feet touched the ground, I immediately heard orders yelled over a megaphone by a female cadre member. She sounded meaner than the guys on the bus. "Find a spot and stand with your feet on footprints that are painted onto the pavement! Face forward! Drop your bag on your left-hand side! Do not gaze! Keep your eyes caged! Have your knowledge in front of your face!" The yelling was authoritative and annoying at the same time. To my left was a large ramp with a sign overhead that read, "Bring Me Men."

Among military institutions, the service academies are unique in that basic training is not run by enlisted drill sergeants but by actual cadets who have just recently been through it themselves. These cadets are one to three years older than the basics so they are a basic's peers—from their own generation. They don't have their authority because of their age, but because of what they know and the rank on their shoulders. A cadet training a basic cadet can be shorter, smaller, and of a different gender, but the basic is required to respect rank, no matter what. Being trained by peers who think in the same way that the trainees think is very effective; the trainer can identify with the trainees and more quickly break the trainee down.

Much of basic cadet training would be a mental struggle: learning all of the knowledge in the little blue book and enduring being hazed by the cadre when it was obvious that the knowledge had not been learned. I was more nervous about this aspect of Beast than I was about the physical demands. I had never been asked to think and learn under such pressure before.

I knew that I had to respect any cadre member in uniform but I wanted to learn what the bars and dots and chevrons on their shoulder boards meant. Standing there in formation while they lined up the other incoming basics, I subtly used one hand to turn the pages of the book until I found the page with an explanation of rank. It looked like a foreign language to me. All of the titles and names of ranks ran together.

Again, the female cadet started yelling into her megaphone, this time about spot corrections. "Cadet German and his team will be walking around to make spot corrections on the way you are standing!

You should have your chins pushed *in!* Your shoulders should go *up, back,* and then *down!* Your feet should be together at the heels and your toes pointing apart with a forty-five degree angle between your feet! Your hands should be cupped with your thumbs pointing downward, unless, of *course,* you are reading your knowledge! You are not even a basic unless you learn to *stand* like a basic!" she yelled through the megaphone. Suddenly there was a barrage of yelling. We were getting screamed at to do just what she had said. Trying to remember it all was impossible. I pushed my chin backward, which caused a sharp pain in my neck and back, and then my shoulders rolled forward. Then I was yelled at. As the cadet yelled at me for my first mistake, my eyes moved and I was yelled at for "gazing off into space." One of these screamers on Cadet German's spot-checking team of about forty cadre members saw that I was looking at the page with cadet ranks. He told me to put my knowledge down and to tell him the second-class cadet ranks. I froze.

"Well?" he yelled in my ear.

"Sir!" I yelled out.

"Sir? What the hell is that? Does that sound like the second-class cadet ranks to *you,* Cadet Wendy?" he asked another cadre member who was now on his way over to me.

"Uh, no it doesn't," Cadet Wendy said. He went on, "So, how long have you been looking at that page, *basic?*"

"For about fifteen minutes. . . . Sir! For about fifteen minutes!" I yelled.

"Fifteen minutes?" Cadet German asked and continued, "and you don't have it memorized yet?"

"No, sir!" I yelled.

From the megaphone came the words, "So, Einstein here has been staring at the same tiny page for fifteen minutes and hasn't even memorized it yet. You better get your asses in gear, people. Turn your brains on. You're at the Air Force Academy now, people. Wake up!" They walked away from me and went to the next victim, a girl who was looking at the phonetic alphabet page that I had been looking at before.

"Phonetic alphabet, go!" I heard one of the cadre say to her.

She began, "Alpha, bravo, charlie, delta, echo, foxtrot, golf, hotel, india, juliet . . ." As she miraculously, continued spouting off the phonetic alphabet, she was interrupted.

"Basic!" the female cadet yelled from the megaphone. "If you're going to recite anything from your knowledge you will start it like this! Ma'am or sir, depending on who you're talking to, the phonetic alphabet is as follows! Or, Ma'am, John Stuart Mill's quote is as follows! Or whatever we ask you to say!"

"Yes, Ma'am!" the female basic yelled out. She went on, "Ma'am, the phonetic alphabet is as follows . . . " She rattled off the entire thing right there, as if she had known it forever. This intimidated the hell out of me. Could she have actually learned it this fast? When she was done saying it perfectly, three upperclassmen swarmed around her. They started asking her how she knew it and how she had learned it so fast. They didn't give her a chance to answer, and their questions turned very mean.

"So, since you know the phonetic alphabet so well, I'm sure that everyone else here should know it too, right? I'm sure that you wouldn't learn the phonetic alphabet without making sure that your fellow classmates knew it too, right? Or are you *better* than the rest of your classmates?"

"No, sir!" she yelled out.

"Well, then I'm sure the rest of your classmates must know the phonetic alphabet." The upperclassmen started picking out individuals and asking them if they knew the phonetic alphabet. We had all been standing still in the hot morning sun for about forty-five minutes in a braced position by then. We were exhausted.

After each person answered, "No, sir," to the question about knowing the phonetic alphabet, they were made to get into the front leading rest—the cadre's word for the push-up position. Before long, every basic cadet was in the front leading rest, our arms numb from holding ourselves still. There stood the female cadet who was being scolded, alone, with everyone else on the ground. "Do you think it's fair that your classmates should have to be on the ground in such an uncomfortable position with you just standing here smoking and joking?" one of the upperclassmen asked.

"No, sir!" she said as her voice quivered. She was almost crying and the upperclassmen knew they were already breaking her.

"Do not lose your bearing, basic!" the female upperclassman yelled into her ear. "You cry right here and you will embarrass yourself, your class, *me,* and this whole academy! Before you want to outdo your classmates and *pimp them over,* think about it next time. Everyone to your feet!" We all got up as fast as we could and let out sighs of relief.

I had learned so many lessons about how to survive Beast in just my first hour at the academy. Again, the rule of thumb was to not stand out. The only way to really do well was to do well *with* everyone else. We would all have to organize and help each other out, I knew. But we weren't allowed to talk to each other, so how would we ever do it? "This flight is ready. March them up the ramp!" one cadre member yelled to another.

"Left! Left! Left, right, left!" someone started to yell to us. "Forward, march!" I was glad not to be in the front of the formation. I just followed the guy in front of me and made sure that my steps corresponded with the cadence, that my left foot was hitting the ground when I heard the word *left.* We marched up the ramp, under the "Bring Me Men" sign. Before my eyes was the Terrazzo of the Air Force Academy. It is called the Terrazzo because of the strips of terrazzo marble interlaced among the concrete slabs that make up the academy's very large quad.

We were marched up to a line of tables designated with letters that corresponded to our last names. Upperclassmen were yelling orders to us as if we were complete idiots, telling us to go to the table with the letter that began our last name and then to pick up our envelope and two green laundry bags. I did just that. Inside the envelope, I found a large card that had all of my clothing sizes pre-typed on it big enough for anyone to see. The card had a chain around it. The upperclassmen yelled out that we should hang these cards around our necks so that our sizes were visible. I did so. Also in the envelope were two cards that said "C-B" on them and that had safety pins through them. The upperclassmen yelled for us to safety-pin our cards to our laundry bags. I noticed that the card around my neck also said "C Squadron, B-Flight." When we were done with this, we were told to put our civilian bags into one of the laundry bags and to carry it with us.

Next, we were grouped together into formation again and marched into various buildings. Down the hallways were stations where we received various vaccines and injections. We were all too scared to speak at this point, so we took whatever shots they were putting in our arms without a fuss. I read my "knowledge" without even putting it down as I received some of my shots. At some of the stations we received sneakers. One particular sneaker station had a window in the hallway wall, behind which a couple of upperclassmen were working. They would throw our sneakers at us as hard as they could. At hydration stations we were forced to drink a Gatorade or a full bottle of water before we could move on. One of the stations had a box lunch and we were given about five minutes to eat it, while standing and facing a wall.

After about three hours of this, we were loaded up with every single thing that we would need at the Air Force Academy for the next four years. I had all my stuff in two laundry bags, from combat boots to dress blues to coats to fatigues to athletic equipment and clothing to a rifle that would be used for drilling. Some things were wrapped around my neck and some were draped over my shoulder and some I just held in the bag. My arms and body ached from carrying it all. The last line that I waited in was for haircuts. Basics filed into a room one by one to have their heads shaved. The barbers took about thirty seconds on each cadet. Just like that, all of my hair was gone.

I went to the bathroom just after I had my head shaved because one of the cadre had yelled for anyone who needed to use the "latrine" to do it then. I used the urinal and then when I went to wash my hands, I looked in the mirror. I remember being horrified at how I looked with a shaved head. My ears stuck out. My eyes were sunken in from being so tired already, and I looked like someone that even *I* would pick on for being so ugly. I was scared at what was going to happen to me in Beast just for looking ugly. I knew I would be singled out. Just after coming out of the bathroom, I was looking for the same cadre member who had been leading me around to all the stations. "Cage your eyes, basic!" someone yelled at me. I froze and a cadre member I had not seen yet came up to me. He looked at my polo shirt. "So what's up polo, are you looking for the country club?"

I thought, *Why is this happening to me right now?* Maybe it was because I had the idea in my head that I would be singled out. Now it was happening.

"What are you doing?" he asked.

"Sir, I'm looking for Cadet German. He is leading me around."

"Oh, well look at this, you're in C squadron, B-Flight. That's *my* flight. I'm Cadet T. David Stork. Don't you forget that name, got it?" he asked with a really strange smile on his face.

"Yes, sir!" I yelled. Cadet Stork led me back to my group and just as I joined the group, we picked up all of our things again and were led back out to the Terrazzo. There were cadre yelling things out from all directions. They were attempting to get the basics to come to the correct lines.

"If you are in C squadron, get over *here!*" I heard one cadre member yelling. I walked toward that voice. When I finally arrived, they were dividing us into flights. I found myself in a line of people who were also listed as "C-B" on their cards. I recognized Cadet Stork standing at the front of our line. I was looking at the other basics in my line, but at that point I was too exhausted to figure out if these were people I would stay with or if we would be shuffled again. I was just glad to be where I was supposed to be. I waited in line for another hour until all twenty-six "C-Bs" had been accounted for. Cadet Stork formed us into three lines and marched us to the dorms. As he led us down the hallway, he told us that if we saw our name on one of the doors, we should walk into our rooms and put our things down. I could not *wait* to find my room and to put down all the weight that I had been carrying.

As I walked, I saw two names on a door tag: Lamb and Lehmkuhl. This was my room! I walked in and put all of my stuff in the corner of the room. I waited a few seconds to see who my roommate would be. Suddenly, a red-headed, overweight guy walked through my door, sweating profusely. "Hi, I'm Patrick. Who are you?" I introduced myself to him and had a sick feeling in my stomach. Was he going to be a problem child? "Oh, my God," he started complaining, "I've never met a bunch of ruder people in my life. This place sucks. I don't know why the hell I came here."

"Shh!" I warned him. "Let's not talk so loud."

"But we can talk in our rooms. It's OK. They said it in the hallway. When we're in our rooms, we're at *rest*. That means we can move, talk, and do whatever we want. We just have to be at *attention* when we're in the hallways. Have you ever read the Bible?"

"What?" I asked.

"The Bible, you know, the Lord's book? Well, here it is." He pulled his Bible out of his green laundry bag and plopped it on the only side-table in the room. "It will help you if things get rough around here." I had no idea what he meant. I had been to church and attended Catholic schools and had even graduated CCD and been a confirmed Catholic, but I had never met someone my own age who kept a Bible handy to get them through a hard time.

"Thanks," I said, just to be polite. I started taking a good look at this guy; he was already grossing me out. He had blackheads popping out of his forehead. He smelled sort of bad, and kept blowing his nose into the same nasty handkerchief. Suddenly, Cadet Stork entered our room. At about five foot seven, Cadet Stork was short compared to me. He had piercing blue eyes and was kind of chubby. He talked with a slight lisp. I could tell that he had probably been picked on pretty hard in Beast and that this was his chance to get back at the world for what had been done to him.

"Are you two going to come to attention when an upperclassman enters your room? Or are you too good for that?" We came to attention. We stood straight up, with our shoulders back and down, our chins pushed in, our hands and feet in the proper position, and our eyes caged. "That's great, you two, but when a superior officer enters the room, you call the room to attention by saying, 'Room tench-hut!'" He yelled this so loudly that it shook me. It took me by surprise that he would yell so loudly, all of the sudden. "Now, why don't we try it? I'm going to leave the room again. You two start smokin' and jokin' and then I'll walk back in. Then you call the room to attention." I couldn't believe that this guy was going to take the time to do this after he had just explained to us what we had to do. He was actually having fun with this. He walked out of the room. We swayed back and forth for a minute waiting for him to come back in. He peaked around the door and said, "I told you guys to start smokin' and jokin'. When I hear you doing that, then we'll finish this drill." Then I *knew* that this guy was crazy.

"So how was your day today?" Patrick asked me.

I answered, "Well, it was one of the longest . . . " Just then, in came Cadet Stork.

"Room tench-hut!" Patrick yelled as loudly as he could. We both came to attention.

"Finally! Jesus. You two are not the brightest crowns in the box. Now, all basics need to change into issue underwear and socks and battle dress uniforms with combat boots. Then you need to put anything you brought with you from home into one of your green laundry bags and set it out in the hallway. Attach one of your many issued nametags to the green laundry bag. Anything on your body that was not issued to you today must also go, including your watch. No basic cadets can wear watches." Cadet Stork left the room.

We followed instructions and changed into fatigues, or BDUs— battle dress uniforms. We then packed up anything we had brought with us and put it out in the hallway. I kept the eight-by-ten picture frame that I had brought with pictures of my friends and family, and Patrick kept his Bible. Patrick was talking to me the entire time about how much he hated the academy already and how he was there for his father and not himself. I just wanted him to shut up. He was drawing attention to us after I had already drawn attention to myself when I got lost after peeing by the haircut station.

I looked at myself in the mirror. I was dressed like a soldier. I had on an olive-drab T-shirt, fatigues, and combat boots. My head was shaved. I had never pictured myself looking like this. My BDUs were already embroidered with my name: Lehmkuhl. It was amazing to me how all of this was ready for all one thousand plus basics who had entered the academy that day.

All of a sudden a girl came into our room. She was about five foot seven, and the barber had hacked off her hair. They didn't shave the girls' heads, but they gave them drastically short haircuts. "Hey, my name is Jodie," she said in a very serious way. I couldn't believe this girl was trying to be serious with me. She wore glasses and, in Beast, they take away a basic's glasses and issue them basic cadet glasses, or BCGs. It was no wonder that BCGs had the nickname "birth control glasses," because anyone who wore them looked absolutely hideous—like a cartoon character. I laughed at Jodie without meaning to. All at once, it hit me how subjugated we all were. We were all being made to look and act in this ridiculous way. I had to release my tension somehow and I did it on her. I just kept laughing with my hand over my mouth. "I know I look ridiculous," she said. I laughed even harder.

"How in the hell did you get *in* here?" I asked.

"Well, we're allowed to move from room to room. I asked if we could. We just have to be at attention in the hallways and put up with any upperclassman who walks by. We also have to *greet* any upper-classmen we pass."

"What do you mean by greet them?" I asked.

"Well, we have to say, 'Good morning/good afternoon/good evening, Cadet So-and-So, B-Flight!'"

"But what if we don't know their names?" I asked.

"Well, then we're screwed. Then we get hazed and yelled at for not knowing their names. But listen. We need to put our clothes and equipment away, but we all have to put it away the same way. We were issued everything from underwear to toothpaste. They don't care how it's put away, just as long as everyone in B-Flight does it the same way. I'm going to show you the way we're doing it so write this down. I'm going to all the rooms to tell people." We listened to Jodie and wrote everything down. She left the room and I felt happy to have met someone normal.

We quickly put our things away just as she said to. It was exciting to have something to do and to know that we were doing it right. This was the teamwork that the cadre yelled about when we were first getting off the bus. Looking at my watch before I gave it away to the upperclassman, I saw that it was about six o'clock. I was getting hungry. I knew they had to be calling us to eat dinner sometime soon.

chapter eleven

THE FIRST SUPPER

As hunger began to overtake me, I looked down at my watch again to see what time it was, but my watch was now gone. I peeked into the hallway to see if my green laundry bag was still where I had put it. Vanished. I didn't like not knowing what time it was. A few more minutes that seemed like hours passed, and then I heard the cadre yelling, "Out in the hallway. Get out in the hallway!"

"Oh, shit," my new roommate said, "here we go." We ran to the middle of the hallway and stood there waiting for others to join us. We stood at attention, looking like total idiots, until something like a single-file line had been formed. Was this what we were supposed to do? An upperclassman came around the corner of the hallway and saw us standing there.

"Oh, my God! What the hell are you doing? Against the wall! When we tell you to come out of your rooms, you will stand against the wall, at attention. You will all line up on each side of the hallway, in the same area. There should be no one standing in front of the alcoves. What is my name, basics?" We didn't answer. "I am Cadet Duncan. I am your flight commander and I control all of your cadre here in B-Flight." That was a name we needed to remember.

C Squadron, B-Flight was housed in rooms down two hallways that made an L shape. At the corner of the L sat a desk that was manned by an upperclassman. The hallway had indentations in the walls about every eight feet. Each indentation contained the doors to two different dorm rooms—the alcoves that Cadet Duncan yelled at us to not stand in front of. "And you two might want to join your classmates in the *other* hallway," Cadet Duncan added. Our section of the L had not been chosen for this particular form-up.

Patrick and I ran to the other hallway and saw our classmates against the wall, at attention, reading their knowledge. There was a space for two more next to one basic; I ran toward it and Patrick caught up and stood next to me. We were all crammed together, reading our small blue books. Patrick's nose was stuffed up and I could hear him breathing out of his mouth next to me, gasping for air. That small run from the other side of the hallway had winded him. I don't think he had trained physically for the academy at all.

"Lamb, close your mouth!" Cadet T. David Stork said as he approached us. "You sound like a freakin' animal! You can't be *that* out of breath already. How high is the Air Force Academy?" The question came as a yell.

Patrick tried to answer, pretending that he knew it before, but couldn't remember now, "Sir! We are . . . "

"Sir, the altitude of the Air Force Academy is as follows! Seven thousand two hundred fifty-eight feet above sea level! Far, far above that of West Point or Annapolis! *That* is how you answer that question!" Cadet Duncan had chimed in. "Lehmkuhl! How high is the Air Force Academy?!" I became stiff and almost choked up.

"Sir! We are . . . " I tried.

"No!" Cadet Duncan interrupted, then continued, "Sir, the altitude of the Air Force Academy is as follows . . . " waiting for me to complete the task.

I had it right this time, "Sir! The altitude of the Air Force Academy is as follows! Seven thousand two hundred fifty-eight feet above sea level! Far, far above that of West Point or Annapolis!" I had said it right.

"That's right!" Cadet Duncan continued. "Lamb here is breathing like a horse. I hope you all got in shape before you came here. Just because of the altitude alone, it will take two weeks until your body is able to adjust and process oxygen efficiently. The more we work on that up here, the faster that process will happen. Don't stand here in the hallway breathing through your mouths. We don't want to smell the breath of a bunch of dirty basics. You all smell bad enough as it is. Now, who has to go to the latrine? Stick out a paw!" Almost every basic in our flight put their hand forward with a clenched fist. I assumed this was "sticking out a paw," so I did it, too. "OK, run to the latrine and get back here immediately!"

We all ran down the hallway to the men's room in the direction that Cadet Duncan was pointing. We had four girls in our flight and all four of them ran to their bathroom. The urinals were crowded, and we had to wait in line to use them. I thought about how convenient it must have been for the girls to use the bathroom, since there were only four of them. I had to pee really badly. I finally made it to a free urinal, opened my BDU fly, and tried to pee. I couldn't do it.

I had never in my life had to urinate in such a stressful situation, around such a large group of people. Every time I had ever gone to the bathroom, even in a public restroom with someone standing next to me, I was able to perform the act pretty easily. For the first time in my life, I was pushing it out, but nothing would happen. I quickly became embarrassed because I had a strong sense that other guys were waiting behind me to use the urinal I was standing in front of. No matter what I thought of, I couldn't release. I buttoned up my BDU fly and walked back out into the hallway. I was in a daze, thinking about how I couldn't pee, completely thrown by it. I decided that it was the overall stress, but it didn't change the fact that I had still had to go in a very serious way.

We all formed back up in the hallway against the walls, reading our knowledge. The upperclassmen did a count and there were only twenty-five of us present. "Who is missing?" Cadet Stork yelled out.

"Sir, my roommate is still in the latrine," said Jodie Turner, the girl who had jumped into our room earlier.

"Who is your roommate?" Cadet Stork asked in a very annoyed way.

"Sir, my roommate is Jane Hemmings," Jodie answered. Cadet Stork ran over to Jodie and put his face in hers.

"I don't care what her first name is! When we ask you to talk about other basics, you address them as Basic Cadet So-and-So! Do you understand?"

"Yes, sir!" Jodie said. "Sir, Basic Cadet Hemmings is still in the latrine."

"Well, that's great!" Cadet Stork started. "I hope she's having fun in there while her classmates are waiting for her. Everyone in the front leading rest!" We all got down in the push-up position. We were extremely tired, hungry, and dirty from the day. "Now repeat over and over again, 'I am waiting for my classmate,' and you better sound off!"

"I am waiting for my classmate!" I yelled out as loud as I could, over and over in unison with all of the other basics in my flight. "I am waiting for my classmate!" I could hear others next to me screaming it louder than I was, annoyed that she was still in the bathroom. This went on for a good minute. My arms felt like they were going to fall off. One of the female basics, Carmen Brown, fell to the floor as her arms gave out. Cadet Hornick, a female upperclassman assigned to our flight and quiet thus far, came to life when she saw Brown fall to the floor.

"Basic Cadet Brown!" Cadet Hornick yelled. "Do not lie on the floor. Get back up in the front leading rest! And why are the rest of you silent? Continue yelling out that you're waiting for your classmate!" We continued yelling it out while Cadet Hornick yelled at Brown for being weak. My ears were ringing from all the yelling.

Finally, Hemmings came out of the bathroom, running down the middle of the hallway. "Hemmings!" Cadet Hornick yelled. "Basics do not get to run or walk in the middle of the hallway! You will walk to the right, as far against the wall as possible! Do you think you're at rest?"

"No, sir!" Hemmings stopped in her tracks. We were all still yelling that we were waiting for our classmate, in the front leading rest.

"*What?*" Cadet Hornick was furious. "Do I look like a *sir* to you?" Cadet Hemmings had called Cadet Hornick "sir" by mistake. It was actually an easy thing to do. Most of the people around us were men and only one in twenty cadre members was a woman.

"No, ma'am!" Hemmings corrected herself.

"We are waiting for our classmate!" we continued to yell.

"You know," said Cadet Hornick, starting to lecture Hemmings, who was still standing in the middle of the hallway while we were in the front leading rest, "it's not that difficult to tell the difference between a woman and a man. What are some of the differences, Hemmings?" The yelling went on and on.

"Ma'am!" Hemmings began. "The differences between a man and a woman are as follows. Women . . . have longer hair!" she yelled, but it had taken her ten seconds just to think of *that* difference.

"We are waiting for our classmate!" we continued to yell.

"No, Hemmings! Not at the Air Force Academy they don't!" Cadet Hornick yelled.

"We are waiting for our classmate!" we screamed louder and louder.

"Ma'am! Women have boobs! Men don't!" Brown yelled. This sounded funny to me, and probably to all of us, but we were so tired and annoyed at this point that no one even thought of laughing. We just wanted up.

"We are waiting for our classmate!" we yelled one last time.

"Get up!" Cadet Duncan yelled. We all got up from the front leading rest and formed back up on the wall. Everyone was breathing heavily and I could smell the sweat and anger coming from all the basics. "Get your knowledge in front of your face! This is the first day at the academy and you are already falling apart! What the hell is wrong with B-Flight, huh? Go down the hall and up the stairwell to the Terrazzo and form up in elements outside the stairwell door!"

As we got outside, we formed up into the same three lines that we were in when they had marched us into the dorms. Everyone was still breathing heavily. I could feel the heat coming off my body and from everyone else's. My BDUs were soaked with sweat around my armpits and around my thighs. "Now, you're going to learn to *dress and cover!*" Cadet Duncan yelled.

The three people in the front of each of the lines were the element leaders. They could stand still, but when he said "dress and cover," the element leader would turn around. Those behind that element leader would move forward if they were taller than the person in front of them, and move backward if they were shorter. Then, on "cover," we would look to our right, and move to the right if we were taller than the person to our right. When we were done "sizing," we would stretch out our right arms, turn our heads to the right, and space ourselves out so that that the three elements were one arm-length apart.

"Dress and cover!" he yelled. We followed his directions and did it well, but slowly.

"Good job. But next time, you'll do it faster. Remember where you are standing. This is where you will march for the rest of Beast. Unless one of you gets kicked out in our academy's twenty percent attrition rate, the people around you are the ones you will always see until the school year starts at the end of Beast."

I was not the element leader but I was first in line behind the first element leader because of my height—six foot two. Standing in front of me was Brian Bowman, two inches taller than I, with bleached-blond hair, tan skin, and a very muscular body. As the element leader, he would turn around often and face me. My nose came to his chin. His neck was muscular, like the rest of his body, and he was always sweating, like everyone else. I enjoyed it when he would turn around. Sometimes he and I would stare at each other and almost laugh. Then he would look away and answer the cadre if they were yelling at him to report the number present. It wasn't a bad position to be in for the remainder of Beast.

Once our flight was formed up, Cadet Duncan marched us to the middle of the Terrazzo where I could see, out of the corner of my eye, some upperclassmen dressed in full service dress by the flagpole. Our flight commander marched us into an opening between all the basic cadets who had arrived at the academy that day. We were all facing the flag. Cadet Duncan began a speech. "Basics! You are B-Flight, a part of C Squadron. There are *ten* Beast squadrons. Each squadron has *four* flights. Because you are C Squadron, B-Flight, that makes you the *sixth* flight of basics. A Squadron A-Flight would be number *one*. This means that, during the school year, you are in the *tenth Squadron*. Tenth Squadron is a squadron of honor! *I* am a member of Tenth

Squadron and so are the rest of the cadre assigned to you. Everything you do is a direct reflection on our squadron. But for now, you are part of *Barbarians* or C Squadron of Beast. Since you're B-Flight, we've come up with a nickname for you all that starts with a B. The nickname is *Battle-axe*. That's right, you are all the Battle-axes! Let me hear you say, "Good evening, Cadet Duncan. Battle-axe!'"

We all repeated. "Good evening, Cadet Duncan. Battle-axe!"

"Good job!" he said. "This is how you will greet any upperclassmen or cadre member that you see until the school year starts. Is that understood?"

"Yes, sir!" we roared. Other flight commanders in flights to our left and right were giving the same speech to their basic cadets.

Cadet Duncan went on as we stood at attention. "Now, I want to talk to you about the Oath of Office into the U.S. Armed Forces. It is where you swear, with your name, to become a member of the Department of Defense. It was explained to you in your application booklets that you would eventually be taking this oath. Get out your knowledge and turn to the page that is titled the "Oath of Office." Read it over for the next five minutes and let me know if anyone has any questions. I turned to the Oath of Office. As I read it, I began to understand how serious this was.

Oath of Office

I, (state your name), having been appointed an Air Force Cadet in the United States Air Force, do solemnly swear that I will support and defend the Constitution of the United States against all enemies, foreign and domestic, that I will bear true faith and allegiance to the same; that I take this obligation freely, without any mental reservation or purpose of evasion, and that I will well and faithfully discharge the duties of the office upon which I am about to enter, so help me God.

"You will need to memorize this and know it perfectly," Cadet Duncan yelled. "When you finish basic cadet training, you will be taking this oath and becoming a real member of the air force. We won't be taking that oath tonight, but you will participate in Taps. When I say "present arms," you will raise your hands to your brows and salute the American flag. Present . . . ARMS!"

I raised my hand and saluted the flag. "Cadre, make spot corrections! Basics, hold your salutes!" The cadre came around to each and every one of us to fix our salutes. There is a proper way to salute, with the part of the arm above the elbow held level and parallel with the ground. The bottom part of the arm, below the elbow, is supposed to be at a forty-five-degree angle from the ground. The hand and the lower arm should be in line, with no bend in the wrist. The flattened hand should be at a forty-five-degree angle from the forehead, with the notch of the straightened hand, between the index finger and the middle finger, resting on the very end of the right eyebrow. It took a few of us a while to do it, but after a few minutes, we all had the same salute.

"Order arms!" Cadet Duncan yelled. "That means put your salutes down and stand back at attention." Half of us had put our arms down at "order arms"—excluding myself. He called out "present arms" and "order arms" about one hundred times, until we all understood what to do when we heard those commands. Suddenly from the middle of the Terrazzo, someone yelled.

"*Group!* Tench-hut!" The entire Terrazzo fell silent. Then the voice said, "Present . . . ARMS!" We all saluted at the same time, including the cadre this time. "Taps" began to play off in the distance, more beautifully than I had ever heard it before. The flag began to be lowered in the sunset light. After the music stopped and the flag was down, the voice yelled, "Order! Arms!" We all put our hands back down to our sides in one crisp motion. I couldn't believe what had just happened. Seeing over one thousand people do this all at the same time, after being at the academy for only a day, was an intimidating and awesome sight. Everyone there had been whipped into enough shape that day to be in formation, dressed and covered, sized, at attention, quiet, and saluting the flag as if we had done it a hundred times. If this was the change in us from one day, what were the next six weeks going to hold?

The next thing I knew, we were marching, all ten squadrons—all forty flights—toward the dining hall. I was relieved because I was so hungry I couldn't stand it. I also still had to piss harder than ever. As we marched toward the dining hall, Cadet Duncan told us that we could run into the bathrooms that were located at the entrance to the dining hall. I couldn't wait. As soon as we got in the door, I saw the bathroom and beelined it out of formation with some others. I didn't want to risk not being able to relieve myself so I ran into a stall. I couldn't unbutton my pants fast enough and started pissing on the wall before I could aim at the toilet. Nothing had ever felt so good in my life.

I walked out of the bathroom and Cadet Stork was waiting for the basics who had gone in to relieve themselves. "All the bathroom basics can come with me and sit at my table. There are nine of you, so that's perfect." I was not happy to see him. I was going to have to eat my first meal with this jerk. I knew meals were complicated at the academy, and my first lesson on how to survive one would be with Cadet Stork. To make it worse, Hemmings had come out of the girl's bathroom and was at our table, too. Among others, we also had Brian Bowman, my blond element leader, and Devin Knight, who I would later learn was a football player who had been recruited to be a quarterback for the Air Force Academy team. Cadet Stork led us to our table. He sat his big, out-of-shape body at the head of the table. We were all standing in front of our chairs. He started grabbing food for himself from the trays that were in front of him. There were chicken strips, a large pot of mashed potatoes, some rolls, and some green beans. He served up his plate and began to eat, ignoring us. Brian Bowman decided to speak up and stuck out a paw. "Bowman, what?"

"Sir, may we please be seated at this time?" Brian asked.

"Wrong." Cadet Stork said, as he took another bite of mashed potatoes. We were all confused. No one knew what to do next. I had my eyes caged, but could see other basics seated and eating around me. I was hungry and started to get angry. We had had a full day and needed to eat, but this cadre member was not going to let us eat unless we did something to make him happy. I was getting angrier thinking about a leader taking care of himself before taking care of the people he was in charge of. I decided to sit down and see what would happen. I took my seat and the rest of the table followed suit to support me.

"NO! Get up. Who do you think you are, Lehmkuhl? You think you can sit down and eat when you want to? You're a *basic*. You're the lowest form of life there *is*." He said all this with his mouth full.

Hemmings tried. "Sir, may I ask a question."

"Nope." Cadet Stork was having fun with this. "You all better get out your knowledge to find out what you need to do at the table." By now ten minutes had passed. It was loud in the dining hall. I could hear yelling from every table. It was a miserable scene. We all pulled out our light blue books. I turned to a page called "Table Decorum," which explained that upon arriving to the table, a fourth-class cadet (or basic) should have three current events memorized in his head to tell the "table commandant." The fourth-class cadets were supposed to pour water for each member of the table and then give juice or milk, or both, to the upperclassmen. The cadets should memorize the drinks that every upperclassmen desired. I immediately grabbed the water pitcher from the table and started pouring water into ten glasses.

"Sir," I asked, "What kind of juice do you like?"

"Lehmkuhl, did you ask to ask a question or are you so special that you get to blurt out whatever question you want?" he answered.

"Sir, may I ask a question?" I asked.

"What?" Cadet Stork was annoyed that I had found exactly what I was supposed to be doing.

"Sir, what kind of drink do you like?" I asked.

He answered in a spoiled kind of way, "I like juice with *no* ice, and I hate milk." I poured him a juice with no ice from one of the three cartons on the table. It was a red berry–type punch. "OK. So the drinks are poured, so you can all sit down, since you don't have any current events yet. You haven't looked at a newspaper today, I'm sure." We sat down. I reached for the tray of chicken strips to pass to the rest of the table. "Lehmkuhl, put those down!" I dropped the tray. "Wow, you must be so hungry that you can ignore all table decorum." I was getting really angry inside. All of the basics that I could see around me were eating. "First of all, you should all turn your plates so the eagle is on the top. You should be staring at your eagle for the entire meal. If you want the chicken, then you ask, 'Cadet Stork, sir, may I make a statement?' Once I answer, then you say, 'Sir, please pass the chicken strips for the basic cadets at the table.' Then I'll pass them." Devin Knight decided to ask for the chicken.

"Sir, may I make a statement?" he blurted out.

"Yes," Cadet Stork answered.

"Sir, will you please pass the chicken strips for the basic cadets?" he asked.

"No, I won't!" Cadet Stork replied, "and you want to know why? Because you can't ask for it the right way. That's not a question. It's a statement. There is no 'will you' at the beginning of the sentence, and you forgot the 'at the table' at the end of the statement." Now I was seriously angry that this guy wasn't letting us eat, so I decided to ask.

"Cadet Stork, sir, may I make a statement!" I yelled.

"Oh, are you angry, Lehmkuhl? You look angry to me," he said. I didn't answer. I just stared at my plate. Brian tried to ask.

"Cadet Stork, sir, may I make a statement?" Brian asked.

"No, you can't." Cadet Stork said with a smile, still looking at me. "Lehmkuhl is upset, so I don't think it's a good idea for any of you to eat on an upset stomach. Why don't you all down a glass of water to make sure you're hydrated, and then fill your glasses back up?"

"Yes, sir!" we all followed order and drank a glass of water and then filled our glasses again.

"Hmm. I think Lehmkuhl is still upset. Let's cool our stomachs down a little more with another glass of water. Maybe that will fill you all up and make you less cranky." We all drank another full glass of water and refilled our glasses.

Just then, some cadre member said, "The evening meal is complete," over a PA system. Just after she announced this, I heard chairs backing up all over Mitchell Hall, the dining facility. Cadre members were making their basic cadets get up. They had all eaten but we had not.

"OK, get up. You're done," Cadet Stork said. None of us moved. We were stunned that we hadn't gotten to eat. "I said get up!" he yelled. We all snapped to attention. He filed us out the door of the dining hall and formed us up with the other members of B-Flight. We were marched back to the dorms and told to shower and go to bed. I didn't even know what it meant for us to shower. How would we get to the showers? Where were they? What if I didn't remember an upperclassman's name on the way to the shower?

Finally, the upperclassmen walked up and down the hall yelling, "Put on your issue bathrobes, and grab your issue shampoo and your issue soap. Put on your issue flip-flops. Grab one of your issue towels. Walk to the shower, take one, and go to bed. You have a *huge* day tomorrow." I did what they said. I put on my bathrobe, grabbed my shower gear, and walked, at attention, toward the shower. Luckily, I didn't pass any upperclassmen. I followed two other basics. I went into the shower; it was a large open room with six nozzles coming out of the walls: three on one side and three on the other. There was a line of guys waiting to get to the next open shower. As one nozzle freed up, that guy would walk toward the dressing area where he had hung his robe, dry off in front of everyone, and leave.

I heard the piercing sound of a whistle in my ear. It was Cadet Stork. He walked into the shower room with a whistle and yelled out, "Every time I blow this, you have to move to the next shower nozzle! When you get to the last shower nozzle, you're done!" Now Cadet Stork was controlling every aspect of our *showers*. He stood there looking at his watch, blowing his whistle every fifteen seconds. We each had a minute and a half to shower. He blew his whistle until every basic was rushed out of the shower. I went back to my room feeling barely clean. Patrick was still in the room.

"Why didn't you go shower?" I asked.

"I'm scared to go," he said with a look of shame on his face. I didn't say anything back. I understood that he was scared to go. At least he was able to eat that day and was able to think more clearly than I was thinking. I couldn't even think about how I was going to sleep. I knew they had issued sheets and blankets to us, but I was afraid of how they were supposed to be placed on the bed. I couldn't think to look in the blue book to find out how, because I was too hungry.

"Shut your doors, it's time for bed!" I heard the cadre yelling. We shut our door and I turned off the light. I climbed up into my bed, wrapped in my robe, and fell asleep.

Out of nowhere, I heard a knock on the door. "Come in," Patrick said. The door opened and it was Cadet Duncan. He flipped a switch and the two huge, overhead fluorescent lights flickered on. I could barely open my eyes.

"No, no, no," he yelled, "basic cadets are not allowed to just sleep any way they want! You *must* make your bed the correct way. There is a full description in your knowledge books on how to do this. No one is going to bed until all the beds are made properly." He left our room and knocked on the door next to us. Other cadre started knocking on doors and waking up the other basics, yelling for them to make their beds properly.

I had never made hospital corners in my life. Patrick told me that his dad was in the navy and had shown him how to do it and that he would help me. I was delirious. I was so hungry and tired that I could barely stand up. We looked in the book and started making our beds. The blue wool blanket had to go over the top white sheet and the white sheet had to have a perfect five-inch fold over the blue blanket. Trying to get it this way was ridiculously tedious and time-consuming. We spent another hour making our beds and I lay down on the floor of the room. About fifteen minutes later, Cadet Duncan walked back in.

"Room tench-hut!" Patrick yelled. I jumped up from the floor and stood at attention. Cadet Duncan inspected our beds.

"This is satisfactory, but we'll work on it some more tomorrow," he said. "Goodnight." Those words were magic to my ears. I couldn't wait to collapse. I didn't want to mess up the job that I did on my bed, so I stayed wrapped in my robe and climbed up into my bed, on top of the covers. I was almost asleep when I heard Patrick crying in the bed adjacent to mine.

"Oh, man, what's wrong?" I asked, as if I didn't already know. If I had had something to eat and had a little more energy, I probably would have been crying, too.

"I can't stand it here," he cried.

"Well, I can't either, but this isn't the academy. We're just in basic training. It's going to be like this for a while, and then we'll be able to walk around freely like the upperclassmen do," I explained.

"Yeah, but I don't even want to be in the real academy. I don't want to be like the cadre. Those are the worst people in the world. They're awful!" He went on to complain about everything we had been through that day, crying with almost every word he spoke. I knew it was going to be a challenge to get him through all this, but I knew I couldn't help him right then. I was to exhausted and I just needed to sleep.

There were no locks on the doors at the Air Force Academy until our sophomore year, when there was policy change to include doors that locked, with each cadet possessing his or her own room key. Everything was done on the honor system, including trusting that no one would break into an unlocked room and steal something. Since there were no locks on the doors during my freshman year, anyone could just walk in on a cadet, who might be in the middle of anything that one does in his or her room. Just as I was drifting off to sleep again, our door opened and closed really quickly. I was in my bed, which was set up like a loft over my desk. Patrick had a similar unit on the other side of the room. I looked down from my bed and saw Jodie, the girl who had come into my room before, climbing up the ladder toward my bed.

"Hey," I said, half-awake, no energy in my voice.

"Hey," she said, "I brought you these from the dining hall. I heard what was happening to you guys. You were at the table next to us and even Cadet Hornick, who was at the head of our table, was commenting on what a dick Cadet Stork was being. I took some chicken strips while no one was looking. I only have two for you because I got some for everyone who was at that table. I shoved them into my BDUs as we were leaving. I know you must be starving so I'll steal some more stuff for you tomorrow." Jodie was my savior that night. I got to eat two chicken strips and they tasted amazing, even out of the crumpled-up paper towel that she brought them in. I ate them immediately after she handed them to me and she climbed down my ladder and walked out of the room. I lay there thinking about how grateful I was to eat something. I thought about how quiet it was in the hallways. I couldn't hear any yelling or sounding off. The two chicken strips must have given me a burst of energy because I felt awake again, as I thought about everything that I had learned that day and what I would need to remember for the following day.

We had no control over anything anymore. We were treated like babies. The only control we had was to help the other members of our flight. Jodie was doing that for others and me. I found that fascinating. Her bringing me that food inspired me to help out my roommate a little more the next day, too. We were all going through separate struggles, so supporting our classmates was a key element to survival. Also, I noticed that no one had been yelled at for supporting another classmate. Supporting someone else was a free move that I could make. I decided to concentrate more on helping others, and trusting that doing so would help me to improve on all that I needed help with.

My first day at the Air Force Academy was finally over. I was a little beat up, but I was alive and hadn't been asked to leave. For a brief second, before I actually fell asleep, I had a positive thought in my mind . . . that I could *do* this.

chapter twelve

FIRST BEAST

I was sound asleep for hours, but it felt like five minutes. No amount of sleep would have made up for the first day of Beast or prepared me for day two. I could hear church bells playing outside my door that suddenly sounded louder and more sinister. The upperclassmen were blaring the song "Hell's Bells" by AC/DC. They had it playing into the hallway on the loudest stereo system possible. No song could wake a person more harshly than "Hell's Bells." The evil beat and music coupled with the screaming voices in the song created a nightmare in my head. Shortly after the song started beating really hard, the cadre began running up and down the hallways banging and kicking on our doors and screaming "Get up. Get up! Get the hell out of bed. Get your boots on. Get your BDUs on. Get out in the hallway, now!"

Adrenaline rushed through my body. I jumped out of bed and started putting on my BDUs from the day before. I became aware of how fast I was moving. I wondered if others were already in the hallway before me. *Was I moving too slowly? Was I lacing my boots up fast enough?* My bones ached from my first day there.

"Get out here *now!*" they yelled, repeatedly.

"Let's go, let's go," Patrick urged. His boots were unlaced and his shirt unbuttoned. "You think we should run out there undressed?" he asked.

"No way," I said. I finished lacing my boots and buttoned my shirt, and, together, we ran out into the hallway. There were already five basics on the floor in the front leading rest. The music was so loud in the hallway that we could barely hear ourselves joining into the chant, "I am waiting for my classmates! I am waiting for my classmates!" The cadre members were banging harder on doors.

"Open these doors! Open them *now!*" Doors flew open all the way down the hallway. Within thirty seconds, all twenty-six of us were in the front leading rest position in the hallway.

"Get up against the wall" Cadet Duncan yelled. The cadre walked up and down the hallway inspecting our uniforms. More yelling ensued. Questions of why boots were not laced and why shirts were unbuttoned were answered with all the wrong responses—any answer to a *why* question was supposed to be answered with a "no excuse, sir," or a "no excuse, ma'am." At 05:30—or 0-dark thirty, a common military term for any early morning call time—no one could remember this simple rule.

We were marched out to the Terrazzo for reveille formation. This formation worked just like Taps formation had the night before, except the flag was going up instead of down. We went through the same drill of saluting until the ceremony was over. We were marched to the dining hall again for breakfast. My stomach had already shrunk so much that I wasn't even hungry. As we approached the dining hall, Cadet Stork ran up to me and put his face in mine. "Are you less angry this morning, Lehmkuhl?"

"Yes, sir!" I yelled.

"Oh! So you *were* angry with me yesterday! You're admitting it!" he said with an evil smile.

"No, sir!" I yelled. He gave me a look as if to say, "I've got your number." This was already turning into a bad morning.

"You'll be at my table again this morning, Lehmkuhl," he said, as he walked away from me.

Brian Bowman, who was marching in front me, said, "Hang in there," under his breath.

"Steal me some food from your table," I whispered.

"OK, I will," Brian whispered back. The meal went the same way it had the night before, except we had a whole new group of people at the table who had not yet experienced the wrath of fat Cadet Stork. I poured his drinks and the waters for the table and got us all seated. I asked for the food in the correct way and actually had everyone's plates filled with pancakes, eggs, bacon, and bread. Cadet Stork found any way he could not to let anyone at the table take a single bite. We were forced to drink several glasses of water while Cadet Stork stuffed his face with food. Finally, the meal was over and we had to get up, leaving our plates and the food on them completely untouched. I wondered if I would have to endure two more meals that day with Cadet Stork because, if I did, I didn't know if I would be able to even stand up by the end of the day.

We marched back to our room and the cadre told us to change into physical conditioning, or PC, gear. This meant putting on an issue USAFA T-shirt, and issue blue shorts, white socks, and sneakers. The cadre members were also yelling for us to put on our wet belts—green belts, about four inches wide, with a canteen attached to them.

No matter what, we all had to look exactly the same. We formed up in the hallway looking like complete dorks. The people wearing BCG glasses looked even more ridiculous than the rest of us. I could tell that I was not alone in having to put my knowledge book up in front of my face to keep from looking at anyone across the hallway from me and laughing. After plenty of training and yelling at us, the cadre formed us up and ran us, in formation, down to the athletic fields. We ended up on the Astroturf field, the football team's practice field. The athletic facilities at the academy are state-of-the-art. Its workout facilities, fields, field house, gymnasiums, and pools are the academy's pride and joy and beautifully constructed.

All the basics and our cadre were now on the field. When we were in athletic gear, the cadre would change out of their intimidating blue uniforms, white gloves, and wheel hats, and put on BDU pants, combat boots, white USAFA T-shirts, and blue berets with a metal propeller-and-wings symbol on the front. They looked even meaner while dressed like this than they did in their blues.

All thousand of us were lined up, dressed and covered on this field, and were made to do various physical training exercises, including jumping jacks, push-ups, sit-ups, and running in place, while periodically stopping to drink from our canteens. One guy, standing on a high podium with a megaphone, led the session.

We would run to the athletic fields for physical training, or PT, early in the morning, but it was still hot. Small increases in temperature felt like huge jumps here because of the altitude, and four or five basics would pass out at each PT session from heat exhaustion and dehydration. I learned in my first few days there that I needed to continue to drink lots of water. Cadet Stork made sure of that at the meals I would have to sit with him.

I would usually get stuck sitting with him for about one or two meals each day for the duration of the three weeks or so of First Beast. Other basics would steal food for me, but it wasn't a nutritious way for me to eat, since I could only have whatever they would stuff in their pockets. I could never steal food for myself because Cadet Stork was always watching me so closely. As other cadets began to get stronger as the weeks went on, my body became more and more emaciated. I was burning more calories than Cadet Stork was letting into my body. Besides a new aversion to urinating at urinals with other guys next to me, I developed a strange reaction toward other people when I was actually able to eat. Throughout basic training, there were some activities when box lunches were served, or when we were allowed to eat at rest in a place other than the dining hall. I would become very quiet when I received my food, turning away from people as if someone was going to try to take the food away from me, and I would eat it very quickly. If I saw others leaving food in their boxes, I would ask them if I could have it. I would either eat it right there or store it in my pockets for another time. I became obsessed with looking for and storing food.

I also became obsessed with saving my energy. Whenever I had the chance to sit down, I would. When I sat, I would put my head between my knees and try to sleep. Not being fed during basic training was taking a toll on my body. I had never before worked so hard, physically, and here I was being denied even half the food that I was able to eat at home. The hunger would also cause a great deal of mental frustration and I would have to concentrate to put it out of my head. I wanted to lash out at a cadre member or cry to someone to *please* let me have some food, but I knew that this would be the end of my basic training experience and me. I would be singled out even further, and run out of Beast by the cadre.

Others were being singled out in other ways—I was not the only one. Anyone who was overweight was made fun of constantly by the cadre: it didn't matter if the basic was male or female. A basic who couldn't finish the run from the athletic field to the cadet area, after a training session, would be hazed by the cadre and then by their own basic roommates back in the dorms. I kept up with the runs and, less enthusiastically, with learning my knowledge, but the lack of food made it very difficult. To me it made sense to expect the most out of the basics, but to expect the best while denying them the basic necessity of food seemed very wrong. I kept my head low and decided that I would do what it took to make it through basic training.

First Beast lasted about two and a half weeks, just three days short of the three weeks I thought it would. Besides the regular hazing at three meals per day, we were taken to PT every morning. We went on long runs every afternoon to acclimate our lungs to the altitude. During all of this, the cadre would constantly attempt to scare us by telling us that First Beast was easy compared to what we would endure as part of Second Beast.

Each day of First Beast included drill practice. Either our flight commander, Cadet Duncan, or another cadre member from B-Flight would take us out on the Terrazzo and teach us the maneuvers of marching, including stopping, quick-time marching or marching in place, turning in formation, flank movements in formation, and eyes right. We also marched with our rifles. We were taught to present arms and order arms with our rifles. The cadre organized competitions for the different flights to see which were the best at drilling.

A few hours were set aside every day for athletics. We were actually released each day to do an assigned sport. We had no choice as to which intramural we would get to play. On the second day of Beast, one of the cadre members came by my room to tell me that my sport was cross-country. Therefore, every afternoon, when we broke from training to do intramurals, I would have to run even more. By the end of the two and half weeks, I had probably lost about twenty pounds. While most of the other cadets were getting bigger and more muscular, I looked like a skeleton. My bones were suffering from all the running and the lack of food. I had painful stress fractures in my feet and shins. I would occasionally ask a cadre member who was overseeing intramurals if I could see a doctor. The doctors sent over to me would tell me that there was nothing they could do about it—that stress fractures were part of all the physical strain I was putting on my body. "Try to take it easy," the doctors would say. They would walk away and I would just laugh to myself at what hell I was in.

There were some downtimes when we could relax. The cadre gave us a half hour per day to write letters home. I would spend this time sleeping and trying to save up as much energy as possible for the next round of physical activity. There was also "element time," when an upperclassman would sit down with each of three elements to talk with us about what it meant to be in the air force. This happened for about an hour per day. I was often yelled at during this time for sleeping. The cadre always caught me trying to shut my eyes for a little rest.

Each day became routine and, after two and a half weeks, even I was ready for a change of pace. I didn't care if the incoming Second Beast cadre were going to be meaner than the First Beast cadre. I just wanted the chance to work with different people.

The morning that marked the end of First Beast finally came. We were told to get up and put on our issue dress blues. It was Meet Your Sponsor Day. Every incoming basic at the Air Force Academy is assigned a sponsor, a family in Colorado Springs that signs up to be part of the cadet sponsorship program. On this day, we would be marched down the "Bring Me Men" ramp. Our sponsors were assigned a certain time to pick us up. They would then take us home, have a relaxed meal with us, and let us spend the night there. It was a perfect chance for basic cadets to meet up with their families, girlfriends, and boyfriends. Before I entered the academy, my parents had found out about Sponsor Day and bought tickets to fly out to see me. I was so excited to see them.

We were marched down the ramp, and there was my new sponsor mom, standing in front of her car with a sign that said, "Lehmkuhl."

"If you see your sponsor, you can go to them now!" the cadre were yelling. I ran out of formation to my sponsor. She was short, with short blonde hair. I walked up to her, smiling, and put out my hand for her to shake.

She shook my hand firmly and said in a British accent, "How are you doing? I'm Tara—Tara Dale." Each basic was given a piece of paper that we had to have our sponsor family sign. I had her sign the paper and brought it back to Cadet Duncan, who was waiting at the front of our flight. I saw other cadets from B-Flight heading toward their sponsor moms and dads. The smiles on everyone's faces were wide and genuine. There was a happy energy in the air. It had not yet registered that I would be leaving the academy for a full twenty-four hours.

I ran back to Tara and she said, "Here, get in the car. Let's get your butt out of here." She grinned. I got into the backseat of her Jeep Cherokee. Tara sat in the front passenger seat next to a man in uniform. I swallowed heavily when I saw the blue air force uniform.

"Hi!" the man said with a smile, "I'm Bob Dale, Tara's husband. We're your sponsors."

"Is that a lieutenant colonel symbol on your shoulder?" I asked.

"Yeah, but I don't want you to freak out," he said, "since I'm just a dentist for the air force. I went in on the medical corps so I'm not all hardcore or anything." They were making me feel totally at ease. "There's a surprise waiting for you back at our house," he said. I didn't know if they were talking about my parents. Maybe they didn't know that I already knew that my parents were going to be there, along with Anne, so I didn't say anything.

"So, you have a British accent. . . . How did you two meet?" I asked.

Tara answered, "When Bob was stationed in the UK for a while, we met there and got married. Then I moved back to the States with him."

"Wow, that's great!" I said. "Good for you two."

"We don't live far from the academy; we're near downtown Colorado Springs and we're almost there," Tara said. I was so excited to be in their car and away from the academy, I didn't care how long it was taking to get to their house. Anyplace was better than being in training. I wondered how crazy I must have looked to this very hip, cool couple. I was skinnier than I had ever been. I was whiter than a ghost from being in uniform every day, and I had a shaved head. I was humbled that they were so nice to come and pick me up and that they would be so cool to someone who looked so pathetic.

We pulled into their driveway. They had a great house on a quiet street. The house was old, probably built in the 1920s, and it was large, with a nice front porch. It was painted yellow with white trim. I opened my door and pushed myself out of their car and when I looked up, I saw the best sight I had seen in two and half weeks. I saw my mother, Allen, and Anne standing on the Dales' front porch. I couldn't control my emotions. Tears started pouring from my eyes. My loving family was there to see me. My girlfriend Anne had flown herself out from North Carolina to be there, too. My mom was the first one to run down the stairs and hug me. We hugged for a while and cried on each other's shoulders. I know they saw how thin I looked and were probably wondering why. I went to Anne and hugged her for a long time, ending it with a kiss. Then I walked up to Allen.

"How ya doin', buddy?" he asked in his Boston accent. He used to ask me the same question every day at home and it was wonderful to hear it again. My heart and soul filled with warmth just from being around them. After going through First Beast, the idea of anyone being gentle or loving toward me was completely foreign and I didn't know how to handle it. I almost felt as if I didn't deserve it.

We walked into the house and my mom told me that she had brought me some civilian clothes to wear around the house. She packed some of my favorite jeans and sweats from home, along with some of my old, comfortable T-shirts and socks, and a sweatshirt that I loved to wear. I asked if I could change out of my uniform right away. "Of course you can, sweetie," my mom said. I went straight into a bedroom that they had set up for me and changed. I walked downstairs and sat down in the kitchen at a large table with everyone. I felt like a human being again. "That's better!" my mom said with a smile.

"So what do you need?" Tara asked. "We have everything. Your mom told us all of your favorite cereals and lunch meats and fruit, and we bought them *all*." The idea of someone offering me food to eat, and for that food to be among my favorite foods, caused me to break down. Food had been my biggest stress since I arrived at the academy. I had tears in my eyes again. Everyone was staring at me.

"What's wrong, buddy?" Allen asked.

"I'm going to leave you with your family," Tara said, and walked out of the kitchen. Bob followed her out.

"Do you want me to leave for a minute, sweetheart?" Anne asked. Anne was always so smart and gracious. She seemed to always know what to do and say. She was raised as a real lady.

"Could you please, Anne? Just for a second?" I asked politely with tears in my eyes. She nodded with a smile and walked out of the kitchen to leave me with my mother and Allen. He was sitting across from me and my mother was sitting to my left, at the end of the table. I had my arms on the table and my mom grabbed my hands.

"What is it?" she asked. I teared up again and told them how much it meant to me that they were there and how much I loved them and missed them. They weren't getting too emotional and I could tell that they were afraid that I was going to tell them that I was going to quit basic cadet training and the academy. I had no intention of doing such a thing and I made that very clear to them. I went on to tell them about Cadet Stork and how he had been starving me for the past couple of weeks. I explained to them that how I looked was not normal and that other cadets didn't look skinny like me. They were furious and asked if there was anything they could do. I told them that, after this Sponsor Day outing, I would be going back to do Second Beast and that I would arrive to a completely new set of cadre. Cadet Stork would be gone. Allen, especially, didn't understand what I was telling him. He told me about his time in the army, when he was in basic training and how meal time was their only free time—when they weren't hazed. They were allowed to take as much food as they wanted as long as they ate it all.

"Take what you want, but eat what you take," Allen explained, was their motto. He asked me how they expected me to perform in basic training if they weren't feeding me. I tried my best to explain the system, but he still found it wrong.

"Well, we're going to spend the next twenty-four hours filling you back up," my mom said. "We're going to give you lots of pasta and carbohydrates so that you can store up some energy and start Second Beast the right way." I loved my parents so much. They always knew how to make me feel better. "You should spend some time with Anne, too. She flew out to see you, honey, and we won't be mad if you two want to be alone. I'm going to get Tara in here and we're going to have a blast cooking for you. How does that sound?" I nodded and smiled. The love I felt for my mom had never been as great as it was at that moment. She was being strong for me, and although I could tell that she was in some kind of back or leg pain, as always, she didn't talk about it.

I pulled myself together and walked out into the living room. Anne, Tara, and Bob were all sitting on the Dales' big overstuffed sofas, talking. I walked over to Anne and reached for her hand. She smiled, grabbed my hand, and got up. I hugged her. "Do you want to go for a walk?" I asked.

"Yeah, I'd like that," she said in a very matter-of-fact way. "Excuse us," she said very politely to Tara and Bob. We walked out the door to the sidewalk and turned left. I held Anne's hand as tightly as I could.

"Thanks for giving me all that time with my parents. I needed that," I said.

"Don't even think about that. I'm glad you were talking with them," she said. Anne was always so selfless.

"I'm sorry I look like this," I said.

"Like what?" she asked.

"Oh, you're being very polite. I look like a freak, Anne!"

"No, you don't!" she said firmly. "You're still the hottest guy in the world, no matter what you say. And there isn't anything they could put you through at that academy that could change that." She was so reassuring and firm in what she was saying. I believed her and felt better almost immediately. Anne was much shorter than me, so I leaned down and kissed her on the top of her head.

"I love you so much," I said. "You make me feel so good all the time."

"I love you, too. I've loved you since the first day we laid eyes on each other on that trip to Europe," she said. "I'm here for you." And Anne *was* there for me. In the past two and half weeks, the basics were taken to the mail room every day, and every day there had been one or two letters sitting in my mailbox from Anne. There was also always a letter from my mom. The letters from Anne counted down the days until the school year would start and basic cadet training would be a thing of the past. She would always write, "Think positive" at the bottom of her letters. My mother's letters would usually tell simple stories of what was happening at home or how her garden was doing. Her stories gave me a mental break from the academy. Every time I found mail from Anne or my mom, my heart would warm up and it would bring a smile to my soul.

As we walked, I explained to Anne what Cadet Stork had done to me and how he had kept me from eating. I told her some of the funny stuff that happened in training that was a little too dirty to tell my parents. I told her about a typical day of basic training and she laughed at some of the things I told her. When she laughed, I laughed, thinking about how ridiculous it all was. During our conversation, the world at the academy that I had been taking so seriously quickly came back into perspective as the crazy, temporary place it really was.

We returned to the house. My mother and Tara had cooked a huge breakfast with every kind of morning food I had ever liked. I stuffed myself with pancakes, cereal, eggs, bacon, and fruit. I took a nap on the couch afterward, and everyone just sat around me in the living room talking and watching TV. Merely hearing their voices put me into a deep sleep.

Later on, we had a huge lunch with delicious turkey sandwiches. I took another nap after that. The purpose of the day was becoming clear: to fill me up and let me rest, and to surround me with quiet, peace, and love.

I woke up from my second nap and I could smell one of my favorite dishes cooking. Cincinnati Skyline Chili spaghetti. My mother had brought some packages of the Cincinnati chili mix with her from home. The smell of this stuff is indescribable. Being from Cincinnati, my family often used to wow New Englanders by making this dish when they were our dinner guests. Everyone loved it. "Oh, my God," I yelled. "Cincinnati chili?!"

"I told you we were taking care of you today!" my mother yelled from the kitchen. I heard Tara laugh.

"This stuff smells amazing! I can't wait to taste it," Tara said.

"Well, we're all in for a treat," I said. Eventually, we sat down for dinner and it became very quiet. Everyone was eating a great meal. I was amazed at how easy it was to eat without people yelling at me the whole time. I kept looking up from my plate to see if anyone at the table had a problem with the way I was eating. No one was even paying attention to me. But despite my being allowed to eat freely, I found myself counting my chews. In basic training, the upperclassmen would count the number of chews the basics took. Six or fewer chews was the rule. No matter how big the bite was that I took, I would swallow it after six chews. Sometimes it was painful, but it was better than being yelled at. Here I was, at the Dales' dinner table, counting my chews and swallowing food before it was ready to be swallowed. I had to consciously change this habit for the time being.

I loaded up on as much pasta and vegetables and bread as I could. I quickly grew tired after dinner and just wanted to go to sleep. The Dales had set up a room for Anne and me and one for my mom and Allen. Anne said that she was tired, too, so we went up to bed.

I knew that this was my only night to sleep well and to wake up in the morning without someone screaming at me and banging on my door. This made me more tired than ever. I think Anne sensed all this because she didn't try to come on to me in any way once we were under the covers together, despite our both being in our underwear. She had been so sweet and gentle to me over the entire day. Anne was lying on her side facing away from me. I pushed up against her and spooned her from behind; her hair smelled good. She fell asleep breathing so softly. I was still awake, thinking about how nice it was to hold such a gentle person who was so sweet and quiet. Here I was with a person who wanted to comfort me rather than challenge me. This was in stark contrast to what I knew I would be enduring the next morning: the start of Second Beast.

I watched Anne sleep and I started thinking about how glad I was that she would never go through what I had just been through. I thought about the type of person who could succeed through basic training and how the experience could seriously ruin a person who did not understand the purpose of the training or who did not understand what to take seriously and what to ignore. I knew I could finish Beast, even with all the extra stress that might be added by an upperclassman singling me out. I felt sorry for the ones who were not understanding the game we had begun to play. I made the decision to finish and win the game, no matter what.

chapter thirteen

SECOND BEAST

Morning came fast, but when I awoke, I knew that I had slept well. I was in the exact same position that I had fallen asleep in. The alarm was ringing in my ear but it sounded like a pleasant symphony compared to the sounds of screaming and door kicking made every morning by the upperclassmen. Anne turned over and looked at me with a smile on her face. It was as if she was saying, *I don't know what to say, and what you're about to go through today is so ridiculous that I don't think there is anything we can do about it but laugh.* I knew Anne's expressions well. In this case, what her face was saying was exactly right. There was nothing that I or anyone else could do to make the day any easier.

I took a shower and dressed in my blue uniform. I looked out the window from the second-story bedroom and admired how "civilian" everything looked. I could see the roofs of houses, yards, and people walking leisurely along the sidewalk, wearing comfortable clothes. I had never before admired how great we, people living in the USA, had it. For at least an entire year, simple creature comforts that I had taken for granted before would be taken away. I would not be allowed to wear civilian clothes. I would not be free to decide where I wanted to go, and I would not get to eat a normal meal, at which the purpose was to relax and get to know whoever I was eating with. My life had changed so drastically with the removal of just a few of life's basic pleasures.

I made my way downstairs and found Allen, my mother, Anne, and Tara Dale in the kitchen. They were all drinking coffee and cooking a huge breakfast. I had to be back at the Academy by ten A.M. We could enjoy a nice breakfast, but then it would be time for me to leave. I started having the same anxious feelings that I had when I left my parents for the first time to start First Beast.

I stuffed myself at breakfast. I felt as if I had gained back a couple of pounds after being at the Dales' for only twenty-four hours. I looked at myself in the mirror after eating; my face had regained a healthy, reddish color. Bob Dale asked me if I wanted my family to come along on the drive to the academy or if I wanted to say good-bye to them at the house. I chose to say good-bye to everyone at the house so that I would have the car ride back to mentally prepare for the start of Second Beast.

I have always hated good-byes, so I kept things short and sweet. By nine fifteen, I was ready to go back. I had to stop thinking about the comforts of home, family, and civilian life, and start focusing on the challenges to come. I thought about other people in my squadron, who were, inevitably, having the same thoughts and anxieties I was. I hoped that the other basics were thinking about me in the same way so we would be more bonded when we were all back together.

When my good-byes were done, I got into Bob's jeep and we backed out of the driveway. My mother and Anne stood on the front porch holding hands, with tears in their eyes. Allen and Tara smiled and waved at me. The scene was all very dramatic and I hated being aware that I was saying good-bye again. "God, let's just get out of here," I said to Bob. In twenty minutes, I was back at the Academy.

After thanking Bob for everything he had done for my family and me over the past twenty-four hours, I did as the upperclassmen told me to and found my way back to my room. As I walked up the "Bring Me Men" ramp, I didn't know that I was in for a surprise. I opened the door to my room and all of my roommate's belongings were gone. His bed was stripped. His desk was cleared. His Bible was missing from the end table. I checked in his closet. Everything was gone. I wondered what had happened. No one had given me any indication that he would be moved to another room. I couldn't believe the possibility that he had already left the academy. We were only through First Beast.

I sat at my desk in a state of confusion. Just then, Jodie Turner came into my room. "We're back!" she said in a totally sarcastic way. "Isn't this *great?*" She had a fake smile on her face and it made me laugh.

"My roommate is gone." I said. Jodie looked around quickly.

"What?" she asked in a very soft tone. "Oh my God. He *is* gone. What do you think happened?"

"I have no idea. But it's scary that someone that I've lived with for two and half weeks is all of the sudden gone. I was starting to like him a little bit. We were commiserating together and he was helping me out with my knowledge so I wouldn't get yelled at so much." Suddenly, we heard screaming in the hallway. It was our new cadre. Our new trainers were upon us, as fresh and ready as our First Beast trainers had been on their first day of training.

"Get out in the hallway!" they were yelling. Jodie quickly ran out of my room at attention to make it back to her room and to meet up with her roommate. I felt so alone. This time I didn't have a roommate to run out into the hallway with. I waited until I heard some others gathered up in the hallway and then I ventured out. The new upperclassmen were already stopping my classmates in the hallway and yelling at them for not greeting them with the proper name, even though there would be no way for us to know their names. We would learn their names by being yelled at for not knowing them. I made it to my classmates and stood at attention on the wall next to them. I pulled my knowledge book out of my pocket and put it in front of my face like everyone else.

The new Second Beast cadre looked more muscular than the First Beast cadre. They wore black combat boots, fatigue pants, white USAFA T-shirts, and blue berets that made them all look like they had just gotten out of airborne assault school or some other hardcore training program. Once every member of my squadron's basic cadet class had finally made it out into the hallway, the new cadre members walked up and down, sizing us up. We looked ridiculous in our blue uniforms next to them—they looked like they could take us on a run until we were dead.

The most physically intimidating one of the bunch began to speak to us as if we were hard of hearing—loudly and slowly. "Welcome to Second Beast! My name is Cadet Chase! Cadet Scott C. Chase! Do *not* forget this name, since I am your new flight commander until the end of basic cadet training. When you see me in the hallway or on the Terrazzo, you will yell at me with a thunderous greeting, 'Good morning, Cadet Chase! Battle-axe!' Is that understood?"

All of us were pumped up and full of adrenaline at this moment and we all, in unison, let out the biggest *"yes, SIR!"* I had ever heard us give. Then it was silent again.

Cadet Chase was about five foot ten, with dark brown hair and a very hardened face with lots of freckles. He stood perfectly still when he talked, yet his eyes moved back and forth. He started up again. "When I say 'go,' I want you to go back to your rooms and get *out* of these sissy blue uniforms that you saw your sweet parents in, and change into Second Beast uniforms. You'll wear battle dress uniform pants, an olive drab T-shirt, and a battle dress uniform shirt with your name embroidered on it. Obviously, you'll wear combat boots with this whole getup. You'll fill your green canteens and attach them to your wet belts. You will always wear your wet belts, with water in your canteens, for Second Beast. One last thing. Grab the M-1 rifle that you were issued on improcessing day. When you have all that together, get back out in the hallway. Now GO!"

We all ran to our rooms as fast as we could. I stripped off my blue uniform and threw my pants and shirt on the floor of the closet. I figured I would get yelled at for that later, but at least I would be out in the hallway sooner. I dressed as he had told us and grabbed my rifle. I ran out into the hallway and realized I was the first and only one out there. I panicked and went to run into another room, but two of the new cadre caught me. They yelled at me for not greeting them and for holding my rifle incorrectly. Before I knew it, I was in the front leading rest, screaming out, "I am waiting for my classmates! I am waiting for my classmates!" Suddenly, there was Jodie, next to me, also in the front leading rest yelling the same thing. It took about two or three minutes for everyone to get out in the hallway. The battle dress uniform was heavier than what we had worn in First Beast, plus we had a full canteen of water on us. By the time they allowed us to get up, our arms were shaking.

"That was pathetic!" Cadet Chase yelled at us. "I think we need to introduce you all to a friend of mine named 'iron mike.' Has anyone here ever done an iron mike?"

"Yes, sir!" one of my classmates yelled out. It was John Cutter. He was a short and stocky guy with light brown hair. I found out later that his father was a judge in small town in Mississippi. He seemed to be the perfect cadet and handled everything the First Beast cadre handed him. He had been through the Air Force Academy Prep School for one full year before entering the Air Force Academy. The prep school was for men and women who were accepted to the academy conditionally—often athletes whom the academy wanted, but whose SAT or ACT scores were too low, or were missing some prerequisite courses. Many prior-enlisted military members were also sent to the prep school before gaining admission to the academy. John Cutter was a football player recruit for the academy who had done his year as a "preppy" before joining us in basic training. At the prep school, he had been through a condensed version of our basic training.

Cadet Chase was impressed that someone knew what an iron mike was. "Show us, Cutter. What is an iron mike?"

John held his rifle above his head, parallel to the floor, with two hands. He got down on one knee. He yelled out, "Iron!" Then he jumped up and switched to being down on the other knee and yelled, "Mike!" He repeated this exercise until Cadet Chase told him to stop.

"Excellent!" Cadet Chase said. "Now I want all of you to do iron mikes until I say to stop." We did as he said. It only took about ten repetitions of iron mikes until people couldn't do them anymore. With heavy clothes and the gun above my head, these were really tough to do. "You all look pathetic!" Cadet Chase yelled. "We have one week here at the Hill and then we're marching out to Jack's Valley for the rest of Second Beast. You *will* be taken to your physical limits out at Jack's Valley, so you'd better work this week at taking our physical training seriously so that you're in shape!"

Our new flight commander was referring to the Air Force Academy campus itself as "the Hill," and he was right to warn us about our march out to Jack's Valley, a piece of land about two miles north of the Air Force Academy. It is landscaped and built for the sole purpose of providing the main elements of basic training that must be completed during Second Beast.

I had read about Jack's Valley in the packet that the academy sent to my home after I had been accepted. After marching out to Jack's, we would go through the mock operation of setting up a tent city, just as soldiers would when being deployed on a mission to a foreign area. Once our tent city was set up, we would live there for twelve days, during which we would endure many long-distance runs wearing full battle gear, and would also complete several obstacle courses. The courses I had read about included a military-style obstacle course, complete with dedicated obstacle course cadre; an NBC, or nuclear, biological, and chemical course; a confidence course; an assault course; a ground navigation course; and a course in shooting two weapons: the M-16 rifle, and the M-9, a nine-millimeter handgun. In addition, our flight would compete against other flights in all of these courses and in some other competitions that the upperclassmen would make up as we went through training.

Second Beast was the part of basic training that many feared the most, but Jack's Valley would be the final frontier of the summer's challenges. The breaks for intramurals that we had in First Beast were now over. Our days were full of training. We learned more marching maneuvers and began learning rifle drills during which we, as a flight, would move our rifles in specific ways, in unison with the others. I never understood why we learned rifle drills. We were a bunch of people dressed up like killers and moving our guns in ways that we would never move a gun in actual battle. We looked like a cheerleading squad. This was among many things I learned in the military that made no sense to me.

Why did we eat meals the way we did, for example—staring at the eagle at the twelve-o'clock position on our plates? I understood the need for discipline, but at a sit-down meal, other, more intelligent training could have been accomplished. After all, this was the only potentially calm time during training. The upperclassmen could have used it to talk to us about leadership or to teach us things about the military in general. Instead, we were busy pouring drinks the *exact* way the upperclassmen wanted us to, and being yelled at for too many chews. I started to focus on the absurdity of many things that we did, which allowed me to transfer my nervous energy about Second Beast into frustration with aspects of the academy I felt were stupid. At least I could control my frustration, and utilize that energy.

On the third day of Second Beast, our flight of basic cadets lost another member. He had decided to quit. The cadre members were supposed to make sure that no cadet was alone without a classmate to fall back on. A three-person room was supposed to be formed if there were an odd number of basic cadets in a flight. Now there were two of us with our own rooms. Cadet Chase came into my room to tell me that I needed to take all of my things down the hall and move in with Basic Cadet Kenny Bass.

This would be the beginning of my social life at the Air Force Academy. Kenny Bass was the basic cadet who had shown the most personality of anyone in the flight and, although we would live with each other for only seven or eight days before marching to Jack's Valley, I was glad to be moving in with him.

Moving all of my stuff into his room was a pain in the ass but some of the other basics helped me. On my first trip into Kenny's room he was jumping up and down, telling me how badly he had to go to the bathroom, but that he was afraid to leave the room because he would get jacked up in the hallway. He told me that he was "brown capping"—he was so close to relieving himself that what he had to relieve was actually sticking out somewhat. I peered at him with a grossed-out look on my face, but he just laughed at me. "What, Lehmkuhl, you've never heard of *brown capping*?"

"No, you can keep that to yourself," I said. Jodie had helped me move a good amount of my stuff into Kenny's room, so she heard the banter between us. She thought it was funny and the more she laughed, the harder Kenny would try to make her laugh, mostly by being silly.

Kenny was shorter than I was, around five foot nine, with reddish-brown hair and freckles. He was stocky and looked heavy. During my first day of rooming with Kenny Bass, I was in awe of how nonchalant he was about the whole academy experience. He was more concerned with making everyone laugh and with having fun than he was worried about the upperclassmen.

We had to leave our room several times that day for meals, marching practice, and different kinds of hazing drills, including a five-mile run in our battle dress uniforms. That night, I felt very tired. I was lying in bed when Kenny came back from the shower. We talked for a while about how much better shower time was now that Cadet Stork, from First Beast, was gone. It was much more casual and there were no upper-classmen getting their jollies by watching us switch shower stalls every fifteen seconds. I started to doze off when Kenny told me that he had stolen some nondairy creamer from the mess hall.

When we said that we "stole" something, we hadn't really—we were just sneaking it without the upperclassmen seeing us do it. Kenny started unloading about a hundred packs of nondairy creamer from his BDU pockets. "Why in the hell did you take all that creamer?" I asked.

"Because it's flammable!" he said, with excitement in his voice that was unusual for an eighteen-year-old.

"Well, what are you going to *do* with it?" I asked, with a good amount of concern.

"Lehmkuhl, we can have all *kinds* of fun with this stuff. I'm going to put it all in my issue mouth-rinse cup and I'll show you how fun it is." He filled the cup with nondairy creamer and walked over to the window of our room. He opened it and grabbed his issue lighter. He started pouring the powder out the window and then placed the flame of the lighter near the falling stream of creamer. The whole quad lit up as the creamer burst into flames. He continued to pour it, making a long stream of fire from our window all the way to the ground. He laughed as loud as he could into the quad and then quickly shut the window and the curtains. Seconds later, I could hear other basics yelling, "Woo hoo!" from all over the quad. Luckily, no upperclassmen would take rooms on the inside of the quads because they all wanted a view. So only the basic cadets could see what Kenny had done.

"Oh, my God," I mumbled under my breath.

"Just relax, Lehmkuhl. You need to have more fun," he said very matter-of-factly, right up in my face. Part of me understood what he meant. I was so frozen in fear and shock by this new life I was living that I had forgotten who I was. I didn't think anymore about what I liked or disliked or what could be fun. I just wanted to do my best and get through this training that I had feared coming to for so many months. I wondered if I needed to relax more. Maybe I wouldn't get yelled at as much in the hallways for forgetting knowledge quotes or upperclassmen's names if I could just relax.

Then again, I was also afraid of getting in trouble. Kenny would be good for me in that he would relax me, but he went to the extreme on many things. He would mouth off to the cadre to such an extent that it was downright insubordinate. Then the cadre would punish us all by holding an impromptu PT session or by making us hold our rifles over our heads during a run. They made no secret about what they were doing to us. The cadre would announce, "This is punishment for Bass's big mouth."

Seven days passed and, once we were familiar with the ways of our new cadre and the ways of Second Beast, it was all about to change yet again. It was time to march out to Jack's Valley. The march out was mellow, although we ran part of the way, so that we were over-heated and sweaty by the time we arrived. Many of the basics were coughing during the latter part of the day. The cadre explained to us that so much dirt and dust would be kicked up out at Jack's Valley from all the training that we would develop what they called "Jack's Hack." It was a cough that would start the day we arrived and that wouldn't go away until about a week after basic training ended.

I couldn't believe we were actually out at Jack's Valley. It was the final hurdle keeping me from my dream of being an Air Force Academy cadet and starting my training to be an air force officer. As the cadre led us to our flight's site and showed us all the equipment that we had to assemble to create our tent city, I felt adrenaline running through my body. By nightfall, we had our tent set up, all the cots in rows along each long side of the tent, and newly issued footlockers at the foot of each cot. We had brought with us all of our other supplies, such as extra BDUs, an issue green sleeping bag, and lots of extra T-shirts, socks, and underwear.

The cadre marched us to the mess tents and while we ate, they told us to get *up* for what we would be doing tomorrow on our second day in Jack's Valley. They didn't say *what* we would be doing, but they were motivating us to do it well. Because there were so many flights of basic cadets out at Jack's Valley, we would alternate in the different obstacle courses. Each day would be different and we had no idea what each day would hold.

We were all marched over to the showers after dinner. They had some skimpy white towels that we were supposed to use to dry our bodies and keep for the rest of basic training. The showers out at Jack's were actual shower trailers that were brought in and then hooked up to running water. There was hardly any hot water and the shower stall was an open room with about six nozzles; however, the cadre would encourage more than that many basics to shower at the same time. Some of us would end up sharing a nozzle with another guy or even two, all in the name of saving time. Then there was a dressing area next to the shower stall that was equally as crowded.

The showers became very nasty very quickly. Dirty socks, underwear, and towels were left on the floors of the showers, which were muddy from all the combat-boot traffic. I think guys were throwing their underwear on the floor that first night and going commando, or without underwear, for the rest of basic training. Besides the filth in the showers, the scene was chaos: twenty-five guys at a time trying to get undressed, showered, dressed again, and brushing their teeth in a space made for about ten of us. One couldn't help being bumped into by the others. I would look across the shower to see five to ten other guys sharing the stall with me, completely naked, except for their dog tags and combat boots, which they were wearing in the shower in an attempt to break them in faster for easier long-distance runs. I did this myself. The sight of soapy water running down all the naked guys' bodies and onto their leather boots led many people to have sexual thoughts. I was under a great deal of stress and my mind remained focused on getting through Beast, but I could definitely sense a sort of sexual tension in the showers, and at times I was, without a doubt, turned on.

About half of the guys were looking down at the floor; the other half were looking at each other's bodies as they washed. I looked down at the floor up until my third or fourth day, when I discovered other guys looking at my body as I showered. One side of the shower area had a row of sinks with a foggy mirror above it that stretched the length of the stall. When I couldn't see a guy looking directly at me, I would find one or two looking at me in that mirror. I did the same thing and also watched myself showering, too. I compared my body to theirs and realized that I was starting to gain muscle and a manly shape that I had only seen in revealing magazine ads when I was a child.

That's when I found it somehow comforting and even recreational to look back at those looking at me as they washed *their* bodies. It was as if I found some feeling of worthiness by having another man admire me, in stark contrast to the mostly male cadre constantly telling me how stupid and worthless I was on a daily basis. As I looked at a guy or several guys looking at me, I felt, without a doubt, that I was doing them the same favor. Equally positive, this was the first time in years that I felt remotely attractive. Although Anne had told me many times that I was handsome, for some reason I never really believed it. I always thought that she and other people were missing something that I saw in the mirror every day—an ugly kid whom everyone talked about and made fun of behind his back. As little sense as it made to me then, my time to experience a sense of my own attractiveness had finally come in the cramped showers of Second Beast.

As I looked at other guys as they looked at me, there were times when either they or I would experience a visible sexual arousal. At that time, both of us would know that it had gone too far, so we would look down for the rest of the shower to control an erection that had crossed some sort of unspoken and abstract line marking what otherwise seemed to be acceptable behavior.

I slept hard that first night. The temperature out at Jack's dropped to about forty-five degrees, compared to ninety-five degrees during the day. The sleeping bags that we were issued were warm, but with hardly enough room to fit a tall body. I would zip mine up and feel like I was in a cocoon. Only my head stuck out of the bag, and I covered the top of it with an issue black stocking cap so that I wouldn't lose my body heat.

Mornings were the same every day at Jack's. They would start with our cadre beating large sticks against the side of our green canvas tents. "Get your boots on!" they would yell. The first morning, it took me longer than almost anyone to get dressed. I listened to the other basics in my tent who told me that we should all sleep naked because the sleeping bags would work better. I never quite understood the theory, but because I saw everyone else slept naked, I did too—but only for one night. On every subsequent night, I put on clean BDUs and underwear and sleep *that* way, with only my boots to put on in the mornings, so that I wouldn't be yelled at for taking too long.

The first morning at Jack's, we were marched to breakfast, taken on a run, and then dropped off with the assault course cadre. I couldn't believe we were doing the assault course on day one. It was supposed to be like the obstacle course, except more intense. The challenges involved more stress, training, and yelling from the cadre than on the obstacle course and, during the course, blanks were shot off from M-16 rifles to increase the intensity. Assault course cadre members were chosen from the Air Force Academy football team, so these guys were not only big, but also athletic. They could have trained right alongside us for hours if they wanted to. We spent what felt like the entire day on the assault course. By evening, we were exhausted. We had crawled through tunnels and over bridges. We had low-crawled through mud swamps. Along with the assault course cadre, we were given pugil sticks—long wooden rods with tough padding on each side—and were forced to battle the cadre with them. We had to run long distances and sprint short distances. Every time we finished a challenge, we had to yell, "Assault course, sir!" If we didn't yell this loud enough at the end, they would make us do that individual challenge over again.

When we were done with the assault course, our regular Beast cadre marched us back to our tents to gather whatever we needed for a shower and then marched us to those trailers. They didn't make us run that night because they saw how tired we were. The only tough part about the march to the showers was that that cadre told us that we would do the assault course twice during our time out at Jack's, to see if we had improved after the first. I tried to think positively, knowing that we had one of the two times already out of the way.

The next day at Jack's was no less brutal. After breakfast, we ran in formation to the nuclear, biological, and chemical course, to teach us what to do if we were ever deployed under this type of attack. We learned how to wear an NBC suit that protected our skin, as well as how to wear NBC headgear to protect our faces, eyes, noses, mouths, ears, and lungs. We spent most of the day sitting on bleachers listening to an instructor talk about all the different ways that our atmosphere could be attacked and how to respond in those situations. After practicing some drills and donning the NBC suit and gear, we were already exhausted from the heat of the day. The suits were made of plastic and rubber and, once inside, our bodies would begin to sweat profusely. We continued to drink gallons of water that day, but I still felt dehydrated.

The finale of NBC training took place inside the NBC tent, where camphor and some other very nasty and harmful chemicals had been released. We filed into this tent, one by one. Again, we had to don the gear before entering the tent. Once inside, a few cadre members stood around in full gear and gas masks. They were saved from the heat because they weren't exposed to the hot sun. After standing in there for a few minutes to see how the suits worked, we were instructed to pull off the head-gear and to try to breathe so that we could see how the suits were protecting us from the actual chemicals. I waited in line and saw basics led into the tent, but also watched in horror as the NBC cadre dragged basics out the other side. Basics were coughing and groaning and trying to throw up. Others were successfully vomiting.

It was my turn to go into the tent. One of my flight cadre members led me to the entrance and I was handed off to an NBC cadre member. He instructed me to put on my hood. I had already put on the suit and my skin was soaked in sweat, since we were waiting in line under the hot sun. I put on the hood and my body temperature felt as if it had risen to two hundred degrees. I was led into the tent and instructed to breathe normally. I could smell some sort of chemical through my mask even though the hood covered my entire head. Just when I started to breathe normally, one of the cadre members inside the tent, who was also dressed in full gear, motioned for me to take my hood off. The hood was zipped to the body of the suit at the neck. With the help of the cadre, I began to unzip the hood from the suit.

As the zipper moved, I could feel the chemicals in the air moving onto my skin. All of my exposed pores were burning. I pulled off the hood and without thinking about it, I closed my eyes tightly and clenched my mouth shut. I could feel chemicals moving up my nostrils and burning them. I could feel all the glands in my eyes and nose purging with fluid. My mouth filled with saliva, my nose with snot, and my eyes with tears. The cadre members in the tent were telling me to try to breathe. I pulled in one breath, and the contaminated air in my throat and lungs caused my entire respiratory system to shut down. I was suffocating and I couldn't see anything. They pulled me out of the tent and dropped me on the ground. I started coughing and spitting profusely, trying to get any last trace of chemicals out of my system and off my face. I lay there for a while and waited for the rest of my flight to make it through the tent.

Our cadre marched us back to our tents and we gathered our things for showers again. A shower had never felt so good. I imagined all of those harmful chemicals leaving my pores and going down the drain.

On the march back from the showers, I remember seeing an upper-classman hazing a basic at a pull-up station. The basic was being made to do pull-ups and, on each one, screaming, "I like girls!" and "I am a heterosexual!" I'm not sure what this cadet had done, but I knew that what he was going through must have been extremely embarrassing as his flight of basics watched.

We went through more courses, including a confidence course on which we did team-building exercises with our flight's basics. We thought of this as an easier course and many of us put as little effort into it as we could while still passing the minimum requirements.

We were put through another assault course and went through the obstacle course twice as well. The obstacle course was physically demanding but not as mentally demeaning as the assault course. We also spent a whole day on the rifle range learning how to shoot the M-9 nine-millimeter handgun and the M-16 semiautomatic rifle. The goal on this course was to gain an expert ribbon by shooting as close to the bull's-eye as possible with the limited number of bullets we were given.

One other whole day was spent on the navigation course, learning to triangulate on a map to find our exact location, with the goal of finding our way to several checkpoints using only our issued military equipment. All of these less intense days were made more challenging by morning rifle runs that would bring us to our limits of physical exhaustion.

Finally the day came when our entire class of basic cadets would march back to the Hill. The march back was actually fun because morale was so high. We knew we were done with Jack's Valley, Second Beast, and Beast in its entirety. For a bunch of people who had been through the most physically demanding experiences of our lives for the past six weeks, we had more energy than we should have had. We were all able to eat more in Second Beast so our workouts actually led to our being more muscular and fit, as opposed to my body withering away during First Beast because of Cadet Stork.

During the march back, we sang many different jodies, or marching songs, which we had learned throughout Beast. Our favorite was "Tiny Bubbles." The cadre would yell out, "Tiny bubbles," and we would repeat, "tiny bubbles." The song continued, "In my beer! Makes me happy! Makes me want to cheer." Then, "Tiny bubbles, in my wine, makes me happy, makes me want to shine." The song would go on and on, with tiny bubbles in every kind of alcoholic drink we could think of. As we marched, I caught glimpses of others in my flight and we smiled at each other, excited to be done with basic cadet training. We wouldn't smile for too long because we still did not want to be caught gazing in any other direction than straight ahead while we marched.

As we arrived back at the Hill, it was strange to feel concrete under my boots. We were marched up the "Bring Me Men" ramp, and then we were stopped once we arrived at the Terrazzo. Everything looked different to me. There were cadets everywhere. All three upper classes were now back from summer vacation, mandatory military summer programs, and summer school classes. They were all in their blue uniforms and, as they walked by us basics, they would laugh at us or make fun of us to our cadre. Some of our cadre would join in and laugh at us too, but Cadet Chase stuck up for us as we came up from the ramp. "These guys are warriors. They did awesome out there!" he would yell back at the ones who were talking to us as if we were little babies as they walked by.

Cadet Chase started to talk. "Listen up! I have some important announcements. You are all now pretty much done with Beast. Give yourselves a round of loud and thunderous applause."

We all cheered and yelled as loud as we could. I could hear our voices echoing across the whole Terrazzo and back. Cadet Chase started again. "Now you are all going to be taken to your freshman-year squadron. Your squadron is Bull Ten, or Tenth Squadron. The twenty-five of you who are still here will make up the entire freshmen-class of the squadron. There are roughly twenty-five people from each of the upper classes. That means there are about a hundred people in a squadron. There are forty squadrons that make up the four thousand crazy-ass people who are here. Does everyone understand this?"

"Yes, sir!" we yelled out.

"Good," he said, "then let's get you down to your rooms. I'm going to march you to the door of Vandenberg Hall. Bull Ten is on the southeast corner of Vandy, as you can call it. The first twenty squadrons are in Vandy and Squadrons Twenty-one through Forty are in Sijan Hall. Once you get to the Bull Ten hallway, search for your new room.

Some of your roommate situations have been changed and you must live with the roommate that the cadre have chosen for you." I had a sick feeling in my stomach about the possibility of being put with a bad roommate. Cadet Chase went on. "All of your stuff has been moved into . . . well . . . *thrown* into your new room. Also on the floor is the bag of stuff that was taken away from you on your first day here at improcessing. When you get to your rooms, get what you need and take a shower. Then get dressed in your blues for a very special ceremony. Tonight, you will take the Oath of Office as a real member of the United States Air Force. OK, is everyone ready to find their rooms?"

"Yes, sir" we yelled with pride, all in unison. With that, Cadet Chase marched us toward Vandenberg Hall. Bull Ten was one flight of stairs down from the main level of the Terrazzo.

As I walked down the hall, I saw a female cadet, but I did not know her name. I figured she was a sophomore because she looked a little younger than the rest of the cadre. I went to greet her with a loud, "Good afternoon, ma'am! Raging Bull Ten!"

She let out a huge, "Shh! Do *not* greet me, basic. I don't want to hear it. And that goes for the whole year. I don't ever want a freshman to greet me. My name is Cadet Kathy Costello and I hate to be greeted. Tell your classmates."

"Yes, ma'am!" I yelled.

"And another thing," she yelled. "Don't ever sound off to me. I like my life to be quiet."

"Yes, ma'am," I said in a normal tone. I continued to walk down the hall, at attention, close to the right-hand wall. I was amazed that there were upperclassmen that didn't want us to yell at or greet them. Hearing that was like music to my ears.

"Lehmkuhl!" Cadet Costello yelled to me. She must have seen my name on my BDUs. I was surprised that she pronounced it right. "Your room is down the hall on the left, just so you don't go walking around like a dumb basic cadet."

"Thank you, ma'am." I said. She was already around the corner and gone by the time I thanked her. Again, after what I had been through, my mind was blown that an upperclassman had just helped me out. I walked down the right side of the hallway, as we were supposed to, at attention, and found my room. The doorplate said "Bass–Lehmkuhl." I was relieved. They had kept me with Kenny. I went into my room to find Kenny already there. He immediately perked up when I came into the room and began showing me the clothes he wore for improcessing day. He had had a T-shirt made that said, "Train Me Please Sir!" I knew at that moment I was rooming with a fairly fearless person. I hung up my clothes and issued items that had been thrown into our room by somebody, while Kenny just sat there and continued to play.

"We have to take a shower," I told him. He didn't seem to listen or care. I gathered my shower stuff and walked down the hall in my issued robe, soap in one hand and towel in the other, just as we were instructed to do.

By the time I finished in the squadron bathroom and returned to our room, Kenny was still sitting on the floor like a little kid, playing with things. "Hurry up, dude. We need to get out to formation," I said. Kenny finally stood up and gathered his things together for a shower and left the room. I dressed in my blues, which were pretty wrinkled. One of the cadre members had told us on the march back from Jack's Valley that we would, in the following couple of days, have the chance to go to the cadet store, or C-store, to buy some essentials, like an iron and an ironing board.

Kenny still had to put on and tie his shoes when the cadre started yelling for us to get out in the hall. I had learned that it was an absolute sin to ever leave a classmate behind, so I rushed Kenny and we ran out into the hall with the rest of our classmates. As we formed up with everyone, I noticed that the upperclassmen had placed us so that half of us were on one side of the hallway and half of us were on the other side. Before putting my knowledge up in front of my face, as I had been taught to do, I looked across from me in admiration at my classmates standing tall in their blue uniforms. We were done with basic training, and these would be our uniforms for the rest of the year and for three more after that.

All of basic training was flashing through my head. I had become closer to these people than I had ever been to any person in my life, besides my parents. I *knew* each and every one of these people in my flight. I had watched them allow others to break them down to crying babies, and they had watched me get the same treatment. I saw all of them improve as the weeks went on, and they saw the same in me. I watched a group of people stripped of their old identities, based on high school and materialistic things like clothes and cars, and have them replaced by identities built on the personal achievements of basic training and the support and respect earned from all the other basics in our flight. I loved each one of them in one way or another, even though many of them annoyed me at times.

We were marched upstairs and out to the Terrazzo and we formed up facing the American flag, just as we had on the first morning of First Beast. All one thousand or so basic cadets were there with their cadre. Each of the forty flight commanders reported to a group commander, who then began the ceremony. He told all of us to raise our right hands and repeat after him. This time, the Oath of Office meant so much more than when we had heard it the first time. I had been hazed enough times to know the oath by heart, so I could recite it with no problem.

We all swore the oath. When we were done, all of the cadre from First and Second Beasts came around us to congratulate us on no longer being basics. We were now fourth-class cadets. (Third-class cadets were sophomores; second-class cadets were juniors; and first-class cadets, or firsties, were seniors.) At the same time, the upperclassmen pulled out our fourth-class shoulder boards and buttoned them onto the shoulders of our shirts. Finally, our blue uniforms looked like those of the upperclassmen.

"Alright!" Cadet Richter, from First Beast, said. "You're cadets now! No more being marched around. You're on your own, but be careful. You have to run only on the marble strips of the Terrazzo. Square your corners when you come to an intersection where you need to turn on a marble strip. And there are certain marble strips that you cannot walk on. You'll find out which ones *real* fast as you get yelled at! Now go. You're free. Well, sort of."

We didn't know what to do. We were all standing there in formation, until John Cutter broke away from the flight, ran to a marble strip, and started running toward Bull Ten. "Get out of here!" Cadet Chase yelled. "And make sure you're double-timing on the strips. The only time you can walk on the strips is if it's raining."

We all scattered. I found myself running back to Bull Ten with everyone else. I was so happy as I ran on the strips behind my classmates. When we ran by upperclassmen who were casually walking on the Terrazzo, we greeted them: "Good evening, sir! Raging Bull Ten!" I was finally a cadet at the Air Force Academy, albeit the lowest form of cadet there was, and I had overcome its "Beast." Now I could put up with just about anything.

My grandmother, Betty Stagg, Women Air Force Service Pilot

With my best friend Jeff Campbell, freshman year, 1993 (I'm on the left)

With my Hell Master, Recognition Night, freshman year, 1993

Assault course march during Hell Week, 1993

Helicopter Incentive Flight during OPS Air Force program, Nettis Air Force Base, Nevada, summer 1994

Dad and Kim Lehmkuhl on Graduation Day, May 29, 1996

Grandma Turner on Graduation Day

chapter fourteen

SCHOOLED

Within two days of the end of basic training, the school year started. The entire class of 1996 was issued new computers, schoolbook carrying bags (all one thousand of us had to have the same bag), our schoolbooks, and our class schedules. We also bought all the supplies that we needed for the school year. Our fourth-class cadet pay was sixty dollars per month, which would provide us with the bare essentials of any smack, or freshman.

Kenny and I went to the C-store together. The rule at the C-store was that we were at ease, meaning that we didn't have to be at attention, but we couldn't talk. To be able to talk, we had to be at rest. Trying to shop without being able to talk to the person I was shopping with was a challenge. Communicating with only our hands and facial expressions as we shopped, Kenny and I agreed on which iron to buy for our room, which cleaners we needed to keep our room in order, and what food to buy to share between us. When we brought our supplies back to our dorm room, we laughed at our ridiculous shopping experience.

Kenny's downfall was his school-issued computer. The year was 1992, so most people had not used, or even heard of, the Internet. Kenny, on the other hand, knew that each of our computers was connected to the World Wide Web, and he was determined to have some fun. I had no idea that we could do anything with our computers other than write papers. Within a day's time, Kenny was showing me what a chat room was and chatting with someone in Australia. I found it neat, but I didn't really understand what the big deal was. I was focused on getting ready for school.

This was my first semester of college and I was in way over my head both in the number of classes I had and their difficulty. My hardest classes were chemistry and history. Back in high school, my advisers had told me to continue with honors biology rather than taking chemistry. This was bad advice, because I was completely lost in my chemistry class. A white-haired man named Colonel Beck, who had no sympathy for anyone who didn't understand the subject matter, taught it. Most of our teachers at the academy were highly educated officers, usually with PhDs or, at the very least, one or two master's degrees.

My other courses were French, which I chose to minor in, math, physical education, and a chemistry lab. I think that because I was so focused on not getting yelled at by the upperclassmen, I would spend all of my free time shining my shoes, ironing my uniform, and studying my military knowledge book of quotes and facts, instead of doing my homework. My concentration level in class was low due to my fear of getting jacked up by an upperclassman, so I never really absorbed any of the history or chemistry lessons that I sat through. I had no idea how to manage my sleep. I was getting about four to six hours per night, maximum, which would lead me to fall asleep during class. By the end of this semester, disaster loomed.

A typical day for a freshman at the academy went like this: Wake up at six A.M. Study the newspaper for three current events to tell the upperclassmen at breakfast. Find out what is on the menu at Mitchell Hall by having one freshman call the office there. Get your schoolbooks ready for that day's classes. Go into the hallway in groups of three and stagger those groups along the hall outside the upperclassmen's doors. Call minutes.

Calling minutes is a fancy way of saying that freshmen were the upperclassmen's alarm clocks. We would stand outside their doors and yell, "Bull Ten! There are twenty minutes until the first call for morning meal formation. I say again! Twenty minutes until the first call!" We would repeat this every five minutes until we got to five minutes until first call. After that, we would run outside on the strips to morning formation. We would go through the reveille ceremony, and then the entire cadet wing would march to Mitchell Hall for breakfast. After we were all seated at our tables, enough waiters would emerge from the kitchen to serve food to all four thousand cadets at once. It was seriously amazing to see. During breakfast, upperclassmen questioned us on our current events and what the meals were for the day. They would complain because someone had poured them the wrong drink or put ice in it when they didn't want ice.

After breakfast, we would run to class. We ran everywhere as freshmen. We were not allowed to walk anywhere unless we were in the school building. There, in Fairchild Hall, we were at rest. Class would go until lunchtime. Then we would run to our rooms to change into whatever uniform Command Post would announce over the loudspeaker system throughout the entire academy. Then we would run back out to noon meal formation. We would all report in while tourists watched us from the chapel wall, as if we were monkeys in a zoo. Then the whole cadet wing would, for the second time that day, march to Mitchell Hall, this time for lunch. At lunch we would be hazed and yelled at for incorrect drinks or for not knowing the knowledge in the new knowledge books that we were issued at the start of our freshman year, called *Contrails*.

Contrails was ten times bigger than the small knowledge books we had in basic training. There was so much to learn and know that it was overwhelming. An upperclassman could always find a question from *Contrails* that an unsuspecting freshman couldn't answer. Then they would train (discipline) the freshman for not knowing the answer with push-ups, iron mikes, or an impromptu run. Of course, when one of our classmates was in trouble, we would all have to join him. That meant that if one person wasn't learning the knowledge in *Contrails*, then all of the freshmen in the squadron were trained for it.

After lunch we would run to more classes until four P.M., at which time intercollegiate athletes would join their team practices, while everyone else would go to intramural sports, which were held every day. I picked water polo because I wanted to try it out. I learned quickly that this was not only a sport that required serious physical fitness, it was a rough contact sport as well. By the end of the first semester, I was able to do pretty well in a match. After intramurals, it would be about six thirty P.M.

We were not required to have formation for dinner. We would run there and sit at any table we could find. Sometimes we sat with upperclassmen who were not from our squadron, but they would usually leave us alone.

After dinner, we had to be in our rooms, sitting at our desks with our doors open, from eight to eleven P.M. for ac-call or academic call to quarters, which was a dedicated study-only time. No upperclassman was allowed to train a freshman during ac-call.

Taps and lights out was at eleven P.M. We were supposed to go to bed then, but no freshman ever did. That was when our free time began. It was our only time to get our uniforms ready for the next day or to finish up a paper or a problem set from one or more classes. Since most of the upperclassmen were asleep, it was also a time to go from room to room and hang out with each other. Kenny and I would usually get to sleep at around one or two A.M., even though we had to wake up at six the next morning.

To make our packed schedules worse, physical education classes were held at the Field House in the middle of the school day; we had to take off our uniforms, dress in the issued physical education outfit, take another shower, put our uniforms back on, and run about half a mile back up to the Hill for more classes.

Our school schedules were set in the first year by the academy. A certain number of core classes had to be taken by every cadet. Both semesters of freshman year were filled with the core curriculum. Majors were chosen in the sophomore year, but there were still some core classes that ran through both semesters of the second year as well.

As there were no locks on the doors at the academy during our freshman year, the upperclassmen could come into our rooms whenever they wanted during the day. When we left for morning meal formation each day, we had to leave our doors wide open for the upperclassmen, who would check to see if our rooms were in inspection order. Just as in First Beast, Kenny and I spent the school year sleeping on top of our made-up beds, under a small comforter.

My phys ed class for my first semester was boxing, a required class for all males at the academy. It was supposed to build confidence, but all it did for me was let me know how much I never again wanted to be hit in the face. I actually did OK in the class because I had long arms and was quick. For the final exam, we had to fight someone for three minutes straight. The guy I fought was about my size and build, and we hit each other in the face pretty good, until we both had bloody noses. Rather than accomplish its proposed mission, the class added nothing but stress to my freshman year.

I searched for a way to cope with the many pressures of the academy. It seemed that when one sort of stress ended by finishing a challenge, another would begin. I realized that the stress of the academy would be ongoing and I had to accept that my time there would never be easy. My need to escape and be myself started taking over. I made homework my last priority, which was a big mistake. I felt the urge to make friends and to have a social clique like the one I had at the end of high school, with people I felt comfortable around.

I knew that some of the freshmen in my squadron were getting out of mid-afternoon jack-up sessions with the upperclassmen by going to chapel or Bible study. Those two things were the only legitimate excuses that a freshman could use to get out of training. I decided that I would go to Bible study, too.

Although I was raised Catholic and had attended Catholic school in my primary years, I learned more about original sin and how awful a person I was born to be rather than studying the verses and teachings of the Bible. As a small child, I remember the nuns at St. Ann instilling in me that I was born a sinner and that I would spend my life trying to make up for that. In contrast, I had been taught that the Bible was supposed to be a good thing for good people, so I figured attending Bible study couldn't hurt. For the first time in my life, I also felt the need to explore the idea of God and where I came from.

I saw a flyer advertising a Bible study class taught by a man named Chaplain Karnes, a Protestant chaplain and also a lieutenant colonel.

Unbeknownst to me, being ignorant of the ways of the world, Chaplain Karnes was a staunch, right-wing Christian zealot. On the first night of class, I walked into one of the chaplain assembly rooms, and there were about twenty other freshmen waiting for class to start. Chaplain Karnes announced that at this particular Bible study, he was going to have us watch a video that we could discuss afterward. Before I knew it, I was watching a video about how gays in America were ruining our country, our military, and our legal system.

Up until this point, the only openly gay person I knew of was Representative Frank, the congressman who had given me my nomination to the Air Force Academy. Even though I had experienced homosexual feelings and thoughts, I never accepted or thought of myself as gay. And to me, Representative Frank was perfectly capable—he didn't seem to be ruining anything. This video painted a much different picture. It portrayed all gays as drag queens showing their genitals in gay pride parades. Then the video went on to claim that gays were preying on the children and youth of America in a plot to *make* everyone gay.

After the video, one girl raised her hand to speak. Her brother had told her family that he was gay, she said, and the family had ostracized him to teach him a lesson "of God." Scarily enough, Chaplain Karnes agreed with her family's decision to throw him out of the house, to take away everything he had. These measures, he said, would have forced the brother to think about his *decision* to be gay. I sat there wondering *what the hell* we were doing talking about gay people during Bible study. I was honestly confused.

When the class was over, as I walked out of the room, a six-foot-two blond guy walked up to me and said, "Can you believe he showed us that video? I think that was really messed up."

"The video?" I asked. "Or the fact that he showed it to us?"

"Both." He said. "Hi, I'm Jeff. Jeff . . . "

"Campbell," I interrupted. "I saw it on your jacket." I had pronounced it like the soup.

He corrected me, "Camp-*bell* is the correct pronunciation. Like the bell at a camp." He had a smile on his face. I couldn't tell if he was kidding.

"OK, I get it," I said. I was happy to be talking to someone who looked cool and normal.

"So, yeah," Jeff continued, "that video was pretty hateful and distorted. I felt like we were watching a propaganda film from Nazi Germany."

"You're right," I said. "You're absolutely right. That was really fucked up." We laughed and shook hands. He told me that he was in Second Squadron, which was two floors above Bull Ten in Vandenberg Hall. I told him that I would stop by later, but I was completely kidding. Freshman were *never* allowed to go to another squadron and, if they did, they would get in *serious* trouble with the upperclassmen. I think they must have had this rule to keep the freshmen within each squadron really tight, so that they would rely mostly on each other for just about everything.

Jeff and I continued to talk about the people each of us knew in each other's squadron as we walked toward the Terrazzo. Freshmen were at rest around the chaplain assembly rooms. As Jeff and I came to the marble strips, we knew that it was time to stop our conversation. Just as we were trained to do, we said good-bye to each other and silently ran on the marble strips, one behind the other, all the way back to Vandenberg Hall.

When I was back in my room, I told Kenny about my crazy experience at Bible study, and that I had only gone there in an attempt to escape being trained all afternoon by the upperclassmen. His answer to my story was simple. "Yeah, well, you're not exactly in the most tolerant environment. They hate anyone and anything that is different here. Hey, have you ever seen the movie *Deliverance*?"

"*Deliverance*? No, I haven't. What's that?" I asked.

"It's this movie that shows the true colors of the backward side of America. These guys who live in the woods who epitomize the uneducated, back-country, ignorant side of America actually end up butt-raping an innocent guy in this movie," Kenny explained.

"But I don't get it. It's the uneducated that usually hate gay people," I said.

"Yeah," Kenny continued, "and the ones who hate blacks and Jews and everyone else. That's the ironic part. The ones who hate gay people the most are probably the ones who fantasize the most about having gay experiences. Their hatred is an outward display of the anger they have about their own homosexual feelings. The gay bashers are the ones who are insecure with their sexuality. Basically, many of them are probably gay."

"Then why was this chaplain showing us this video that would turn *anyone* against a gay person?" I asked.

"Because he's a *bigot*, too!" Kenny yelled. "Or maybe he's a flamer!" Just then it hit me. This was one of the first moments in my life of real *free* thought. It occurred to me that all people were fallible. Even the clergy that I had grown up with could have been wrong about so many things. Up to this point in my life, I had blindly trusted every leader I had encountered, including priests, policemen, teachers, and even my basic training cadre. Kenny had made me realize that not everything is what it seems. I felt, at that moment, that I had sheltered my own mind from thinking about the world around me. I hadn't formulated my own opinions on so many issues, including gays, abortion, religion, and even war.

I knew Kenny wasn't gay. He talked about girls and "pussy" whenever he could. I started to verbalize my thoughts to him. "It's really messed up that this 'man of God' showed us something so horrible. I mean, those people in the video were celebrating a pride parade and the video made it look like they were criminals. What does that have to do with my being closer to God? What does that have to do with the military?"

Kenny answered, "Well, a lot of people say that letting gay people into the military would lower morale. It would bother the people who hate gays."

"But they only hate gays because they were *taught* to hate gays," I yelled.

"Right," Kenny yelled back. "That's what's so ridiculous about what you went through tonight. We have excluded a group of people from the military not because they aren't fit to serve, but because ignorant people have a problem serving *with* them. So we're excluding a group of people who are able to serve to protect people who dislike gay people. It's ridiculous. We don't exclude black people because there are racists in the military. No. We tell the racists to get with the program and to get over it. But we won't do this for gay people."

I had never in my life discussed gay people in a serious way. I had never thought of the word *gay* in any other way than as an insult or a derogatory term. However, on this night, I saw a group of actual people, in a video, who defined themselves as gay, and who were having a peaceful demonstration that wasn't hurting anyone. Yet, they were being chastised just for being themselves. The dialogue in the video made no sense when applied to the images on the screen. The dialogue talked of sinful, hateful people who wanted to change the world to a "gay and ungodly place." As I ironed my uniform for the next day, and as I brushed my teeth, and even after I went to bed that night, I continued thinking about gay people, and I couldn't get the thought of them out of my head.

The next morning, Jodie came into our room and we were sharing current events from the paper to announce to the upperclassmen at that morning's breakfast. I asked her if she knew anyone who was gay.

"Are you still on this, Lehmkuhl?" Kenny asked, slightly annoyed. I told Jodie about the video I had seen the night before.

Her response startled me. "Well, what did you expect from a bunch of Jesus freaks?" she asked. Kenny laughed.

"What?" I asked.

"Honey, haven't you learned by now that it's the Jesus freaks who are the ones with the problems in this world? It's everyone else who is just going about their business, being who they are, and living their lives happily. The Bible thumpers are walking around in a tizzy telling everyone how wrong they are and that they need to change to avoid going to hell. Look at the video they showed you again and compare those gay people with the Jesus people. Then you'll see who's *really* ruining this world." Jodie was on a roll. I could tell she had thought this through and was pretty passionate about it. "And they're always so smug, the Jesus freaks. They tell everyone that they don't hate the sinner, just the sin. As if that's any nicer than hating the sinner. They're still *judging* everyone . . . which, by the way is supposed to be a mortal sin."

Jodie started mocking them. "Oh, I *forgive* you for being a sinner." She made a face and then pretended to talk to a Jesus freak. "Please don't bother forgiving me. I'm doing just fine . . . so leave me alone. And leave the gays alone, too." Her theatrics with this were making me laugh, and I think it was mostly in relief of all that had been weighing on my mind about the inequity of all that I had witnessed with Chaplain Karnes the night before. What Jodie was saying actually made sense when I applied it to this religious leader showing us the video. I felt like she had partially helped me sort out my own thoughts and opinions. The problem was the hater, not the gay people. She was blaming our current policy of exclusion on the values of fundamentalist American Christianity. But the academy was a military and government institution that should accommodate all American religions. *How could it have such an exclusionary and unfair policy based on any religious belief at all?* I wondered.

Jodie continued. "My sister goes to Mizzou—you know, the University of Missouri, where I'm from, and I was walking on campus with her last year and these two guys were holding hands, walking in front of us. I asked my sister what they were doing. My sister told me that they were a *gay* couple. As I watched them together, I started to understand it. They were just like anyone else. And I told my sister that. I said, 'They're just like anyone else. There's nothing wrong with them. They're in love. It's just as beautiful as a straight couple being in love.' My sister agreed with me."

Jodie's story, after Kenny's speech the previous night, really affected me. To hear two people whom I greatly respected talk about gay people in a positive way left me reconsidering the negative connotations I had always associated with the word *gay*. What else had I merely accepted in my life that I needed to rethink? I suppose this kind of soul searching happens to many people when they reach college age, but I sensed that most people at the academy did not think like Kenny or

Jodie. "People here hate gay people. I saw it in their eyes as we discussed the video last night," I said.

"Yes. You are at the U.S. Air Force Academy. This is one of the most conservative places on the planet. You're not in a free-thinking sort of place, so watch what you say to people," Jodie warned.

For years I had always associated the word *conservative* with positive ideas. For me, the word meant safety, responsibility, and maturity. For the first time in my life, I saw the destructiveness and hatefulness of people who considered themselves conservatives.

So many cadets at the academy were Christians. They walked around with Bibles on Sunday, dressed sharply in service dress, which was the most formal uniform we owned. Many cadets wore bracelets on their wrists that said "WWJD"—what would Jesus do?—as if they had an idea of what Jesus would do about anything in a present-day situation. As the school year moved on, Kenny and I continued to talk about the very strong religious overtones that thrived at the academy. Kenny, who was very educated on the Bible, showed me quotes from different chapters that completely contradicted each other. He showed me how the story of Jesus was of a man who associated with the very people everyone else hated. Through Kenny, I developed an understanding and a respect for this man named Jesus that I had never found in my CCD classes. I thought about how we should all try to be like him to attain a peaceful, spiritual level of existence with our fellow human beings. I thought about how, if Jesus were here today, he would most likely support gay people, the ones who were hated and misunderstood by so many. I imagined him warning people not to judge or chastise any of God's creations and giving the human race the assurance it needed to accept gay people as brothers and sisters.

On the flip side, being educated about Jesus left me confused by people's actions at the academy. How could religion and this warped form of Christianity be used to spread anxiety, hatred, and fear of others? Why had religion become something that made one cadet, or person, better than any other?

These questions pervaded my mind for the entire school year. I began to watch people and develop strong opinions about their behavior. I became more and more irritated, knowing that these people walked around so smugly with their Bibles, but clearly seeing how judgmental, closed-minded, and ignorant they really were beneath their Christian facades. It bothered me that they didn't have the sense to question their own belief systems or that they didn't bother to see the damage that they were causing so many people, every single day. I would go to church on Sundays and, for the first time ever, really listen to what was being said and pay attention to what was going on. In the world of religion, I realized how many myths and rules man himself had actually conjured up to suit his own ideals, prejudices, and dislikes, while continuing to call it all Christianity.

Pointing out the hypocrisy of these so-called Christians became somewhat of an obsession for Kenny, Jodie, and me. We would pick people out of our squadron who wore Christianity on their sleeves and criticize their actions. We had a lingering respect for their right to their beliefs because all of our criticism happened privately among us and behind their backs. If these so-called Christians ever became angry, frustrated, or impatient, we had a sort of self-satisfying fun in our rooms, acting out confrontations with them. "Now c'mon, what would *Jesus* do in this situation?" In our own defense, we only picked on the ones who showed disdain for those of us who didn't want to attend their Bible studies or the ones whose overzealous pursuit of Jesus gained them a higher standing within the academy system. Since we all agreed that Jesus was a person to respect and emulate, rather than someone to use, we found this behavior particularly disturbing.

Despite the academy being a government-run institution that should cater equally to all American religions and cultures, most of the air force officers who taught our classes were openly proud fundamentalist Christians, and we began to notice a sort of wink-wink system between cadets and officers who shared their pursuit of the same type of Christianity. This environment of religious nepotism would eventually become more than something to disapprove of; it was something to fear as a driving force in a machine that would stop at nothing to suppress the diversity that existed within the walls of *their* Air Force Academy.

chapter fifteen

A SYSTEM, A MACHINE

The cadet system was set up to handle everything itself, including accountability for formations, good grades, the physical fitness of all cadets, and, most important, the punishment and discipline of those cadets who strayed outside the regulations. Cadets even policed their own honor code: "We will not lie, steal or cheat, nor tolerate among us anyone who does." Cadets accused of an honor violation are brought up in front of an honor board made up primarily of cadets, who decide if the accused are actually in violation, and what the punishment will be. Usually, the punishment for a confirmed honor violation is to be kicked out of the academy altogether.

On top of self-governance, each of the forty squadrons had an officer, an Air Officer Commanding, or AOC—assigned to it. When cadet matters reached a point at which intervention was required, the AOC would take over and make final decisions. In the spirit of the military system, a chain of command existed, so that a squadron AOC might take his or her decision to the Group AOC, who was in charge of the ten AOCs in each group. Squadrons One through Ten comprised Group One at the Academy. Squadrons Eleven through Twenty comprised Group Two, and so on. The cadet wing comprised the four cadet groups.

The Bull Ten AOC was a man named Captain Mendez, who was as unusual as an AOC could possibly get. A hispanic man in his early thirties, Captain Mendez had more feminine mannerisms than Ru Paul. He was slender and he would often talk about watching his weight and his "sinful" obsession with M&M's. When he walked, he swished in the same way that supermodels do when they walk down a runway. His voice was high and he had what I considered a stereo-typically gay lisp. He exuded feminine sensibilities as well as homo-sexuality. Somehow, none of the other officers seemed to notice, I think because he was married with kids. His wife was a large woman, and we cadets figured that he was in a marriage of convenience. Although we were sure he loved his wife and kids, we were heavily of the opinion that he was gay.

"Mithter Lehmkuhl," he would say, "how are thingth going with you thith morning?"

"Sir, they're going great!" I would say enthusiastically and in a manly way, almost in an attempt to make up for his being *so* girly. I wanted to bring some sort of military bearing back into the conversation.

Of course, to make it all the more confusing for everyone, Captain Mendez was also a Christian. He kept a Bible proudly displayed on his desk and absolutely loved it when cadets would announce that they were holding Bible studies in their rooms.

Captain Mendez would often intervene and assign punishments for regulation violations, which cadets preferred not to deal with. Regulation violations were different from the honor violations of lying, stealing, and cheating. Reg violations, as we called them, were less of a big deal, and included things such as not keeping your dormitory room in inspection order or your hair being too long. Punishments for regulation violations included tours or confinements, and always restriction until the punishment for the violation was served.

Marching a tour meant going out on the Terrazzo on weekends in full service dress with a rifle over your shoulder and walking in a square of terrazzo marble strips for one full hour. That was one tour.

A confinement meant that a cadet was confined to his or her room for one full hour on the weekend, with the door open, in service dress, with the room in perfect inspection order, working on schoolwork or military activity, such as shining shoes, ironing uniforms, or cleaning the room.

Restriction meant that normal cadet liberties, such as using the squadron TV room, wearing civilian clothes on weekends, or leaving the academy on passes, were taken away.

If a cadet was caught smoking in a dorm room, for example, the punishment was 10/10/Y, or ten, ten, and yes. This meant that the cadet was charged with ten tours and ten confinements; the "yes" meant that the cadet was restricted until this punishment was served. A cadet could knock out about ten to twenty tours or confinements in one weekend, depending on what mandatory military activities the cadet had to do with the rest of the cadet wing. A larger punishment might take almost an entire semester to fulfill. Cadets given more than one hundred tours during their entire academy careers were called centurians. These were usually the fun people at the academy, with good senses of humor—at least that was my experience in meeting and talking with centurians.

Captain Mendez would get upset with the squadron if he found himself having to give out too many reg violations. Sometimes he would come out to formation to tell us how disappointed he was and how we needed to shape up. One day, at morning meal formation, Captain Mendez even went so far as to increase the severity of punishments from there on out by telling us, "The house of pain is *open*." To us, this sounded like, "The *houth* of *pain* ith *open*," said in the most nonthreatening and feminine way imaginable.

That day was historic in Bull Ten because, after that, everyone in our upper class would quote his words to us: "The houth of pain ith open!" This would always make a freshman in our squadron crack up during a training session, so the upperclassmen would use it sparingly.

One freshman, in particular, often made fun of Captain Mendez. His name was Seth English, one of my fellow Bull Teners, and he was sort of feminine himself. Seth was about six foot two, good-looking, and athletic, with dark hair and eyes. His feminine qualities were, however, endearing. Seth's father was a colonel who had stopped by a couple of times during our basic training. I was surprised by the stark difference between Seth and his dad. Colonel English was big boned, with a deep voice, and seemed to be the epitome of masculinity, whereas Seth was thin, physically well cut, and sort of gentle.

Every Thursday, the entire cadet wing was instructed to wear flight suits instead of a blue uniform. The academy called it War Fighting Awareness Day. I guess we were getting into the spirit of those pilots who actually wore flight suits because they flew for the air force. Flight suits were extremely comfortable and tailored to our bodies. They were so nice to wear, in fact, that most of us would not wear underwear on flight suit day. While joking about free balling in our flight suits, or going commando, as we called it, we'd ham it up even more. Seth would get excited after putting on his flight suit in the morning and would usually end up in Kenny's and my room, along with Jodie, talking about how good he looked. "Look at me!" he would say effeminately, "My waist is so small and my hips are so wide that I look like a *girl* in this flight suit!" We would howl and quote his words whenever we got the chance. "Sir! My waist is so small and my hips are so big that I look like a girl in this flight suit!" That became Seth's fun tagline—something like an ism.

By the end of our first freshman semester, we all had isms we were known for. Jodie was known for her ability to confront people on their hypocrisy. She was especially good at this with the Christians in the squadron. Her strong personality, loud voice, and good laugh made her a great person to be around. She would get silly with me much of the time. She also loved to come into our room and make announcements. "I have an announcement!" she would yell at the top of her lungs in a sarcastic imitation of how we always had to sound off to the upperclassmen. "Three of us are all walking to dinner. Would you like to come with us?"

I would play along. "Are we taking the Mercedes or the Rolls-Royce to dinner?" I would ask her in a British accent, for no reason at all.

She would laugh at the British accent and pick up on it. In her own British accent, she would say, "No, we're not taking the horseless carriage this evening . . . we're taking the mare."

"The mare?" I would ask. "Which mare?" again, in a British accent.

"Oh. Well, we're taking the gray mare, of course. Yes. So, load up the gray mare, because we're ready for dinner." Then she would leave the room and Kenny and I would laugh to each other. This kind of interaction was very common between Jodie and me. We often came up with random skits, on the fly, that no one seemed to understand but the two of us. Kenny would always tell me that she and I were in love with each other, but I would deny it, saying that we were just friends.

Kenny's isms were his random acts of destruction, like the incident with the nondairy creamer. He would do anything that was out of the ordinary to make us laugh. One night he announced to the freshmen that it was grilled cheese night. I walked in from intramurals to find Kenny cooking at a makeshift kitchen he had set up next to the sink in our dorm room. All rooms had two beds, a nightstand, a counter with a sink in the middle, and a mirror above the sink. Kenny had propped up the iron that we used to iron our uniforms, with the hot part was facing up, using it as an electric stove. At the C-store, he had bought bread, butter, cheese, and aluminum foil, which he draped over the iron, on which he was cooking the grilled cheese sandwiches. The room smelled amazing. Even though I was annoyed that he was doing this, I was so hungry I couldn't get mad at him. I hadn't had grilled cheese in forever. Within an hour, not only did we have the whole freshmen class of Bull Ten in our room, we also had upperclassmen in there asking if Kenny would make sandwiches for them.

Despite all the fun, Kenny wasn't a good roommate for me. He was a huge distraction from my studies. I was already having trouble keeping up with the large amount of schoolwork that we were assigned every day, but Kenny would never keep the room as a place of sanctity suitable for studying. I would often go to others' rooms to do homework, but then I would end up talking to *them* instead of doing my work. What I really needed was a quiet place to study with no other people around me. My need to be social was really to blame for my bad grades. By the end of my first semester at the academy, I had earned a grade-point average of 1.4. I made a D in chemistry, which was a double-period class—so that gave me *two* Ds on my report card. I got a C in math, a D in history, a B in French, and an A in boxing—which counted for peanuts in the scheme of my GPA. I had really failed myself and I felt terrible about it. I had never before earned a D. The only time I had earned a C in any class was in an English class in high school, and the teacher and I didn't get along. With the subjective grading in an English class, I knew she had just given me that grade out of spite.

I could have done better in chemistry. It was my fault. I was always tired in that class from lack of sleep and too much socializing in the squadron. I slept through almost every class. When I was awake, I was too tired to comprehend what the instructor was saying. History class was sort of the same way. This class required a great deal of reading and the ability to understand chains of events. That semester we focused on the wars of the world since the beginning of recorded time. Although I was attending a military academy, I wasn't very interested in war. I thought of the Air Force Academy as a place to study new technology and the frontiers of space, rather than a place that should involve itself with the study of past conflicts. I didn't have the maturity to understand or care why wars affected us in our present-day lives.

French was easier since I had taken four years of it in high school. I didn't even try and still ended up with a B, but my struggles with my other courses prevented me from excelling. Math was the same way.

Cadets with GPAs of 2.0 or below are put on academic probation, or ac-pro, as we called it. They remain on ac-pro until they bring their grade point average to 2.0 or higher. Ac-pro meant being restricted every weekend of that semester—which didn't mean much to freshmen, because other than being granted two separate one-night passes during the semester, freshmen couldn't leave the academy grounds. Other than a loss of dignity, I hadn't missed all that much by being on ac-pro. However, this was the first time in my life that I felt like I had totally failed at an academic challenge, and I didn't understand how to fix things. I saw other freshmen with 3.5 GPAs and wondered how they did so well and why I did so poorly. I certainly had an incentive to clean up my act in the coming months, however. The Academic Review Committee, or ARC, had warned me that being on ac-pro for more than one semester, was almost certain grounds for dismissal.

My first semester at the Air Force Academy was finally over. I had only been home once, over Thanksgiving weekend. Anne and I had promised each other that we would spend Thanksgiving together, but by the time Thanksgiving weekend rolled around, I had been so over-whelmed by the academy that I had lost touch with Anne. Since basic training ended, she was writing me letters only once a week instead of every day. Freshmen had phone privileges only on Sundays. Some weekends had gone by when Anne wasn't available when I called her, so we would wait two weeks to talk. On top of not communicating, I had been through so much mental stress that I had changed person-ally. Despite my bad grades, I had actually gained a tremendous amount of confidence. Things that I didn't want to think about or that weren't a priority for me were put on the back burner for my own sur-vival. As much as I loved Anne, my relationship with her was not a pri-ority. I didn't know why that was, but I often thought about how I would only go through the motions of a relationship with Anne to please everyone else, including her. I thought about how I never really felt a strong passion for her, or why I didn't cry when I had to leave her the way I had cried when I had to leave my best friend, Ben Sil-verman, back in Massachusetts.

I slowly pushed Anne away as my identity continued to build, and as I became a serious person with more confidence and integrity. Any person developing those qualities would not spend time doing some-thing that wasn't truly driven by free will or passion. A person with those qualities would make decisions that were true to his own heart. That's exactly what I was doing. My true self was emerging, albeit slowly and carefully.

By Thanksgiving break, I was feeling similarly isolated from anyone outside the academy. I think this happened to many cadets. I felt that even Anne, Ben Silverman, my brother Bobby, and my parents would never understand who I had become. They wouldn't understand what I had been through because they would never get to go through it themselves. They would not understand the craziness and the isms that we had all developed in our freshmen class of cadets in Bull Ten. They would never understand "load up the gray mare," or why that would even be funny to me. They wouldn't understand the complicated bond that I had developed with my other classmates, or why only *we* truly understood each other.

One Sunday, before Thanksgiving break, I built up the energy and courage to call Anne to tell her that I would be going home to my parents during my break and that I didn't think it was a good idea for us to see each other. Anne cried and cried. I cried too, but for her, not for myself. I didn't know why I was ending our relationship, but I knew, inside, that it was the right thing to do. Over the phone, Anne and I had broken up. A large weight had been lifted from my shoulders.

For Christmas break, I didn't want to go home. I had gone home for Thanksgiving. My parents still lived in the trailer. I knew I didn't want to go back to that place ever again. Now that my confidence had been boosted, it occurred to me that, as a kid, that trailer, and all that I went through in high school because we lived in it, had stripped so much of my confidence away from me. I decided to go to my brother's house for Christmas. This would be a two-and-a-half week break and I wanted to be in a place I was comfortable. My brother lived in Valencia, California, at this point, and had done very well for himself in the auto sales business. He had a beautiful home and nice cars. He took nice vacations. He had made wonderful friends and had had great experiences. My brother had certainly become the most fabulous and successful person in our family, in my eyes. I went to be with him. He let me borrow his car if I needed it, and his girlfriends were seriously fun to be around, so I loved it there.

I spent Christmas vacation doing what I needed to do: vegetating. I watched television, drank beer, swam in the pool, lay in the sun, and ate whatever I wanted. I also entertained my brother and his girlfriend with stories of the academy. Their favorite story was that any time an upperclassman saw one of the freshmen doing something wrong, upperclassmen would always start a training jack-up session with, "Oh, my *GOD!*" with the word *God* spread out over several seconds. They would ask me to tell them stories of all the times I had been in trouble with the upperclassmen over the past semester. I would tell them what I was doing wrong and how, all of the sudden, I would hear, "Lehmkuhl! Oh, my *God!*" My brother and his girlfriend laughed harder than I had ever seen them laugh. They were most fascinated by what I got in trouble for, and what a big deal was made over such menial violations.

They were also fascinated by the privileges of seniority at the academy. Freshmen were allowed to have nothing in their rooms other than what had been issued to them on their first day there. Sophomores were allowed to have stereos in their rooms. If a freshman were caught with a stereo or any sort of music-playing machine, including a small portable player, it was the worst thing that could happen to us as a freshman class. The upperclassmen would lose their minds and punish the entire Bull Ten freshmen group with physical training, restrictions, and confinements. They continued to howl in laughter as I told them these stories.

Once, our freshman rooms were raided by the upperclassmen, and two freshmen were caught with a pet mouse. When I told them this story, they started laughing really hard before I even finished. They yelled out, "Oh, *my God!*" as they laughed.

I continued telling them how a junior could have not only a stereo, but also a plant! Seniors could have all those things plus a television in their rooms, so that they would no longer have to watch their favorite shows and movies in the squadron television room.

As I watched them laugh at all of these stories, I started laughing with them. It was good for me to see how funny it all actually was. So much of it required a sense of humor. I thought about taking so many things I went through at the academy less seriously, and not letting its unusual rules and regulations bring me to a place of fear or worry or doubt. This new state of mind would surely help me upon my return to the Hill.

chapter sixteen

NATHAN

After Christmas break, I flew from Los Angeles to Colorado Springs and, just as I had witnessed on my first flight to the academy, the entire plane from Denver to Colorado Springs was filled with cadets. I needed to reestablish the mind-set required to survive this next semester as a freshman. In flight, I pulled out a piece of paper and wrote down all of my goals for the next semester.

- Study every night, and explain this need to my new roommate
- Don't take hard training personally; don't take it too seriously
- Eight hours of sleep per night
- Continue to understand my life

As I wrote, it occurred to me that just a few short months ago, I wouldn't have been mature enough to put my thoughts on paper. I was truly changing. On that same plane ride I thought about things like time management, stress management, working out at the gym, laughing with my friends, and getting more sleep. Time management? What was happening to me? Whatever it was, I liked it, and I was motivated for the next semester's challenges with a better under-standing of how to meet them. I returned to the academy, both in body and spirit.

With the change in semester, our cadre gave us the opportunity to pick new roommates. There were a few switches, but not many. I asked to be removed from Kenny Bass's room, even though the guy had become like a brother to me. Jodie lived with a female cadet named Carmen Brown during the first semester and asked to be removed from her room. Carmen was a very small cadet who struggled like no other to keep up with us physically. Jodie had listened to Carmen cry about her performance during the entire first semester.

Jodie, who was recruited to play tennis, was an amazing athlete and could outrun most of the guys in our squadron, so she was not matched up with the right roommate. Her two other roommate choices were Jane Hemmings, a girl with the military bearing of a tomato who was always in trouble for screwing up, or Shannon Everett, a women's volleyball team recruit who was rather rough around the edges and had many isms that annoyed Jodie. Shannon ended up being the best choice for Jodie, but the lesser of two evils.

Kenny Bass's new roommate was Kory Stamp, whose previous roommate had been kicked out for medical reasons. At six foot two, Kory was an athletic guy. He was loud and stubborn, with brown hair and brown eyes, and always had an intense look on his face. He already hated everything about the place. Rules that had no rationale behind them were his pet peeve. He was also at odds with the academy's Christian and religious teachings. Kory was from a liberal part of New Jersey and didn't understand the lack of diversity of the academy. Minorities made up about fifteen to twenty percent of the cadet wing; everyone else was white. He hated how gay people were a constant object of jokes among cadets.

My new roommate was Nathan Nixon, who was left without a roommate because his old one had decided to leave after the first semester. Nathan's GPA was 3.5. He was smart and knew all of his required military knowledge from *Contrails*. He stood about five foot eleven, had dark hair and brown eyes. Nathan had been recruited to play baseball, but had injured his shoulder in basic training on one of the challenge courses and couldn't play, so he focused more on his long-term dream of flying airplanes for the air force. Nathan's grandfather, like my grandmother, was a pilot in World War II, and had always shown enthusiasm for Nathan's attending the academy and, eventually, becoming a pilot.

Nathan was excited to have me as a roommate. He had seen me struggle through the first semester and always tried to help me when I had trouble with my studies. He made it very clear that, as my roommate, he was going to help me out of my first-semester rut. He talked about all of my extra training by some of the upperclassmen and told me how much he hated those upperclassmen for doing that to me and others. Here was someone who was instantly on my side. In the first few days of the semester, I asked him, "Why are you being so nice to me?"

"Because I think you've got a lot to give and because I just want to be nice to you," he answered. I found myself with the best roommate I could ever have asked for. He promised to make me study and to get some sleep. In a militaristic way, he controlled everything in our room, and I needed that. He handled the alarm clock, he turned on the lights in the morning, he helped make my bed and iron my uniforms. He quizzed me on our required military knowledge every night. He would tell me when to go to bed at night and, because he was carefully watching my school load, he decided what I should try to finish and what I shouldn't before going to bed. Sometimes Nathan would get mad at me for not following his advice when it came to these things, but the majority of the time, I followed his wishes because I knew he was on my side and wanted the best for me.

Nathan told me about his very serious passion to fly. He wanted to pilot the F-15 and knew everything about this particular plane. He couldn't wait for the summer after freshman year, when all cadets were given the opportunity to take Soaring—the program during which cadets learn to fly a sailplane. He told me that his only reason for being at the academy was to fly. He didn't care about any other aspect of our training and wrote it off as ridiculous.

Although Kenny Bass was no longer my roommate, I didn't and couldn't stay away from him. I visited his room almost every day just to say hello. There was always something crazy happening in his room so it was nice to laugh at whatever he and Kory were doing, then to have the luxury to leave whenever I wanted so I could go back to my own room and study. Kenny and Kory were perfect roommates. They laughed at each other's jokes and they both loved and hated the same things and people in our squadron.

Jodie was not so happy with her roommate. She complained to us that Shannon snored too loudly at night. Her stories about how gross Shannon really was would make us laugh. By this time, love relationships started to develop among our freshmen class. Jodie's roommate, Shannon, was already seeing a football player. He would wait for days to sneak into our squadron, and come to see Shannon in the middle of the night. She would get depressed and have crying spells if he didn't come as often as she liked. Jodie hated having to listen to her cry and whine about her boyfriend.

Sneaking around to others' dorm rooms in the middle of the night became our method of seeing each other. As we made more and more friends from other squadrons, this "sport" became a necessity. We went to great lengths to make it safely into others' rooms. If we were caught, the entire freshmen class in our squadron would be restricted for a month as punishment for our breaking the rules.

By mid–second semester, our own real group had formed. Nathan Nixon, Kenny Bass, Kory Stamp, Jodie Turner, Seth English, and I became a tight-knit family. We were always in each other's rooms and, when we could, we would run around the academy together in the middle of the night. We had a good set of lies already made up just in case we were caught. Our best lie was that we were on a spirit mission—outings that freshmen went on in the middle of the night to do something to the campus that everyone would see at morning meal formation. Spirit missions were encouraged by the upperclassmen. For instance, if a football game was coming up, we would decorate a firstie's car with air force decorations and dress up a small wagon with the opposing team's logo or art. We would set the two props up in the middle of the Terrazzo for all to see the next morning. If we were ever caught, we would say that we were on a spirit mission for any number of reasons, such as to celebrate an upperclassman's birthday, or engagement, or simply to raise the morale of the cadet wing. We would get our lie straight before we all went out.

Nathan was the most conservative one of the group. He made sure he had plenty of sleep and didn't often go out with us to roam the academy at night, but he always promised to back up our lies. He was from Stillwater, Oklahoma, and a fan of country music. I told him of my love for the Grateful Dead and that, when we were allowed to have a stereo in our room, I would be playing a lot of the Dead. "What's so great about the Grateful Dead?" he asked once. Never again would he wonder who the Grateful Dead were or what they were about after I told Nathan about going to my first show.

It was back in 1988. My best friend Josh and I were with my parents in Maine during the summer after eighth grade. On our way into the town of Norway, where our summer house was, we saw people who looked like hippies walking along the side of the road. As we drove by the Oxford Plains Speedway in Oxford, Maine, we saw huge signs advertising that the Grateful Dead were in town for some weekend concerts. My brother had told me about a Dead concert he had gone to in 1986. He said it was an incredible experience. He explained to me that the Grateful Dead put on shows, not concerts. I would eventually understand the difference.

I figured that a band with a name like the Grateful Dead had to be a hard-rock band, or maybe even a death-metal band. Seeing all these hippies on the side of the road completely fascinated me. Some of them were beautiful men and women, holding up signs that read, "Need one ticket." Many of them were hitchhiking and some of them were doing it half naked. We even drove by a few women with their shirts off. That made us laugh, but my mother cringed.

My parents were visibly *not* happy with the invasion of the Dead and their Deadhead followers. Their obvious disdain for this group of people made me even more fascinated by them, so I decided that I would do anything to hang out with these Deadheads at some point over the weekend. We were only in eighth grade so we didn't have cars, but I knew some kids who lived on the lake where we water-skied. These kids were a couple years older than we were so they had their driver's licenses. On the Saturday following the Friday night that we had arrived in Maine, I told my parents that Josh and I were sleeping over at my friend Mike's house. Mike had a room above the detached garage of a house on the lake. Many of the kids on the lake had spent numerous nights there and we used his room as a hangout to smoke cigarettes and drink beer that older kids bought for us. That evening, Mike drove us to the Oxford Fairgrounds. We didn't have tickets but we all had cash on us. We found two guys who were selling extra tickets and we bought ours for about $20 apiece.

The first thing we noticed when walked into the show was the parking lot, where there were rows of people selling things out of the backs of their Volkswagen buses, from veggie burritos to necklaces to tie-dyed T-shirts. They were running the whole parking lot like it was a functioning hippie community. Josh and I were in awe of the sight. We noticed the smell of pot in the air. Many people were stoned and, consequently, were the most gentle people I had ever met. Guys and girls alike were walking up to me and Josh asking us if we were brothers. They would tell us how good-looking we were and would say things like, "You two have *good* karma coming your way." People were hugging and kissing everywhere. Everyone was smiling and people were talking about good energy and bad energy and all of these crazy concepts that I had never thought about.

We met two girls our age walking around the parking lot. They told us that they were camping out at the show for the weekend with their friends. They invited us back to their setup to meet their group before the show. They were very nice to us but Josh and I were nervous. This was our first time venturing into a situation in which we would meet total strangers and talk to them. The girls offered us some punch from their van. We were hot and thirsty and drank the punch. "How was the punch?" one of the girls asked us before they both began to laugh.

"It's good! Do you have any more?" I asked naively.

"Oh," one of them said, "you don't want anymore than what you had, believe me." I didn't know what that meant but I had to ask the next question.

"Well, are we going to be OK?" I asked.

"Yes, babies, you will be fine," she answered. Josh and I were a little freaked out, so we left their little setup and agreed to keep a close eye on each other because the girls were acting strangely about the punch they gave us.

We walked into the show and realized that the Grateful Dead was already playing on stage. We found our seats, but no one was sitting down. Everyone there was up and dancing. I had never seen people dance the way they were dancing to this music. They were swaying back and forth with their hands in the air and their eyes closed. It looked as if the music was actually moving the people. We were sitting at a midlevel height in the stands, so I could see waves of music moving over the crowd. I don't know if it was my imagination or if it was real, but I could swear that Jerry Garcia, the lead guitarist of the Grateful Dead, was actually tailoring his ever-changing guitar riffs to the movement of the crowd. The crowd was actually deciding how the music would go. This made for an energy and feeling, among the thousands of us, that took away all of my anxieties and fears about being there.

As I continued to move myself with the crowd and the music, feeling happier, healthier, and more a part of this world than I had ever felt, I noticed that it was snowing! As I looked more closely at the people in the crowd, I could see that they were all throwing marshmallows in the air out of their own individual bags. They threw them up in the air to the different beats of the song. As I stepped back to take in the whole scene, I realized how beautiful the flow of marshmallows really was. The music the band was playing seemed to be secondary to everything else that was going on in the crowd. The love and smiling and happiness were enough to make a person never want to leave the show. I made an attempt to focus on the music and I watched other people around me mouthing the words to the songs. I listened to what they were singing about. The songs were very folksy—all about the Wild West and different lessons that can be learned in life. I was completely taken by this experience and this band.

From that day on, I loved the Grateful Dead. I bought their albums and would randomly meet others who liked the Dead, too. We would trade bootleg tapes of the many different shows that were played around the world. Throughout high school, I did whatever I could to see a local show. There was no judgment at a Dead show. No one cared if anyone was black or white, gay or straight, or how they were dressed. Ever since my first show, I felt educated enough to understand who Deadheads were and I wouldn't ever let anyone make fun of them. It was as if I were on a personal mission to defend Deadheads against people who would talk about them in a negative way. Those people were usually the ones who had never met a Deadhead, and who had never taken the time to understand what Deadheads were all about.

* * *

In the same story to Nathan, I briefly mentioned how I felt about gay people and the opinions I had formed after talking with Jodie and Kenny. I told him of my thoughts about treating everyone with respect, similar to the feelings I had experienced when I saw that first show. I knew that I would stick up for gay people in the same way that I had always stuck up for Deadheads. Being older and more mature than ever, I knew also that I would stick up for gay people against anyone, no matter who they were. Nathan seemed kind of lost when I mentioned my opinions on gay people, but he seemed to completely understand my feelings for the Grateful Dead.

I concluded my Grateful Dead story by telling Nathan that I had decided that being at the Air Force Academy was not going to stop me from appreciating and loving the Grateful Dead—whose shows couldn't have been more different from the academy experience and from what was being taught there. He looked up at me with a sincere look of fascination and intrigue on his face. "Wow!" he said. "Dude, that sounds awesome. Take me with you to a show someday, OK?"

I nodded as we looked into each other's eyes. I think I was more fascinated than he was at that moment. I was speechless. Here was this very masculine, deep-voiced athlete from Texas who was actually listening to me tell him about something that was important to me. He had hung on my every word, looked me directly in the eye, and smiled as I described everything. Despite his being in an air force uniform, I saw that his interest in my story had nothing to do with the air force. I saw that he actually understood my love of the Dead. I could not have been more appreciative and grateful for my roommate than I was at that point. We continued to talk for a while about how different the people who like the Grateful Dead were from people at the Academy.

"But if you like something like that, how can you like being here?" Nathan asked.

"I don't know," I said, "I need both, I guess. I like the discipline of this place. I think I needed it to shape up my life. But then again, I like the idea of people being hippies and simply loving each other without the bad energy of war and capitalism around them. There is something to be said for people talking about love and treating each other well. Here at the academy, I've learned what it takes to defend our country. It's a whole mind-set of being in a defensive mode of living—always looking out for someone to hurt us. In a way, it's like constantly living in fear. A Dead show is just the opposite. Everyone is looking to help each other and assumes that everyone else is nice. I guess I like to fantasize that's how the world could be."

Nathan sat there listening to me. "Imagine if there was an academy with *this* kind of discipline that wasn't based on war?" I continued. "If it were based on making peace in the world. The U.S. Peace Force Academy. Its graduates would travel the world on missions to help others and they would be paid just as much as we are now paid to wage war in the name of *defense*. What if *it* were given the same amount of money that this place gets from the government? What would the world be like? What would our country be like?" I asked.

Nathan thought about my questions and said, "Unfortunately, there are leaders of countries out there who are not peaceful people. Left unchecked, they'll take us over."

"I wish there was a way. But for now, I'll continue at the academy and go to as many Dead shows as I can to keep my life balanced," I said.

"Well, after what you just described, you'd better take me with you," Nathan said as he smiled at me. I smiled back.

During the second semester of freshman year, Nathan mentioned the Grateful Dead many times, telling me he couldn't wait to hear their music. Although Nathan was the conservative one in our group, he was obviously willing to open his mind to new things, which, to me, made him very intelligent. He hadn't been exposed to much when he came to the academy, but he was smart enough to know that there was a world worth knowing outside his own. I think the real reason we all loved each other within our small group was because, like Nathan, all of us had something to learn from the others. Even though each of us was unique, our commonality was that we had open minds, and we were ready to learn and change.

I continued to study French and by chance, Jeff Campbell, whom I had met in Bible study, was in my class. We sat next to each other and hung out together before and after those classes. We spent time together on weekends, too, becoming better friends. He went to chapel every Sunday and I went with him, just to try out the academy's Protestant services. We also hung out together in Arnold Hall, the recreation building, where there was a coffee shop and restaurant called Arnie's at which freshmen often gathered. Jeff and I would bring our homework to Arnie's on weekends and sit there for hours in our uniforms, talking about everything in the world.

I began to look forward to my time with Jeff so much that when we couldn't hang out, I would get upset. By this time, we freshmen had figured out all the places where we could meet and socialize without getting in trouble. We were at rest in the library, the school building, the chapel, the athletic fields, and Arnie's. Over time, I introduced Jeff to Seth, Jodie, Nathan, Kenny, and Kory, and he had as much fun with them as I did. Whenever I did anything with my Bull Ten gang, I would try to include Jeff as well.

Jeff was taking his mandatory boxing class during the second semester. Unlike me, he developed an instant passion for the sport and made boxing his intramural choice. He even decided to compete in the Wing Open, which was the huge yearly boxing match held by the Air Force Academy. Jeff became obsessed with training for this competition. He talked about the upcoming Wing Open often and I would let him know how supportive I was of him and how confident I was in his abilities. I even made sure my friends from Bull Ten were behind him, too. Sometimes I would ponder how I had become this close to someone that I met and bonded with at Bible study over a horrible antigay video played for us by Chaplain Karnes.

My Bull Ten friends and I went to Jeff's preliminary boxing matches to support him. We had given him a family away from home that would support his efforts. I loved how happy Jeff was when he was around all of my friends and it made me happy to see him smile.

Sometimes when we watched his boxing matches, I would see Jeff getting hit in the face and bleeding from his nose or lips. It made me sick to watch. I would get so upset that I had tears in my eyes. There was nothing I could do about it except to try to hide it from the rest of the gang. We all knew each other very well by this point, so when they saw me so emotionally distraught, they would say something. "Relax. He's OK," Jodie would say while consoling me, but with a confused look on her face, looking me in the eye, wondering why I was getting so emotionally distressed.

"You're not crying are you?" Kory and Seth would ask.

"No, I'm not crying," I would claim. "I'm just not used to this." Kory would look at me like he was really worried about me. Seth looked at me like he was intrigued, as if he knew something that even I didn't know.

Nathan was the only one who wouldn't say a word. He ignored the tears in my eyes and made comments about the fight. "Jeff's kicking this guy's ass right now. Look at him go. He's in better shape than ever now." He would focus on Jeff and not me, even though he could see that I wasn't enjoying myself.

After one of the qualifying matches, when I was finally alone with Jeff at Arnie's, I asked him if he wanted to keep fighting all the way up to the Wing Open. I reminded him that there would be more adrenaline flowing at that fight than ever before. "But my adrenaline will be flowing too," he said. "And why do you care? This should be *fun* for you to watch. I'm doing all the work. You're supposed to be supporting me."

"Yeah, Jeff, but your face," I blurted out.

"What about my face, Reichen?" he blurted out in the same tone. I was stunned. He was staring me down as we sat across from each other in this booth at Arnie's. He had a look of confusion and maybe a little anger on his face. I didn't know what to say.

"Do what you want," I said quietly and looked down at my food. There was a ten-second pause, and I could see out of the edge of my eye that he was staring at me while I ate. I worked as hard as I could to push my tears back into my eyes. I thought about other things. I thought about what my brother and dad would say to me for acting this way. I knew I was acting like some worrisome mother rather than as a friend to Jeff. I hid my emotions the best I could by immediately detaching myself from Jeff at that moment. I needed to look back up at him and see someone that I didn't care for at all.

"Look at me," he said. I looked up and my eyes must have been red. "You need to get over this anxiety about my boxing matches. I need for you to be able to watch me and support me like everyone else." I thought Jeff was going to tell me that I was freaking him out too much and that he didn't want me around him anymore. I was assuming the worst. Instead, he was concerned about me and wanted me to adjust so that I could hang around with him more easily. He really cared about me. This realization warmed my heart more than any moment I had had with Jeff up to this point, but I remained calm and held my emotional distance from him.

"Don't worry, I'll be alright," I said. "I'm being stupid. I don't know why I get this way with you, but I promise it will stop." I looked back down again. Jeff continued to stare at me, trying to figure me out.

Lunch didn't last much longer. We talked about a few other things and went back to our rooms. When I walked into my room, Nathan was there. "What's up?" he asked.

"Nothing, why?" I answered, knowing that Nathan wanted to talk about Jeff.

"Just know that if you ever need to talk to me, about *anything*, you can," he said. That was enough for me to hear. I loved how Nathan didn't push the issue. I knew at that moment that Nathan would be OK with anything I needed to tell him, and that was a comforting thought. "Do your homework. We've been having too much fun this weekend and you need to have everything done for tomorrow morning," Nathan warned. He was right.

I sat down at my desk to do my homework and thought about what had happened over the day. *What* was *the issue?* I thought back to my lunch with Jeff. I thought about the moment that we got up from the table and left each other to run the strips back to our squadrons. I thought about what I looked at when I said good-bye to him. I looked into his eyes and at his lips. I looked at the slight stubble on his face. I looked at his beautiful blond hair. As we parted, I had an urge to hug him, but didn't. I had an internal wish that he would pull me behind some wall and kiss me before we parted, but he didn't. *Wait. What did I just imagine in my head? OK, I imagined that Jeff and I were making out in our uniforms and couldn't let go of each other.* I thought about it more. I was letting my mind go. *We were hugging passionately and rubbing our faces against each other. His mouth would pass my ear and he would tell me that he loved me and I would tell him in his ear that I loved him more than anything I had ever seen in the world. Then we would kiss again. I would kiss his mouth, his lips, his face, his eyes, his ears, and all the while his body would be pressed up against mine. We would both start crying because it felt so good.*

"Nathan, I'm in love with Jeff!" I said as I turned around in my chair, breathing hard as if I had just been holding my breath. "Please don't. Please don't!" I begged. Nathan jumped up from his desk where he was doing homework and got in front of me.

"Stop it! It's OK! Stop! Don't do what?" he asked sternly. I was still sort of hysterical.

"Don't. Please don't tell anyone," I begged as I continued to breathe heavily. "What the *fuck* is wrong with me?"

Nathan was now kneeling on the floor in front of me while I sat in my desk chair. He had his elbows on my knees and his hands around my torso. "Shh," he said gently. "Shh. Calm down. It's OK. It's OK. I'm not going to tell anyone. It's OK. No one's going to know. No one's going to hurt you. Shh." Nathan studied my face as I tried to pull myself back together. We looked at each other for a good ten minutes before I was able to speak.

"I'm at the academy and this is my chance to make a whole new life and now what? I'm falling for some *dude?*" I asked, feeling sorry for myself and holding back any tears.

Nathan spoke again. "Maybe you're not falling for him. Maybe this is just some sort of strange crush you have on Jeff, but because he reminds you of something from your childhood you're reacting this way. Why, do you think you're *gay?*" he asked. This was a loaded question and both Nathan and I knew it.

Here, my roommate, who had made very clear his negative opinion of gay people, was asking me if I was gay. Over the school year, he had told me of several people that he thought were gay because of the way they looked at him or by the way that they couldn't handle certain athletic activities. He told me how those people freaked him out. We had these conversations during the same time period that Kory, Jodie, Seth, and Kenny would talk to me about the lack of diversity at the academy and how ridiculous people were who hated blacks, gays, or any other minority group. In stark contrast, Nathan would be in our room talking about how gay people scared the hell out of him. I wanted to have a peaceful existence with my roommate so I had avoided saying anything back to him.

Now, I felt I had blown any chance of Nathan having any continued respect for me. "Nathan, what I just told you about Jeff is something I really feel. I don't know why. I have thought about controlling these feelings and I've tried *every* way possible to control them. I'm not a bad person. I'm not some freak. I'm just me. But I know the feelings I have for him are real. And before you say anything, you need to listen to me." Nathan nodded yes as he looked at me very intently. I continued. "We've talked about gay people in the past and we always talk about them wanting to butt-rape other guys or that they must be crazy because they could possibly find a guy's hairy ass attractive. It's not like that with me. It's not like that at all. With Jeff, it's more about just wanting to be around him. Yeah, I'll admit that I want to kiss him or feel his skin on mine, but I don't think about having butt sex with him. I just care about him more than I've ever cared about any guy or girl in my life, and I don't understand why. I think I went through this last year with a friend of mine in high school named Ben Silverman. So I've done this before. Fuck, Nathan! What the fuck?"

"Listen to me," Nathan said, "I've never dealt with anything like this before. And here *you* are, my roommate, who I have a ton of respect for, telling me that he likes another guy. When I've talked about gay guys in the past, I've pictured exactly what you just described. Freaks! But I would have *never* ever thought that anyone that I know would tell me something like this. You are blowing my mind right now. But at the same time, I can tell you that I'm OK with it." I really tried to pull myself together as Nathan continued. "I'm not gay and I have no desire to be with a guy, but somehow when you're telling me about Jeff and your feelings for him, I am listening and I can't believe it, but I'm OK with it. I don't know why, but I just am. I'm not going to tell anyone. You're just as confused about this as I am. I can see that. So take it slow. Figure this out. I'm here if you need to talk."

I was so very lucky to have Nathan as a roommate. He went back to his desk to finish his homework as if everything were normal—like we had just cleaned up some grape juice that spilled on the floor, rather than cleaning up an emotional coming-out by his roommate. I thought about Nathan and how strong a person he truly was. It was amazing to me. If I had had any other roommate, this could have been a complete disaster. I trusted Nathan more than anyone and it was a good thing that I did, because I had to.

To cheer me up that night, Nathan told me that Seth and Jodie had come in earlier asking where I was because they were going to take a run through the tunnels that night. This is something we had always waned to do. Running through the tunnels was completely illegal, but this maze of hallways built more than three stories below the academy was something we had all heard about, but had never actually seen.

That night, the four of us ventured out and explored the tunnels. What we saw was absolutely wonderful. What we didn't know was that, very soon, those tunnels would be a place we would come to know all too well.

chapter seventeen

RECOGNITION

Every cadet at the Air Force Academy must go through the grueling times of basic cadet training and freshman year. There is no such thing as transferring to the academy from another college and entering as anything other than a basic. Every cadet is required to go through the entire system, from improcessing day to graduation day.

Every year in April, a Hell Week is scheduled, during which the freshman class's privileges are brought back to those of basic training. Watches are taken away; so are blue uniforms. Freshmen are required to wear battle dress uniforms again and are put through a more intense week of training than they experienced during basic. Not only are their usual basic training cadre brought back to do the training, but *all* upperclassmen join in, including the sophomore class, which gangs up on that year's fourth-class cadets.

Hell Week training is meant as one more rite of passage before freshmen can be treated as human beings by the rest of the cadet wing. As dreaded as Hell Week was, we were all looking forward to it because, at the end, we would be "recognized" into the cadet wing— known as real cadets, instead of as smacks or doolies or plebes, as the upperclassmen then referred to us.

With recognition would come many privileges. We could walk around everywhere at rest. We would never again eat at attention. We would never again have to run on the Terrazzo's marble strips. We would never have to refrain from moving or talking as we wished. After recognition, we could have stereos in our rooms and go to bed whenever we wanted. We would no longer have to call minutes in the hallway in the mornings to wake up the upperclassmen.

At the start of the second semester of freshman year, each fourth-class cadet was assigned a sophomore mentor. Since this mentor did less mentoring and more hazing, the third-class mentor was called a hellmaster. A hellmaster's freshman was called his hellchild. A hellmaster could choose his or her hellchild, and the selection process was fought out by the sophomore class in each squadron.

My hellmaster was a sophomore named Kendall. We had gotten along well throughout the year. He was another tall, dark-haired, good-looking guy with blue eyes. The way that he trained me just seemed to work. He motivated me on squadron runs, and pushed me to become more athletic through working out at the gym and swimming laps. He helped me with my knowledge more effectively than any other upperclassman. He was patient and didn't like to yell. I definitely responded to his more intellectual approach to training.

When the sophomore class announced who our hellmasters were going to be, I was very happy. Kendall would be the one to give me my extra training in the weeks leading up to Hell Week and would monitor my performance closely during that final week.

Kendall wasn't the only one who would provide extra training, however—and not all of the extra training we received was legitimate or sanctioned by the academy system. There was a group of upperclassmen who went around at night and woke up freshmen, leaving a piece of paper in their beds that ordered them to go to a certain place in the cadet area, where they would find another note or object that would lead them to the next step. Basically, they were sending freshmen on scavenger hunts—on steroids. During the missions, the freshmen would be put through extra, and sometimes scary, physical training. I ended up being the target of one of these particular training quests, but mine didn't take me anywhere other than a few doors away from my own dormitory room.

About two weeks before recognition, two male upperclassmen came into my room and woke me up. They were wearing battle dress uniforms with their BDU caps, and black bandanas around their mouths. "Lehmkuhl, do you want to be recognized?" they asked.

"Yes, sir," I whispered.

"Get down out of bed," they ordered. I was nervous about the challenges I was about to be put through but at the same time, I imagined that they were Bull Ten upperclassmen who had trained me every day for the past year and, for that reason, I could feel safe with them. I stepped down my ladder and, because I always have slept naked out of habit, scrambled to find my underwear. I put on my underwear and, before I knew what was happening, they had put a laundry bag over my head. Instinctually, I immediately tried to get the bag off my head, but they surrounded me and forced my arms down. One of them spoke into my ear through the laundry bag, "Don't be a pussy. Just do what we say and you'll get it out of the way before Recognition Week."

I had heard stories about this kind of middle-of-the-night training, but I couldn't believe it was now happening to me. I had no idea it was coming. At any moment, I could have ended this nightmare by yelling and waking Nathan, but I would have had to make a big scene since Nathan could sleep through just about anything. I stopped moving my arms and decided to calm down. Out of necessity, I imagined that whoever had me in this position was someone I could trust, and that gave me some sort of comfort. I couldn't have been more wrong.

The two guys directed me out of my room with nothing on but my underwear and the laundry bag over my head. I felt carpet under my feet as they led me down the hall. I wondered who else could see me or if they were getting away with this without anyone knowing. I wondered what time it was. I had walked only a few feet down the hallway when I was spun around and then directed to walk some more. I had no idea where I was at this point. I was led into another cadet dorm room. I was standing there, feeling no one touching me anymore, and suddenly I felt the wind getting knocked out of me.

Before I even realized that I had been punched in the stomach, I fell to the floor and tried to take the laundry bag off my head. "Don't even fucking try!" they yelled in a whisper. I lay on my side, on the floor. After a few seconds the laundry bag was quickly pulled off my head and an elastic headband was put around my eyes. Now I felt more naked than I did before.

"Get ready to do some push-ups," one of them said in a whisper. "Get in the push-up position *now*, Lehmkuhl." I followed orders and was propped up in the front leading rest. I could see out of the bottom of my eye that a small votive candle had been placed under my chest. It made my chest hot but wasn't unbearable until they had me doing push-ups. On the down stroke of the push-up, I would feel the candle almost burn my chest and then I would push myself back up in relief. I had done as many push-ups as my arms could take and was holding myself up, above the candle. *What was I going to do now?* I thought about falling on the candle. Although the wax would burn me at first, I would put out the flame. My arms were shaking. The two guys above me were whispering. My body started to arch so that my pelvis was getting close to the floor. "Get your butt up, Lehmkuhl! What the hell do you think you're doing?" I straightened out my body as much as I could and all of the sudden, one of the guys pulled my underwear from my hips to my knees. The crazy part was that I could feel him doing it from underneath me. The other guy was next to my face and said into my ear, "Now come down slowly to the floor." I lowered my body and I was relieved to feel that the candle had been taken away. As I went down, my chest hit the bare chest of one of the guys and my exposed penis went into what felt like the mouth of the guy underneath my legs.

The sensation that I experienced at that very moment is difficult to describe. With a warm man's chest under mine and my legs all over the body of another guy, a feeling of extreme pleasure came over me all at once. At the same time that my body was stimulated, my mind was telling me that I didn't *want* to enjoy it, knowing that it was all forced. After such fear, anxiety, stress, and muscle fatigue, it was almost as if these two guys had thought of the most relieving and pleasurable thing

I could experience at that moment. After I lowered myself and felt the two guys on and around me, I lay as still as I could, trying to think of what I should do next. *Can I fight this? Are they going to hurt me?* I thought to myself.

The guy under my chest was lying perpendicular to me and he had placed his arms over my back to hold me in place. I lay still for about a minute. His chest felt warm and kind of sweaty, and I could feel some clipped chest hair against my bare chest. My breathing became harder and deeper. I couldn't control the fact that these guys were turning me on. I became aroused and I felt myself growing inside the guy's mouth. Although it felt good, I was trying to fight it in my head. I didn't want this to feel good in any way. I reached around to remove the headband from my eyes but the guy in front of me wouldn't let me take it off. I closed my eyes.

"You *love* it, don't you, smack?" the guy in front asked. "Answer me. You love it. You love it, don't you? Oh, yeah. You love it." I didn't say anything. I felt like it was a trap, even though they would be in just as much trouble as I would for saying that I liked it. The difference was that I didn't know who they were, but they knew exactly who I was. They had me in the most intense physical situation that I had ever been in.

I decided to try to release myself from them, so I pulled up with my pelvis, but the guy there followed me up with his head and mouth still around my penis. I moved back down. I was so sexually aroused, yet feeling so violated, that I didn't know what to do. I struggled to move away from them but they held me tighter. The motion of getting away felt so good between my legs that I kept moving up and down. It only took me about two minutes to come, and when I did, the guy in front of me had turned his body somewhat so that my face was on his chest. I must have given him a hickey on his chest as I sucked on his skin while I came. Right after, they rolled me off them and put the bag back on my head. One of them sat me up on the floor and held my head and chest while the other slipped some sort of shorts onto me. I was stunned, tired, and in a daze. They led me into my room and shut my door. I crawled into bed and fell asleep, sort of shaking and sort of delirious.

The next morning, I woke up to our room alarm. As usual, Nathan got out of bed and shut off the alarm. He told me to get up. "What are you wearing?" Nathan asked. I was warm and didn't have the sheets covering me but since Nathan knew I slept naked, he wondered why I was wearing boxer shorts. I looked down to see boxer shorts with camouflage on them. Being freshmen, we weren't even allowed to have any sort of civilian clothing in our rooms, so this definitely looked out of place.

"These two guys came into our room last night. They took me out of here and beat the shit out of me." I knew I wasn't ready to tell Nathan what happened to me after that, so I skipped it. "Then, they took my underwear and put these on me while I had a bag over my head."

"Fuck you," Nathan laughed.

"Nathan, I'm serious," I said.

"You're telling me that someone took your underwear, dude?" he asked, still laughing. "It had to be one of us in Bull Ten. One of the freshmen, playing a trick on you."

"No, it wasn't a freshman. It was two upperclassmen. They told me that I had to go through this now instead of during Recognition Week," I explained.

"Dude. Are you kidding me?" he asked.

"No, Nathan. Fuck. Never mind," I said and rolled over. I looked down at my boxers again and pulled them off. On the inside of the elastic band at the top, written in black magic marker, was written, "WE KNOW ABOUT YOU." I wanted to vomit. I put the shorts under my pillow and pulled the covers up over my head. I doubled over as if my stomach were in pain. Nathan was getting ready to call minutes to wake the upperclassmen of the squadron.

"Get out of bed, dude. You're going to be late," Nathan warned. I didn't want Nathan to ask any more questions. I thought that if I told him about the boxer shorts and the whole story, he would feel like he was in danger simply because people knew about me. I thought that he would be worried that people would think that *he* was gay because he was my roommate. I walked down my ladder, facing away from him. I wiped my eyes and continued to look down while I put on my uniform.

I could still feel the dried semen and saliva on me as I put on a new pair of underwear. I didn't want to try to wash off in front of Nathan and I definitely didn't have time to take a shower. I felt gross. I wondered who had done this to me. I wondered if they had done it to anyone else and how the hell they were getting away with it.

Worse, I thought about how good it felt to have my chest up against another guy's chest and how good my legs felt on the stubble of the guy who took care of my lower half. My first sexual experience with a guy had happened and it was nothing like I had fantasized.

As I stood in formation and saluted the flag, looking at hundreds of men dressed in uniform, just like me, I stared at the backs of their heads and thought about how creepy it was that two of these guys had done this to me. But who else might have been watching the whole thing happen? I felt sick to my stomach again. I wondered, *How in the hell did these guys know?* Maybe they had seen me in the shower and just liked me. Maybe Jeff had told them. Maybe Nathan had told them. None of these theories really made any sense to me.

At this point in my life, I had no concept of gaydar, the ability to tell if someone is gay just by looking at them and maybe exchanging a few words. If I had known about gaydar, maybe I could have written it off—these guys were gay and detected enough of a gaydar signal from me to know that I liked guys.

For the rest of that week, I could not get the experience out of my head. During the day, I was freaked out by it, but at night, I would find myself fantasizing about being with them again. I felt guilty and disgusted with myself for having those thoughts. Then I would stop and remind myself that they punched me in the stomach before they did what they did. The experience had not happened in a healthy situation. *So why would I want to be with them again?*

I became desperate to clear my head and wanted to tell someone about it. I thought about going to counseling, but any counselor at the academy would have made a huge deal out of it, and that is not what I wanted. I didn't want an investigation or for anyone to be punished. I just wanted to talk to someone about my feelings. Besides, I wouldn't have been able to tell a counselor everything anyway. If I had in any way indicated that I had come during the situation, or that I liked what had happened, I would have been labeled a "homosexual" in my military record, and all that I had thus far earned in the air force would be taken away from me. I knew the chaplains were the only people at the academy who had absolute authority to keep a secret, if they wanted to, but I was afraid to go to them after the creepy experience with Chaplain Karnes and his antigay video. Even if I told the story as a victim in the scenario, I might still have been investigated, and then labeled as gay. There was no place for me to go for help.

The Uniform Code of Military Justice, or UCMJ, is a set of laws, rules, and regulations that establish proper conduct for military personnel. Punishments for breaking UCMJ laws are, in many cases, much more harsh than punishments for breaking the same laws in the civilian world. Homosexuality and homosexual conduct are still considered incompatible with military service under the UCMJ. Punishment for homosexual conduct can land a member of the military in deep trouble and result in harsh punishment, such as a less-than-honorable discharge. Sodomy is also considered a crime under the UCMJ and, if proven, can result in severe punishment, depending on the perceived severity of the offense by the military court system. The military environment allows for homosexuality to be grossly unacceptable. Jokes about the hurting and killing of homosexuals are widely accepted in the U.S. Armed Forces and are even used to gain a military member recognition as a macho or socially responsible and acceptable person.

Like all the other stress and trauma that I went through at the academy, my forced sexual experience soon faded from my mind because new stresses and challenges took its place. The only way I could survive at the academy was to continually erase problems from my mind so that I could handle those challenges the future held for me. I was already in that mode of mental survival, so this situation was no different for me.

Before I knew it, Recognition Week, or Hell Week, had begun. Classes ceased, so all that existed at the academy was raw military training by the upperclassmen. There was still snow on the ground at the start of April, and the upperclassmen used it to their advantage. I did my fair share of low-crawling, running, and push-ups in the snow. We went through the obstacle course again.

We did about ten "fashion shows" in the hallway. The upper-classmen would command us to get into service dress or another uniform. Then, once we were out in the hallway they would train us for having problems with the way we were wearing them. They would make us do push-ups or iron mikes for things that were wrong. Then they would tell us to run back into our rooms and get into BDUs. Then they would call us back out into the hall and train us again. It gave them a chance to yell at us and create stress, and was an excuse to make us do more physical activities.

My hellmaster, Kendall, trained me hard during the whole week. He yelled at me but had a twinkle in his eye the entire time. He was being cooler than ever and motivated me to really push my limits. I *wanted* to work hard for him because I could tell we had a mutually respectful relationship. At the end of the week, we were all spent physically, emotionally, and mentally. I could tell that the upperclassmen in our squadron were proud of us.

In the last ceremonial event of recognition, we were all marched up to the squadron assembly room, or SAR as we called it, and lined up in a row facing the wall. Then we were ordered to do an about-face. When we did, our hellmasters were staring us in the face. They pulled us aside to our own private place in the SAR and each gave us a little speech. Kendall told me how proud he was of me for handling Hell Week so well and said that he had a feeling that I would be a great addition to the academy and to the air force. When a freshman is recognized, he or she is given a pin with the symbol of a prop and wings tied together to be worn on the cadet flight cap. It's a symbol of being a legitimate, recognized cadet of the academy. The prop and wings has two pins on the back that can pierce fabric; two "frogs," or backings, are placed on the pins to hold them in place. When the prop and wings are set onto a cadet's chest, punched into the breast muscle, and left there for a while, it puts two small holes in the cadet's chest—and turns the wings into "blood wings." Kendall asked me if I wanted blood wings, and I told him yes. As he punched them into my chest, the sharp pain paled in comparison to the adrenaline rush I experienced from making it to recognition. I wore my blood wings for about thirty minutes, and then put them on my flight cap in my room.

The rest of that night was truly amazing. Walking around the academy and the hallways of the squadron at rest felt like a dream. My gang and I walked across the Terrazzo to dinner at rest, and couldn't believe how absolutely wonderful it felt. We were proud of what we had accomplished, and we were proud of each other.

The feeling that a cadet at a service academy experiences when he or she reaches a milestone such as recognition is indescribable. We had experienced a similar feeling at the end of basic training and we were experiencing it again. Something that we had worked so hard for was not to be taken lightly and, if pushed, we would go to great lengths to protect all that we had earned.

Everything had been taken away from us when we arrived at the academy, and on this day, it was returned to us. But the message was clear: the only thing that we truly owned on Recognition Day was pride in ourselves. We were born again into a people of greater strength, character, and integrity than we had ever imagined we could become.

No cadet would make it easy for another person to take away the status he or she finally held by accomplishing so much. What a cadet earns by way of hard work, sweat, and tears is sacred, very personal, and to be protected at any cost.

chapter eighteen

WINEFEST

Things were looking up at the end of that second semester. My grades had improved and I was looking at a GPA of 2.8, which was great, considering my previous 1.4. This would take me off academic probation for the start of my sophomore year.

Sometimes, on Sunday nights, the academy would entertain foreign visitors or special-interest groups with large dinners in Mitchell Hall, complete with lobster, steak, and wine. Seth would always find a way to be invited to these dinners and sneak out a couple of bottles of wine in his backpack when the meal was over. It was illegal for cadets to drink in the dorms, so it was a big deal to hide these bottles of wine in our rooms. We were very careful about not being caught.

On one weekend night, Seth, Jodie, Kory, Kenny, Nathan, and I had an overnight pass to use, so we decided to ride with Seth to his house. His father, Colonel English, was stationed locally, so he had bought a house in Colorado Springs. Seth's parents weren't home that weekend and we had the house to ourselves. Seth had told some other Ninety-sixers (the year we would graduate) that he was having a little get-together, so they ended up joining us as well.

Before arriving at the house, I had Seth take me to a CD store and I used a new credit card to buy a couple of Grateful Dead CDs. We had about sixteen bottles of wine for twelve of us and every one of us got hammered that night. Seth's house had an inground pool that was heated so we all went swimming, too. The house and pool were pretty awesome because they overlooked the city of Colorado Springs. At night, the lights of the city were beautiful, especially when viewed from a warm pool filled with my friends, drunk on wine.

In the pool, we were up to our old tricks of imitating different upperclassmen in our squadron. Jodie and I were the best at this and had a great time mocking their voices and their pet peeves. "Ooh, those cadets are swimming in a pool and having fun. This has to stop. Ooh!" we would yell while making faces and clenching our fists, and then we would laugh our asses off. Everything we did was funnier because we were drunk. This was my first night of any sort of real college experience. Nevertheless, we were all so tired from our school week and so conditioned to waking up at the crack of dawn that we went to bed early that night. Jodie and I took Seth's room. I put the Grateful Dead in his CD player and we went to sleep to the peaceful and soothing music that I loved so much. Jodie liked it, too. "Ooh," she said before we went to sleep, "those cadets are male and female and are sleeping in the same bed. Ooh!" We laughed again, hugged each other tightly, and fell asleep.

The next morning, as we ate Seth's cereal and milk, we talked about how much fun we had all had together the night before. We talked about how cool it was to drink the leftover wine, and we vowed to do it all again.

"Let's call it WineFest," I said. A few people laughed. "No, I'm serious. We're harvesting the wine from the academy. It's WineFest, and we'll do it once a semester."

"WineFest it is," Seth said with a smile on his face. WineFest would happen again and I would make sure of that, but next time, it would be even more fun, with more people, and more wine.

chapter nineteen

SURVIVAL MATES

The school year ended with a solid week of finals and the anticlimax of having to clear out our rooms and put all of our stuff into storage. That sucked. Rooms had to be cleared out because of summer programs that occurred over the summer. There were three segments of summer programs, each lasting three weeks. Two of the segments were taken up with military summer programs; one was allowed for vacation time. However, cadets could give up a vacation segment and fill it with another summer program, such as a summer school class or an additional military program.

The military programs available depended on a cadet's class. For incoming sophomores, or third-class cadets, there was a mandatory training program where we learned survival and deception techniques to protect us from an enemy. Other programs for the summer included Soaring—or training to fly and solo in an engineless sailplane—and Jump, which was the academy's free-fall parachute training.

That summer, I had been assigned first Soaring, second vacation, and third survival activity training. First Soaring was the worst to be assigned because there was less of a chance of picking up a normal amount of wind for training flights at that time of year. I went through one week of classroom training and then, when it was time to actually fly with

Soaring instructors, who were also cadets, the wind was always too strong for us to go up.

It usually took about ten flights with an instructor for a cadet to be proficient enough to fly and land a sailplane alone. I ended up getting only about six flights in two weeks and didn't get a chance to solo. Luckily for me, that summer Nathan did end up soloing in Soaring. He took it on as a full-time extracurricular activity during sophomore year, becoming a Soaring instructor—and I was able to go up in a sailplane any time I wanted to. That year, Nathan and I could take a plane up any weekend, and he would let me fly or I would tell him to fly and to "make me high." With that, Nathan would pull the plane up for a few seconds and then drop us down fast so that I felt like I was floating for a good minute.

Second vacation was my three weeks to escape the academy for the first time since the semester's end. Again, I went home to my brother's house in Los Angeles instead of visiting my parents. I didn't want to go anywhere near the trailer park that had created so much strife in what I now considered my previous life. The hardest part about visiting my brother was explaining to my parents that I didn't want to come home. They thought there was nothing wrong with where they lived, which had been their sentiment when I was in high school, and I never understood how they didn't grasp what living there had put me through.

After three weeks of plenty of rest and relaxation, I had to go back to the academy for survival training. Almost every cadet I knew was afraid of survival training and every incoming sophomore at the academy was required to pass it. I used to envy the class ahead of us for having already completed it. We would hear their horror stories of starvation, sickness, frostbite, and physical abuse.

Our survival training was made up of many parts, including classroom training for about a week. The second week was the survival portion of the program. It was a one-week journey through the woods of the Colorado Mountains. We were given a backpack filled with certain food items, including meal replacement bars, two meals ready to eat, or MREs, iodine tablets to sterilize the water in our canteens, and a live rabbit, which was given to us halfway through the program. The only water available was the water we would take from streams and rivers, and the rabbit was an eventual meal for my survival mates and me.

Each team was made up of several people. The purpose was to simulate being shot down from a plane in enemy territory. The scenario was that we had successfully parachuted out of our planes with our survival packs, which is what we would live from for about a week. In our survival pack was a map of the territory that we had supposedly been patrolling in our airplanes. With the map and our compasses, we were supposed to navigate our way to predetermined checkpoints that we were, in the scenario, briefed on before our mission flight. The checkpoints of interest on the map included places to find water, food, and, in particular, partisan camps where we would find supplies and friendly people sympathetic to the American mission of the scenario's war. The "partisans" were interesting people. As we approached the camps, these cadets, who acted as partisans as they were trained, would react to us in many different ways. Some would be extremely angry when we approached their camps. Others would be delighted to have us there. Our part of the training was to learn how to ingratiate ourselves into the camps in order to gain the supplies that we needed. We also had to learn how to live at the camps without giving away our location to the enemy. The classroom training that we had in the week before the survival hike taught us these techniques.

Throughout the paths that we were navigating were other cast members of the program, who were chasing us. They were cadets posing as enemy soldiers out headhunting the Americans, who they knew had been shot down. It was nearly impossible to make it through the entire program without being captured by one or more of the enemy. Once they captured our group, they would beat us up by hitting or kicking us while we were forced to lie or sit on the ground. Sometimes they would take a rope and put it around our necks and shake us violently until we answered their questions.

Eventually, we were supposed to attempt an escape, as we were taught during training, either by force or by slipping away quietly when they were not paying attention. Luckily, on our attempt, we slipped away without needing to use force. We had our opportunity to escape after being thrown in a truck and let out a few miles down the road. The enemy had asked us to collect firewood for them in the immediate area, so we banded together and snuck off quietly. They made a ruckus when they realized we were gone and started shooting off their weapons, but we lay low and moved farther away to safety.

The other guys on my team were athletic and could handle the harsh conditions of the program. They were extremely focused on surviving and so was I, so we worked well together.

Eventually, there came a point when we had to eat the rabbit. I had given it a name, which was not a good idea. Watching "Jerry" die didn't do much to keep up my morale, nor could I eat his flesh or any meat offered to me by the others.

The program eventually led us to being detained in a concentration camp. Every person in the program was eventually thrown into this concentration camp. The first thing I found myself dealing with at the camp was the will not to freak out, because we were being transported there in a closed truck with breathable bags over our heads. I just closed my eyes and hoped for the ride to end as soon as possible.

By the time I got to the camp, I was burning up. It was far from comfortable to be standing inside the truck, or even outside in the hot sun, wearing BDUs, with a bag over my head. But the discomfort was just beginning.

The first thing they did to me at the camp was throw me into a wooden box that was four feet high by four feet wide by four feet long. My body barely fit in the box, so I was shoved in there like a pretzel. I do not like to be hot or restrained, and I especially do not like the two together. I don't know how I survived this because most of my experience in the program has been erased from my mind. I would guess that this is because it was such a stressful time that I have suppressed it for my own good.

I had most definitely developed an eating disorder during my freshman year from the upperclassmen not letting me eat at meals. I would hoard food in my room to eat later, but would never eat it. I always felt like I had to have enough food stashed away in case someone kept me from eating a meal. Therefore, the lack of food became my biggest fear in the program. I spent so much mental energy on ignoring my hunger that I didn't focus on much else.

I can remember only a few moments and experiences from the concentration camp. One was when I was put into a cell for what might have been a few days. I had completely lost track of time. The cell was cold and completely dark and black except for a tiny bit of light that came from under the door. There was a speaker in the cell playing, at full blast, the sound of a woman singing a song that sounded like screaming in an Asian language. It went on for hours and hours. Sometimes they would change the sound to a low rumbling, with water dripping in the background. I was completely delirious and out of my mind in this cell. There was a single coffee can in the cell for me to defecate and urinate into. I was in there long enough that I had to use the can for both. After using it, the cell smelled awful and made me nauseous beyond description. I threw up, so I had to endure that smell also. At one point, whoever was working the cell block pulled me out of the cell. My eyes burned from the bright overhead lights that shone on me in the hallway of the cell block. I could barely open them. I remember a black guy yelling at me and telling me to take off all of my clothes as he kicked me. I took them off and they took my clothes away. I was sitting on a hard cement floor, naked. They told me to lie on the floor and, as I did, I noticed I was lying next to about ten other naked guys. I was scared to death. At this point, I had lost all memory that I was in a mock situation, which they had warned us might happen. I really believed that I had been taken to another country and that I was a fallen pilot.

As we lay on the floor, they instructed us to close our eyes. When I did, I felt someone grab my genitals as hard as they could. I was hungry, tired, scared, and confused, so instead of fighting him off, I clenched my eyes shut and just took whatever they were going to do to me. In my head I was thinking that I just needed to take one moment at a time, and get through *that*.

With one hand around my penis and the other hand around my throat, he asked me some questions, to which I responded with only my name, rank, serial number, and date of birth, as I had been instructed to do in training. This *always* upset the staff of the camp. Right after answering, he let me go and stood up. Before I knew it, they were pouring buckets of ice water onto all of the guys who were lying on the floor. Everyone let out what I can only describe as a man-scream as they tried to suppress the feeling of the shockingly cold water.

"Shut up, Americans!" they yelled at us. Soon after leaving us lying in puddles of cold water, they picked us up and threw us back into our cells with no clothes on. When I got back into my cell, I noticed that the horrible smell was gone. They had sprayed out the vomit and emptied my coffee-can toilet. The floor was wet and cold. I sat there shivering, counting the minutes until my body dried off. I rubbed my skin to make the water go away faster. Then I moved around the cell and lay on different parts of my body so I wouldn't feel the cold, wet cement on one part of my body for any length of time.

To pass the time and to combat boredom, I plugged my ears for a few minutes and then unplugged them for another few minutes to fully hear the screaming coming through the speakers.

I was finally dry and felt a sense of calm come over me. I was aware of my hunger but it wasn't painful anymore. My mind was controlling my needs to eat, to be warm, and to be clothed. As I became more comfortable, I stared more and more intently on the light coming from under the door of my cell. I tuned out the screaming and began to hear a tapping rhythm that somehow sounded like someone was talking to me. As I followed the tapping, I watched in awe as the light under the door became a stage in a theater. As I rocked back and forth, the light rays changed under the door and I started to see people and animals on a stage that I was imagining. They were all dancing and moving to the music, doing an entire show for me. I absolutely loved what I was seeing and I would have done anything to make sure it didn't stop. I started humming to the tapping. I'm sure that I continued watching this for over an hour.

Then, suddenly, one of the staff members kicked my cell door so hard that the sound made me jump back in my cell and hit my head on its four-foot-high ceiling. That woke me up. I looked down at the bottom of the door and failed to see anything but light. The stage had disappeared. I was heartbroken. I felt my eyes fill with tears. All at once I felt hunger moving over me. I had a throbbing headache. Was it from hitting my head or was it from not eating? Or was something else wrong with me? "Help!" I screamed from my cell.

"Help me! Let me the fuck out of here!" I yelled at the top of my lungs. Silence. No one could hear me. I must have been in there for over two days. Even if I were naked and beaten after being dragged out of the cell, I would have been happier than sitting in the dark anymore. I thought about how awful it would be if they had forgotten about me. *What if I were left there for dead?* All of this was running through my mind at once. I was in a state of panic.

Tap. Tap. Tap. Tap tap. I heard the tapping that I had focused on during the imaginary play under the cell door. It suddenly occurred to me that this was another prisoner tapping to me in an algorithmic tap code that I actually understood. It was the tap code that we had learned in classroom training! I counted the taps. "Are you OK?" they tapped.

"No, I'm feeling really strange. Hallucinating," I tapped back on the wall that the tapping was coming from.

"Don't worry. I am, too," the person next to me tapped. All at once, I felt amazingly better. I felt a burst of energy inside me. I had just found out so many things. I could communicate. I was not alone. Someone else was going through what I was going through. I wasn't crazy.

"How long have we been in here?" I tapped.

"I don't know. Feels like a year now," he tapped back.

"Are you naked?" I tapped.

"No. I was. They just gave me my clothes back," he tapped. I was glad to hear that. Maybe I would get mine back, too.

Just then, my cell door opened and I was blinded by fluorescent light from the hallway. It burned my eyes. I turned away. The same black guy reached in and pushed me by my bare stomach to the back of the cell. He threw my clothes and boots back at me and shut the door. One of the boots hit me in the face. I didn't care. I was frantic. I searched through the clothes, blinded by the darkness, to find my underwear. There it was! I put it on first. I couldn't get dressed fast enough. I found only one sock but I put that on next. I pulled my pants over my legs. They felt so good. All I could think about was being protected from the cold floor underneath me. Soon, I was fully clothed. I wrapped my arms around myself and sat in the corner, with my legs crossed. I felt warmth forming in and around my body. I needed rest. I tried to sleep, but I repeatedly heard screams or noises that prevented me from dozing off.

My cell door opened again. A pan was slid in the doorway by a woman's hand. It was a metal tray with a quarter loaf of bread and an apple on it. I saw both of these in the light and then the door slammed. Was this a trick? I didn't know what to do. I scooted forward and reached toward the door. There was the bread and the apple! I ate all of it in about a minute flat. I ate every *bit* of the apple, including every seed, the core, and the stem. By the time I finished the bread, I felt completely full. My stomach must have shrunk to the size of a golf ball. I could barely finish the small amount they gave me but I forced it down because I knew that I needed it to survive.

My next memory is of being in a courtyard with two wooden guard towers on either side of it. I don't know how I got there. It was the middle of the night. There was barbed wire along the top of the fence that surrounded the yard. I was moving gravel with a metal rake. I had a guard yelling at me to work harder. I was tired, weak, and could barely stay awake or stand up. There were other "prisoners" around me doing other kinds of work. I saw two guys carrying boulders from one end of the yard to the other. They were dropping the rocks and moving very slowly. I saw one guard pushing a guy down a hole in the ground. As I looked closer, I realized that he was being pushed down on top of other prisoners who were further down in the hole! Then the guard put a wooden lid on the hole and stood on it as they all yelled from below for him to please stop pushing on it.

My next memory has me sitting in a classroom with a bunch of other prisoners. The staff, wearing all-black BDUs like the mock-enemy soldiers who had caught us in the woods, were asking us questions with guns pointed at us. There was a video camera set up, taping us. "What kinds of food do you eat in America?" they asked one guy.

"We eat hamburgers and cheeseburgers and pizza and . . ." the guy continued on in a dreamy state, fantasizing about eating again. After he answered, they made us all put our heads down on the desks of the classroom. We had our heads down for what seemed like an hour. If anyone moved, they were threatened with being shot by the camp staff. After a while, a guy came back in with a tape in his hand. He put it in the VCR, and on the TV played a clip of us being interviewed in that classroom.

The interviewer asked the prisoner, "What do you get to eat in the prison?" The camera shot moved to my fellow prisoner saying, "We eat hamburgers and cheeseburgers and pizza and Coke and big breakfasts. . . ."

"Stupid American!" yelled the guy who had inserted the tape. He laughed and told us that this was the tape that they would send back to our news media to let America know that we were being treated well in prison.

My last memory of the prison camp was the night of liberation. I was doing my job of raking gravel with an armed guard standing next to me when I heard the sound of M-16 semiautomatic rifles shooting all over the camp. The camp staff started shooting back with their AK-47s. There must have been blanks in the rifles since it was a simulation but it felt all too real. I hit the ground as fast as I could. The guard who was monitoring me fell down next to me. He had been "shot." His rifle flew out of his arms and part of it was lying on my hands, which were cupping the back of my head.

Men dressed in sharp BDUs broke into the camp. There was a helicopter overhead shining its searchlights onto the camp through the night sky. Guns were firing everywhere. "Are you alive?" one guy yelled to me. "I'm an American soldier. We're here to get you out!"

"Yes, I'm alive!" I yelled.

"Stay here!" he yelled back at me and ran away. This simulation was so real that it was scary. Soon, the American troops had completely wiped out the mock-enemy in the camp. Medical personnel were carrying out some "wounded" American soldiers on stretchers. After about an hour of gathering up all the prisoners, lining us up, and putting us into formation, they yelled out the commands that I was so familiar with for morning and noon meal formations at the Air Force Academy. They dressed and covered us so that we were sized appropriately in formation. I looked at the guys I was with in the yard of this concentration camp. Everyone looked tired, dirty, and skinny.

One of the rescuing soldiers went to the flagpole and lowered the flag of the country that we were supposedly in, the same flag that was sewn on the uniforms of all the mock-enemy soldiers. The soldier attached a United States flag to the rope and began to raise it high in the middle of this awful concentration camp. I couldn't hold back my emotions. Tears were pouring out of my eyes. Someone in the crowd, probably one of the soldiers, started reciting the Code of Conduct for Members of the Armed Forces of the United States, which I had had burned into my head during freshman year at the academy. Everyone else followed along, holding back so much emotion.

I am an American, fighting in the forces which guard my country and our way of life. I am prepared to give my life in their defense.

I will never surrender of my own free will. If in command, I will never surrender the members of my command while they still have the means to resist.

If I am captured, I will continue to resist by all means available. I will make every effort to escape and aid others to escape. I will accept neither parole nor special favors from the enemy.

If I become a prisoner of war, I will keep faith with my fellow prisoners. I will give no information nor take part in any action which might be harmful to my comrades. If I am senior, I will take command. If not I will obey the lawful orders of those appointed over me and will back them up in every way.

When questioned, should I become a prisoner of war, I am required to give name, rank, serial number and date of birth. I will evade answering further questions to the utmost of my ability. I will make no oral or written statements disloyal to my country and its allies or harmful to their cause.

I will never forget that I am an American, fighting for freedom, responsible for my actions, and dedicated to the principles which made my country free. I will trust in my God and in the United States of America.

When we finished reciting it, almost every person in formation had tears in his or her eyes, including me. Suddenly someone ordered, "Present arms!" We all saluted the flag and just as we did, someone started playing the song "I'm Proud to Be an American" by Lee Greenwood over the camp loudspeaker. We listened to the whole song in the salute before they began playing the national anthem. After that, I had chills running through my body. "Order arms!" was called, and we brought our hands slowly back to our sides, standing at attention.

After the formation, we were ordered to relax. I sat on the ground and put my head in between my hands. I couldn't believe what I had just been through. I looked up and around me at the camp and imagined what real prisoners of war go through. I had been there for only a matter of a few days, but there are POWs who have lasted *years* in captivity, getting much worse treatment than I had experienced.

I have never forgotten my experience and will always have more respect for the survivors, as well as the not-so-fortunate prisoners of war who have been captured while serving on a mission for the United States.

I had learned a great deal in survival school. Once a person is captured, it doesn't matter what he or she was fighting for or whether the mission was right or wrong. The captured person has one thing to think about and that is survival while in captivity. The mental challenges that I endured for just a couple of days were nothing compared to those about which I've read in the stories of past prisoners of war.

One particular story is that of Captain Lance Peter Sijan, who was shot down during the Vietnam War. All cadets at the academy are issued a book describing his captivity. After being shot down, he evaded capture for six weeks. He was captured and then escaped, only to be captured again. He died two weeks later in Hanoi. What he endured after being shot down was much more harsh than any of the experiences I had in the survival program. I am forever grateful, however, that I was able to experience something similar to what POWs go through—and to be able to appreciate the feeling of being rescued from such a nightmare.

chapter twenty

SOPHOMORIC

My second summer at the Air Force Academy was over. Within a matter of days I found myself back in the cadet bookstore buying everything I needed to start class the next day. Sophomore year was supposed to be the hardest technically, so I wasn't looking forward to it. The nice part, however, was that I wasn't a freshman anymore; eighty percent of my stress was lifted. I was a recognized cadet and ready to succeed.

While I was doing my summer programs, the new year of basic cadets were going through basic training—being tortured and hazed by the incoming juniors and seniors as part of *their* mandatory summer programs. I was looking forward to working as a Beast cadre member the following summer. I wanted to work First Beast because I wanted to be part of a new basic's first impression of the Air Force Academy.

I had finished moving all of my belongings back into my room in Bull Ten. Nathan was my roommate again, and we were glad to see each other after such a crazy summer. We had a better room than the previous year because we were further down the hall from the squadron desk. Even though we didn't have a room with a view on the outside of the quad, it was quieter down at the end of the hall and away from all the action.

A sophomore manned the CQ, or charge of quarters, desk at all times. The squadron was L shaped, and the CQ desk sat in the corner or joint of the L. Our sophomore class of the squadron now had to decide who would sit at the desk, and when. We had no phones in our rooms, so the only squadron phone was at the desk. Often, cadets gathered at the CQ desk to read the squadron message board. The board had four columns on it, one for each class in Bull Ten. Announcements were written on it throughout the day and it was our responsibility to check the board for important messages. I hadn't paid much attention to the new freshmen in Bull Ten because I was busy moving into my room. In fact, Nathan and I avoided a lot of interaction with the rest of the squadron, which, for us, became a major theme of our existence at the academy.

I'll never forget the first time I walked down the hall and one of our new freshmen stopped, at attention, in the hallway, trying to read my uniform's name tag, and said, "Good afternoon, Cadet . . . Lehm . . . Lehm . . . Lehmkuhl! Raging Bull Ten!" What a moment that was. I didn't know what to do. So, being the nice person I was, I said, "Thanks," and walked on by.

Thanks? I thought to myself afterward. *Why did I* thank *him?* I decided, at that moment, that I wanted to be one of the upperclassmen who asked the freshmen *never* to greet me in the hallway. I found the whole tradition pointless and really annoying. When I was a freshman, I hated hearing the sound of freshmen yelling in the hallways. Even more annoying were upperclassmen who actually demanded they be greeted. I wondered if it built up their egos to hear someone greet them. I would choose a quiet life from here on out, at least as quiet as I could make it. I really needed to focus on my schoolwork.

* * *

Being a sophomore meant that I could roam to other squadrons. I ended up hanging around in Jeff Campbell's squadron quite a bit and met all of his friends there. Jeff and I became better friends during the first semester and planned to do some skiing together that year since we had more weekend passes and I was no longer on academic probation.

One weekend when Jeff was really feeling homesick, we both cashed in a weekend pass for a much-needed break from the academy. I rented a car and we drove to Nebraska, where he is from. Our drive was long, so we didn't have much time there. We stayed with his parents for a couple of days, and all was well until I had to meet Millie, his girlfriend from high school. Jeff had told me stories about her and how they had a high school romance and then sort of ended the relationship when he went to the academy. Millie and I met over lunch with Jeff on Saturday and it was awkward. I could tell she didn't like me; it was almost as if she was jealous of me. I, in turn, didn't much care for her. I sensed that she and I were in competition for Jeff's attention.

I guess she had lots to be jealous of because Jeff and I slept together in his bed during the entire weekend. His mother and father had kept his bedroom exactly as he had left it. It was filled with Jeff's high school memories and trophies. Being in Jeff's room with him was a pretty crazy experience. I felt like I was back in high school, sleeping in the room of some guy I secretly had a crush on. Behind his house were acres of cornfields that seemed to start just outside his back door. Next to his bed was a glass slider that looked out onto the corn. Coming from the academy, a weekend in this very wholesome environment of corn and high school sweethearts and football memories made for a really nice change of pace.

From the moment I had set foot in Jeff's house, I felt like a free spirit. After a long day of touring all of his old haunts, Jeff and I went to bed, but I couldn't sleep. For the first time, I was sleeping next to him. We were both in our underwear. I couldn't help but be completely aroused the entire time. Looking back, I can't believe it didn't hit me that I was gay. Here I was, fantasizing about Jeff and me being totally naked in his bed, rolling around wrestling with hard-ons, doing whatever we wanted to each other.

"Jeff, wake up," I whispered. He turned over and looked at me.

"You're not asleep, man?" he asked.

"No, I can't sleep. Stay up with me. Let's *do* something." I said.

"Like what?" he asked.

"Like I don't know! I'm restless. I need to get rid of some energy." Before I finished saying that, something came over me and I jumped on top of Jeff with my whole body. I rolled him over onto his back. His hands were outside of the covers so I grabbed them and started trying to pin his arms down above his head. He was laughing and fighting me.

"What has gotten *into* you?" he asked as he started wrestling me in the bed. I was getting what I wanted. He rolled over and got on top of me and pinned my hands down. His big body was pressed against mine; I could feel his boner, and I know he could feel mine. In his defense, he may have just had a leftover boner from sleeping, but it still felt great. In fact, it felt so great that I almost had an orgasm right there. I knew I couldn't lie there with him on me anymore or else I would lose it, so I wriggled my way out from underneath him and ran over to the sliding glass door.

The moon was bright that night, shining on the corn and into the bedroom. I looked down at my light blue boxer shorts; my hard-on was showing, plain as day. I looked back at Jeff. He could see everything. He was lying there on his back with one hand behind his head, looking at me. He looked hot lying there, showing me his armpit. I had to think fast. Even though I didn't know *what* I was doing, other than being playful, I swung open the glass sliding door. Cold air flew into the room.

"What are you doing?" Jeff asked as he sat up in his bed.

"Come with me," I said.

"Where?" he asked.

"Running through the corn in my underwear!" I said as I darted out the door.

"Jesus, Reichen!" I heard him say. I looked back, and he was following me. The ground was cold under my feet. Parts were muddy, but it was mostly hard packed. The corn was hitting my body pretty hard but it was shockingly refreshing. I was yelling and hooting as I ran. "You are such a freak," he yelled as he caught up to me and tackled me. We fell into a bunch of stalks as we landed, wrestling again in our bare skin. It was cold out but Jeff's body was warm, and I knew I must have felt the same to him.

Jeff got off me and ran back toward the house. I grabbed myself and did what I knew I had to do, which was finish off the orgasm that had been on its way for hours. It took me about all of two seconds. I ran back to the house, and when I got in the door I found Jeff cleaning his feet off with a towel. I did the same and we got back into bed. We were breathing heavily and were still kind of laughing as we lay down. I was exhausted from all the anxiety that I went through before running through the cornfield so I went to sleep quickly and slept like a baby. I didn't even have to hold on to Jeff or touch him. My mind was completely satisfied with all that had happened in the past hour.

We didn't have any more experiences in his bed, but I didn't care. That first experience would last me a lifetime. That next morning, we drove back to the academy and never talked of it again.

The semester dragged on. For Thanksgiving, I again went to my brother's house in Valencia, California. He had a party on Thanksgiving eve and invited a bunch of girls whom he claimed wanted to meet me. I was still very awkward around women. Although I had found a connection with Anne, I didn't do well with heterosexual romance. I wanted to be friends with women but that was about it. My brother would always ask me why I never talked about girls and I would just tell him that I hadn't yet found *the one*. That was something that he could understand so it worked for a while. But that night I *did* end up hooking up with a girl. She was one of the girls from his office, and after my experience with her, I was a god in my brother's eyes.

I had a couple of drinks, took this girl into my bedroom, and performed orally on her for about two hours. Then, once everyone had left the party and gone to bed, I took her out to my brother's poolroom and asked her to get on the pool table. I climbed on top and had sex with her. Although the sex was fun and athletic, I can't say that I actually felt anything for her. I was going through the motions but there was no passion in it. As hot as she was, she didn't do anything for me. I was more turned on by watching my male body do what it was doing than I was turned on by her body. Even while I was doing it, I thought back to Jeff and how I would rather be wrestling him than doing anything at all with this girl. Nevertheless, she told everyone at work and it got back to my brother. Soon I was a stud to my brother and his whole circle of friends and coworkers.

I spent Christmas break with my brother as well that year, but we didn't stay in Valencia. We went up to Lake Tahoe for five days. Bobby was always very generous with me when I came home on vacations. He spoiled me most of the time. His Christmas presents were always the nicest material things I've ever had: brand-new skis, skiing equipment, and beautiful clothes. That year, he rented a ski chalet on Lake Tahoe. We skied until we dropped. At night we hung out and drank beers, catching up on the year's personal news. It was always fun to spend that time of year with my brother, especially since he tried to make my birthday extra special, because many people forgot about it: the day after Christmas can be a tough day to be born unless your family really pays attention. Their extra attention on my birthday, coupled with their celebrating my "half birthday" every year on June 26, made it fine for me all my life.

When I arrived back at the academy for the second semester of sophomore year, I again vowed to do better in school. I had earned about a 2.8 GPA for the first semester of my sophomore year. This was the semester when our AOC, Captain Mendez, wanted us to get more involved with the freshmen and their training. The last freshman that I ever allowed to greet me in the hallway with a loud and thunderous "Good afternoon, sir! Raging Bull Ten!" was a cadet smack by the name of Allen Ladd. He was one of the only freshmen with whom I actually had a conversation—if only in order to let him know that I never wanted to be greeted again. I had asked him to spread the word to the rest of his freshmen in Bull Ten and, within a day, no one was greeting me. I was impressed that he had spread the word so quickly, and that all the freshmen knew who I was.

When I was required to train the freshmen on weekends, Cadet Ladd and I always seemed to end up in the same places. I would train him in my own way, which was very lenient compared to some of my other classmates, who were complete "tools" to the poor freshmen. I would watch some of my classmates, who had not done so well themselves in basic training and during freshmen year, train the new freshmen with a vigor that made no sense to me. How could they expect so much from the freshmen when they, themselves, couldn't produce half of that when *they* had been freshmen? I lost some respect for a lot of people when I saw that.

A better way to train the freshmen would have been to be honest about one's own past performance and to explain to the freshmen how they could do better. That's not how it happened. It seemed that the biggest basic training "strugglers" or "strivers," as we called them, were the worst when it came to putting the freshmen through hell when those strivers were finally in power. Strivers became tools, right before my very eyes.

Training weekends sucked for the sophmores as well as the freshmen, because our class was expected to do all the main training for the upcoming recognizable class. Usually, a training weekend would be in association with a football game weekend or a parade weekend. Weekends that included all of these activities were called triple-threat weekends. "Triple" was for a football game, a parade, and a Saturday morning inspection, or SAMI—which we pronounced *Sammy.*

A Saturday morning inspection rolled everything absurd about military discipline into one ridiculous morning. SAMIs were especially challenging for the freshmen. I remember being a freshman and having upperclassmen come through my room with white gloves. They would find some surface that I didn't even know existed in my room, wipe the finger of their white "inspector glove" along it, and then hold the now-dirty finger in my face while looking disgusted. We would have spent, literally, seven or eight *hours* getting our room to a point of operating-room cleanliness, and this tool of an upperclassman would find something wrong with it. Then we would be yelled at and trained in our rooms for an hour or so for being so messy.

Parades, as they were called, were formations of the entire cadet wing out on the academy parade field. We would march onto the field in groups by squadron and line up. A gun would go off, everyone in the stands would clap, and we would all salute. Then everyone in the stands would clap again and we would all march off the field in perfect dress, cover, and pace. It was simple really, but because we all had to be in parade dress, which was the most uncomfortable and goofy-looking uniform we had, everyone hated parades. As cadets, we were always given more to do than we could possibly handle, from homework to military training to athletics, and time was our most precious commodity. Most of us would rather have been in our rooms catching up on work than marching in a parade. Morale was low on parade mornings.

But for me, worse than a parade *or* a SAMI was a goddamn home football game. Game days sucked, again, especially for freshmen. The entire cadet wing would have to march onto the Air Force Academy football field in service dress. Sometimes the wait to get onto the field would leave us standing in the hot sun, in the all-polyester service dress uniform, for an hour or more. After marching onto the field, we would all salute at the same time. Then the crowd at the fully packed stadium would clap. Then we would be released and be ordered to run, not walk, but run like crazy people to the section of the stands set up for cadets. However, if the Air Force Academy scored a touchdown, the freshmen had to run back down onto the field and do push-ups in the end zone. Even worse, freshmen had to stand for the entire game. I remember being jealous of the upperclassmen because, even though they were sweating their asses off in service dress, they were at least allowed to sit down. Needless to say, I developed a hatred of going to football games. I had so much on my mind and felt that they were such a waste of my time that I could not have cared less about who won.

Nothing put me in a worse mood than a triple-threat Saturday. Imagine waking up to a parade—*if* you had gone to sleep at all the night because you were trying to clean your room—then coming back and changing into service dress for a SAMI. Then, to top it all off, marching onto the football field to be tortured in the sun and watching a game you don't care about for a good four hours. When the game was over, cadets were put on those well-painted Air Force Academy blue-and-silver tour buses and brought back up to the cadet area. That ride was miserable, too. All I could smell were guys sweating into overly dry-cleaned polyester, which never smells good.

At least triple-threat weekends were better as a sophomore, but I would find myself getting into a bad mood just because I hated the whole concept. Sophomores' rooms were still inspected, but by juniors and seniors and, since we were all recognized cadets together, the inspections were much more lenient than they had been freshman year.

Sophomores were slated to inspect the freshman rooms and expected to be the hardest on them. I was not one of these tough sophomores. I would go into a freshman room and they would call the room to attention, but I would tell them to relax. Then I would pick up a picture or something they had pinned neatly on their cork-board and have an interesting conversation about it with them. Instead of training them for things that they had, most likely, tried their best at anyway, I tried to get to know them better in a more inti-mate setting. Not every upperclassman had to be a tool to them. Plus, this was my own way of rebelling against the SAMI and the triple-threat weekend.

I was definitely developing into a different person. I had become quietly rebellious and it was showing more every day. Cadets are eighteen to twenty-two years of age, which is usually one of the most rebellious times in a person's life. I needed *something* to rebel against. My pet peeve was military tradition or training that made no sense. *Why are we doing it this way?* or *Why do we do this at all?* were questions that I asked on a daily basis. The answer was always the same and it made me mad.

"Because we've always done it this way at the academy," they would answer. Allen Ladd, whom I trained more than any other freshman, understood my disgust with some of the things we did that had nothing to do with preparing us for a military profession. When it came time to choose hellmasters and hellchildren, we had both chosen each other.

I would train him over the next few months in the same way that I would have wanted to be trained. I would be hard on him only to test him mentally and athletically, but I wouldn't have him memorizing quotes that didn't mean anything or wouldn't make him a better cadet or officer. I wouldn't deny him food. How could I expect him to perform for me if I didn't offer him basic nutrition? If I woke him in the middle of the night for training, I made sure that he had had ample sleep the night before or earlier that day. If I did train him physically, I would do whatever he was doing, with him because, when I was a freshman, I couldn't *stand* upperclassmen who would make me do long runs and an ungodly number of push-ups that they couldn't possibly handle themselves. I wouldn't teach him the sixteen-count rifle maneuver because there was no reason to, and it would never be used.

Allen Ladd was a good-looking guy. He stood at my height and had dark hair and blue eyes. I came to know him well from training him.

For the second half of Allen's life, he was raised in a wealthy, right-wing, Republican, fundamentalist household. He told me stories of his father funding large political figures and their visits to his Los Angeles mansion by famous republican political leaders. His father held onto the full antigay, anti-anything-outside-the-norm sentiment that I had come to despise as I knew my world better and better every day.

Allen knew I was intolerant of people who closed their minds to alternative ideas or homosexuals and he knew that my friends were intolerant of them also. As a freshman, he would never give his opinion to me, but I would wonder what he would say to me if he could speak freely. I wondered if we would actually get along after he was recognized.

As we came closer to Recognition Day, I took Cadet Ladd on a few motivational runs. We got closer to each other on a mental level as the training went on. It was imperative that we didn't let down the trainer–trainee relationship. He always called me "sir," as all freshmen had to address upperclassmen. I always called him "Cadet Ladd."

Fraternization, or the development of a friendship, between any upperclassmen and a freshman, was illegal, and could sometimes be grounds for being kicked out of the academy. The rationale for this rule was to teach cadets not to fraternize with enlisted people after graduating. Enlisted people enter the military right out of high school and are not required to have a college education or officer's training. Officers must have a four-year degree from an accredited university or service academy, and must have military training to be commissioned. If the officer isn't from one of the service academies, he or she must have four years of Reserve Officer Training Corps (or ROTC) training at an accredited university, on top of an educational degree. In the active duty U.S. Armed Forces, enlisted people and officers must maintain strict business and chain-of-command relationships to ensure orders are followed at all times. I understand the rationale because, in the military profession, people's lives are at risk, so the need to do a job correctly is at the highest level.

During one particular week about four weeks before recognition, I had taken Cadet Ladd on two motivational runs. The first night, I took him on a run to Flat Iron, a large hill that looked like the face of a clothes iron and that was almost impossible to climb. We went with another freshman, with another sophomore running beside me. It was a tough run and it challenged all of us. I had woken Cadet Ladd at midnight to take him on that run, and we didn't go to bed until about two thirty in the morning.

Ladd could handle anything I put in front of him. I trusted him. We were both pilots with training from an early age—mine from my grandmother and his from his father. Along with me, he was also a member of the Cadet Aero Club, for cadets who were private pilots. He had a passion to fly and so did I. I saw a certain gleam in his eye that fascinated me. Maybe I was physically attracted to him but at that point, I wouldn't have acknowledged it because I had not ever admitted to myself that I could ever be attracted to a guy. Gay wasn't an option for me. I had blocked out what happened to me with the masked upperclassmen during my own recognition, and I made excuses as to why Jeff always left me feeling crazy and horny. I tried to believe that I was just a horny guy, but not gay.

I liked the way that Allen would sometimes answer my questions sarcastically. He would stand up to me and follow through when I put the pressure on him to perform. He played water polo, as did I, and on the athletic grounds, there were no ranks between cadets, so we were able to get along with each other. There, I was able to get an even a better sense of his personality.

Later that week, just days after the Flat Iron run, I woke Cadet Ladd to take him on a run down to the parade field, where the bleachers were. The parade field was a good place to take a freshman on a run because it was a wide, open space, the grass was nice for doing exercises, and the bleachers served as a place to run up and down stairs for an extra leg workout.

As at other times, I knocked on his door in the middle of the night and made him put on his BDUs. With his rifle and mine, I ran with him across much of the academy grounds and then down to the parade field, where I made him do push-ups, flutter kicks, and iron mikes, all while he repeated knowledge that I deemed necessary for a recognized freshman to know.

This night would be like no other. After some strenuous physical exercise, I stood there yelling at Cadet Ladd for continually making errors in repeating the quote by John Stuart Mill that all fourth-class cadets are required to memorize. Our voices were ringing across the parade fields and the academy grounds.

I felt strange for making things so hard on him that night but I wanted to keep our trainer/trainee relationship in perspective for both of us. It was cold and windy that night, but we were both sweating. We came to a point at which we weren't communicating well; I think it was because I had completely worn him out, physically and mentally.

I asked him to repeat Mill's quote again and, this time, he recited it perfectly, despite screaming it at me with anger and frustration in his voice. I smiled at him. I was exhausted, too. We were standing there quietly. I had nothing else to yell at him for. I realized that we had locked stares. I held my stare and he held his; I wasn't really sure *what* we were doing. This went on for about a minute and as it did, my heart began to race.

Suddenly, Cadet Ladd threw himself toward me and, before I could raise my hands to push him away, he was hugging me in a tight embrace. His whole body was pushed up against mine and his head was buried into the left side of my neck and shoulder. I let out a huge breath of air and in moving my arms forward as fast as I did, I prepared to push him away from me. Almost instinctively, I relaxed and just held him like he was holding me. I felt my blood temperature change from warm to hot as my heart worked harder to push it through my veins.

I could feel his heart against my chest, beating just as strongly. We stood like this for probably thirty seconds, but it felt like hours.

Finally, he let up on his grip and backed away somewhat. I grabbed his upper arms and moved him even further away from me. We were looking into each other's eyes again. At that moment, I realized that I was utterly and totally attracted to him with every part of my body, inside and out. Yes, I had been attracted to guys before, but this time, I was looking at him like a viable and possible chance to finally feel mutual intimacy with another man.

Then I thought to myself, *Stop it, this is ridiculous. He's a freshman.* I was battling these thoughts back and forth in my head, but the fight was futile. For the first time in my life, there was no denying that I was sexually turned on, not only by a guy, but by men in general. I don't know why I came to that conclusion at that particular moment, over all the moments I had gone through at the academy; I just knew it all of the sudden. I was completely overwhelmed.

I realized, too, that I was as hard as a rock and that I could feel my pulse in my pants for the first time in my life. This was an intense moment. I was staring at him with crazy sexual thoughts running through my head and I swear I could hear, see, taste, and feel all of his sexual thoughts toward me. I had never, *ever,* felt anything like this before—not with my girlfriend, nor any girl that I had ever gone out with, and not with any guy that I might have had a crush on in the past.

I knew I had to stop this experience, even though I could have taken it to its limitless possibilities. I broke away from our stare and I turned around to walk away from him on the parade field. "Jesus!" I yelled, under my breath, facing away from him. After walking a few paces away, I turned around and looked to find Cadet Ladd facing to his right, toward the academy, standing at strict attention. I didn't know what to do other than to end this situation.

"Let's head back up to the dorms," I said.

"Yes, sir," he answered. He started running up to the dorms and began chanting one of the air force jodies, or marching songs that keeps a soldier in step with the rest of the squadron. He picked the most grotesque jodie that we had taught him in basic training:

Went to the playground.
Where all the kiddies play.
Pulled out my machine gun.
And I began to spray.
Left right, left right, left right, kill!

I couldn't figure out why he would sing that particular jodie after what had just happened. Maybe he was trying to make himself more butch after such a strongly intimate situation with another man. The "Left Right Kill" jodie was something that we only sang sarcastically, and everyone found it disturbing—a type of sick humor that we used to mock the worst parts of the military. I couldn't take him singing it anymore. "Shut up, Ladd! Just run," I snapped at him, as we made our way back up to the Hill.

We arrived at the dorms and I escorted Cadet Ladd back to his room. As I opened his door I looked at him with confusion. Only his blue eyes told me that he was confused, too. Then he said, "Goodnight, sir."

I shut the door behind me and walked down the hall in a daze. I needed to talk to someone. I knocked on Jodie Turner's door to announce my arrival and walked right on in to her room. She was asleep.

By now, Jodie was the girl in my squadron to whom I looked for advice in all things crazy in my life. I respected her. After all, Jodie was someone who would carry another guy's rifle, along with her own, just to make sure the squadron finished a basic training run. She was a star tennis player with the face, body, and hair of a supermodel. She had a strong spirit and I think, over time, I realized that I had been strangely in love with her ever since we met on that first day of basic training, when she ran into our room wearing her "birth control glasses." It was a different kind of love, but if there were ever a girl whom I could marry, it would be her.

Luckily, her roommate, Shannon, was gone on an intercollegiate basketball game trip so we had the room to ourselves. I woke her up and told her I needed to talk to her.

"What is it, sweetie?" she asked in her raspy, sexy voice. I sat her down and turned on the lights and told her what had just happened to me with Cadet Ladd. After the whole story, she sat there quietly for a few minutes looking at me. I was afraid of what would come out of her mouth. Would she tell me that I was going to be in trouble? Would she shun me for being attracted to a guy? Finally, she got smile on her face and began to talk.

"You got aroused by him?" she asked, in a sort of excited way.

"Yes, I did. It was crazy," I said.

"This is awesome," she said very matter-of-factly. "You're gay." I couldn't *believe* she just said this to me.

"I'm not gay!" I snapped at her, even though deep down, I almost knew that I was. I wasn't even close to being ready to admit something like that to anyone else. "This is a crazy, messed-up situation." Just then, Jodie pulled out a bottle of black-labeled rum. I looked at her like she was crazy but she just smiled at me.

"You need a drink, baby," she said.

"This is great," I said. "Now I'll get kicked out for an alcohol hit along with a fraternization hit!" She laughed a little and we drank a lot. Over about thirty minutes, we each had about ten swigs from the bottle, feeling good and relaxed, and probably a little drunk. Then Jodie made one of her announcements.

"We need to go to his room right now," she said.

"What? Are you *crazy!*" I yelled, turning it into a whisper by the time I hit the word "crazy."

She explained that I needed to go talk to him to get this cleared up and to find out what happened. She had me frightened that he would tell someone about our embrace on the parade field and get me kicked out of the academy. In our rum-induced wisdom, we eventually decided to make the journey down the hall to Cadet Ladd's room.

We opened the door. There lay Cadet Allen Ladd, asleep in his bed. Ironically, Ladd's roommate, like Shannon's, was away on an intercollegiate sports trip.

We entered the room and shut the door behind us. We stood still for a while until our eyes adjusted to the dark room. Jodie walked away from me and climbed up the ladder to his bunk. I couldn't believe she was going to wake him. I decided to roll with the punches and handle whatever would happen next. "Ladd!" she whispered. "Ladd, wake up!"

"Yes, ma'am!" he yelled, and jumped forward off the pillow in his bed.

"*Shh!*" Jodie and I both whispered as harshly as we could while we waved our hands to shut him up.

"What's going on?" Cadet Ladd asked.

Jodie spoke quietly, "Cadet Ladd. I know what happened tonight on the parade field with Cadet Lehmkuhl. I just want you to know that it's all okay, but more importantly, I just want you to know that I know. Actually, more importantly, Cadet Ladd, is that I need you to know how much I *love* Cadet Lehmkuhl and how far I would go to protect him." Cadet Ladd sat there, silent. Jodie climbed down the ladder and motioned for me to open the door. We left the room together.

"Why did you tell him that?" I asked.

"It felt like the right thing to do," she said, "because I don't want this guy turning you in and ruining your life. I want him to know that someone who cares about you very much is on your side and that you would have an alibi if someone were to accuse you of something. "*That* is between me and Cadet Ladd now." She smiled at me and put her arm around me as we walked down the hall to my room. "You're going to be okay. You have nothing to worry about as long as I'm around. We'll deal more with Cadet Ladd later on. Like after recognition."

I went to bed that night, thankful for Jodie and her strong will. But beside that, I remained awake for hours fantasizing about Cadet Ladd. My mind ran wild. I thought about having sex with him. I thought about sharing special moments with him. What surprised me most was that my thoughts about this *man* felt more natural and proper than any similar thoughts I had had in my prior life, about women.

chapter twenty-one

ENLIGHTENMENT TO ABOMINATIONS

It was a shame that such a new and amazing experience between the two of us had to end in such feelings of guilt and fear. Heavy sexual intimacy between two cadets or sex in the dorms was illegal and we all knew it. Nevertheless, sex happened, and it happened *all* the time. Yet, no one did anything about it. Sex was untouchable in the unspoken cadet code of things. But by sex, I mean heterosexual sex. That was OK and easy to digest for all of us eighteen to twenty-two-year-olds.

Fraternization was another activity that we all knew was prohibited. But if an upperclassman truly wanted to be with an underclassman, and other cadets found out, they wouldn't say anything. Sex at the academy between men and women, and between, say, a junior male and a freshman female, was completely tolerated by a large percentage of the cadet wing. The small percentage of cadets who were against it, and who would actually turn someone in to the AOC for such an act, let everyone know that this was their stand on the issue—and everyone knew to keep those people out of the loop.

I never once, at the academy, heard a male cadet argue that women shouldn't be allowed to serve in the military because it might lead to sex. I never once heard a female cadet say that men shouldn't be allowed to serve in the military because it might lead to sex. When sex happens and hinders a mission, the two offenders are dealt with appropriately.

However, whenever the issue of gay people was brought up with the same cadets, especially ultraconservative religious people or fundamentalist Christians, they would tell you that gay people shouldn't serve in the military because it might lead to sex. They would also tell you that gay people might frighten those who don't like gay people, which would break down morale.

Were these people serious? If the fact that sex between men and women isn't a reason to keep women out of the military, then why is it a reason to keep gay people out of the military?

If the presence of women in the military upsets the men who don't want women there, or if it upsets the men who are too distracted by the sexual possibilities created by the presence of women, why isn't *that* a reason to keep women out of the military?

As a military community, we have been trained to think that keeping women away is no longer a possibility at all. The masses have been trained to accept or, at the very least, tolerate the presence of women, and to be sensitive to their needs and their contributions, as they very well should.

Top-ranking military leaders today just don't want to do the same for gay people. They *know* that they are vomiting up the same excuses to keep gays out of and segregated within the military that have been used for years to keep women, blacks, and gays from all sorts of equal military service in our country and in many other countries. With all of these minority groups, military commanders complained in the past that the morale of those who didn't want that particular minority group near them would be broken down and, by logic driven only by bigotry, ignorance, and lack of education, those complainers would always win.

The fact that I was tempted to have gay sex in the military is no reason to make an excuse for the exclusion of gay people from the armed forces. It's simple. When we put young adults together, whether they are straight or gay, there is a distinct possibility that they are going to have sex. To single out gay people as being deviant, when heterosexual sex is pervasive in the military, is absurd. To single out gay people for exclusion because of the kind of sex they want to have is equally absurd.

Gay people are equally capable of avoiding and refraining from sexual situations as straight people are. In the military environment, if sex must be avoided, then gay people can be asked, just as heterosexual people are asked, not to have sex with other military members of consequence. Punishments can be the same for heterosexual and homosexual military members if the sexual relations they have create problems for a mission.

When hateful, ignorant, uneducated groups and individuals use sexual relations as excuses to bar gay people from any sort of equal rights, including military service, they are displaying a lack of knowledge about people and life in the military.

To this day, I cannot write the word *Christian* when referring to the purveyors of hate who call themselves "Christians" without being tempted to use quotation marks. A basic study of Jesus the Christ would show anyone that, whether they believe Jesus was the son of God or not, he was, at the very least, a person who had reached a supreme spiritual level. He reached that level by forgiving everyone, including his worst enemies. He also reached that level by loving and accepting people from all walks of life. A religion based on following the sentiment of Jesus the Christ cannot leave behind the basic philosophies of love, acceptance, and forgiveness.

But many who preach Christianity do so based solely on words written in the Bible. After being translated so many times, the words in the Bible remain up for interpretation—and thank God, since many verses in Bible actually contradict each *other*. How someone can use a book that continues to be interpreted by different groups in completely different ways to further the robbery of rights from gay people should make no logical sense to anyone. It makes no sense that anyone would think his or her particular interpretation is absolutely correct, especially when that interpretation contradicts the very spirit of the Bible: to further the basic tenets of Christianity, including forgiveness and love.

And how can we select only certain verses of the Bible to follow? Burning animals in sacrifice and killing people are promoted, and "abominations" such as eating shellfish are essentially forbidden by the Bible, while Jesus himself is never documented saying anything about homosexuality.

Using Bible verses to cause pain, suffering, and even death for gay people should be considered an abomination by all of us.

* * *

The Air Force Academy's general population remained in a backward mode of thinking while I was there. The religious machine was alive and hungry among its cadets, officers, instructors, and, of course, its clergy. Tolerance for anything against "Christian" doctrine at the academy was dealt with strongly and ruthlessly, but quietly. By my sophomore year, I knew how it was. I was looked favorably upon for attending a cadet's privately held Bible study—which made it not so private at all. A quiet accounting of who was a Christian and who was not always seemed to be taken by upperclassmen and our AOC. Not only did I feel like I was forced to *believe* in their form of Christianity, but I felt that I had to go one step further and be conspicuous about my belief in it all. I had to be showy.

One way that many cadets would do this was to buy a Bible holder— a leather cover that slipped over a Bible, zipped up, and even had handles for easy carrying. This was a regular phenomenon at the academy. One might have mistaken this "Bible holster," as my group of friends liked to call it, for a daily planning book or even a purse if it were seen anywhere else. But when you saw one on a cadet's desk, in class, on the table while eating a meal, or sitting on the bunk in their dorm room, you knew that this cadet was an upstanding, God-fearing Christian.

All of this behavior is related to the antigay environment at the Air Force Academy and in the air force. The military is a perfect place for continuing the belief in the "sissy factor" of gay men. While I attended the academy, anything that was not masculine or militarily driven was considered "gay." The word was used hundreds of times per day by everyone there. Even *I* used the word to describe things. "This homework assignment is gay," one might say to describe something that completely sucked. The word *gay* became more than a term for all things sissy, but also a general derogatory term. An actual human being who was admitted to or was caught being gay was considered to be a lower form of life.

Coming out as a gay person was not an option at the academy. Being caught as a gay person was even less of an option. So what were the choices for someone who found himself having gay feelings? One choice might be to rape a male freshman cadet in the middle of the night who you think might enjoy it. I have enough insight now to understand why those guys did that to me and I have actually forgiven them and, even further, felt sorry for them and the mental anguish that they must have lived in every day. I find myself feeling sad and angry when I think of those cadets who *were* gay at the academy, and who committed forced sexual acts in order to fill their need to be with a man. They had been brainwashed by the academy and society to detest their own thoughts and behavior.

There was no place to go for a cadet who wanted to talk about his or her gay awakening. There was no authority figure, or even counselor, whom anyone could go to, and this was a tragedy for many. The feelings of self-hatred that were bred by the academy environment and by the people who had raised these young adults to hate themselves brought many people to the brink of suicide. Not being able to talk about their feelings led others to leave the academy, denying the country some amazing military officers.

When America allowed women into the military, we ensured the availability of counselors and leaders to whom women could go if they had issues that were affecting their job performance. In addition, we educated our troops on the woman's experience in the military and made them attend mandatory sexual harassment training so that they knew what not to do and why not to do it. We, eventually, did the same thing for racial minorities by putting military members in diversity-training classes.

When I was at the academy, if cadets wanted to talk to someone about their gay feelings, they would spill their story to someone they thought they could trust and would quickly find themselves in the hands of the Air Force Office of Special Investigation, or the OSI, as we called it. The OSI would then start an investigation on that member and any other member that they may have named when they originally went for help. The investigators were trained to find out if a cadet was admittedly gay or if he or she had committed any homosexual acts.

The U.S. Armed Forces are governed by the words of the Uniform Code of Military Justice, or UCMJ, which are the laws by which every military member must abide. There are laws in some of the United States that say that sodomy, or the act of using the sex organs in any other way than for penile–vaginal sex, is illegal. The UCMJ law is interpreted the same way and, in addition, is very clear about the prohibition of homosexual acts. Someday soon, we will *all* see how barbaric these laws were and will scoff at how backward we were to keep alive, in military policy, any sort of wording that regulates what someone prefers sexually.

> *From the actual UCMJ Code:*
> *TITLE 10 > Subtitle A > PART II > CHAPTER 37 > § 654*
> *Policy Concerning Homosexuality in the Armed Forces*
>
> *Policy.—* *A member of the armed forces shall be separated from the armed forces under regulations prescribed by the Secretary of Defense if one or more of the following findings is made and approved in accordance with procedures set forth in such regulations:*
>
> *(1) That the member has engaged in, attempted to engage in, or solicited another to engage in a homosexual act or acts unless there are further findings, made and approved in accordance with procedures set forth in such regulations, that the member has demonstrated that—*
>> *(A) such conduct is a departure from the member's usual and customary behavior;*
>> *(B) such conduct, under all the circumstances, is unlikely to recur;*
>> *(C) such conduct was not accomplished by use of force, coercion, or intimidation;*

> (D) *under the particular circumstances of the case, the member's continued presence in the armed forces is consistent with the interests of the armed forces in proper discipline, good order, and morale; and*
>
> (E) *the member does not have a propensity or intent to engage in homosexual acts.*
>
> (2) *That the member has stated that he or she is a homosexual or bisexual, or words to that effect, unless there is a further finding, made and approved in accordance with procedures set forth in the regulations, that the member has demonstrated that he or she is not a person who engages in, attempts to engage in, has a propensity to engage in, or intends to engage in homosexual acts.*
>
> (3) *That the member has married or attempted to marry a person known to be of the same biological sex.*

The same misinformed people who wrote the above codes also wrote codes touting the need for good order, longstanding elements in the military, and unit cohesion, all of which have been used as rationale for excluding gays from the service. Yet, like the Bible, many of the lines of code contradict themselves, leaving this section of the UCMJ code a blaring example of nonsensical babble passed down from one uneducated person to another.

In the civilian world, sodomy laws are loosely enforced and, usually, only in special cases. However, when the military says that someone will be prosecuted for sodomy, it means it. Not only will it prosecute someone for being gay, but it will hunt someone down and probe the situation for as long as it takes to find someone who is committing the so-called crime. The purpose of this, I would guess, is to root out all the gay people in the military who are supposedly breaking down morale.

The military's Don't Ask, Don't Tell policy is ineffective in preventing these types of witch hunts. Besides encouraging members to hide and lie about their sexuality, it almost dares other military members to *make* someone profess their homosexual feelings so that the ensuing witch hunt will be that much more intense.

The investigation process to root out homosexuals is inhumane and humiliating for the person being investigated as well as for anyone else involved. Once one is under investigation for being a homosexual, the terror can begin with the member being pulled from duty, immediately.

For cadets, this means being pulled from classes, athletics, and military training and separated from their peers. Then, after a full investigation, cadets can be dragged in front of a military court-martial and trial to have their conduct evaluated by anyone whom the military decides can be present. All of it is documented in their personal military file, which can haunt them forever. Sentences can range from an acquittal and reinstatement into service to removal from the service with an honorable or less-than-honorable discharge to punishments as harsh as jail time. The lucky ones are let go from the service with an honorable discharge: cadets put back into the service are thrown into an environment of torment with no support from their peers.

Once cadets reach their first day of class junior year, they are officially obligated to finish the academy and, after graduating, to serve a certain number of years as an active-duty service commitment to pay back the cost of an education at the academy. For cadets or academy graduates found guilty of homosexuality with a discharge, not only are their military careers ruined, they are subject to recoupment as well. Recoupment is when the military demands that the member who benefited from an academy education pay back its cost. When I was there, they used to tell us that our tuition amounted to over $75,000 per year. Assuming that it costs considerably more today, recoupment fees can total hundreds of thousands of dollars.

Is it really necessary to put people through this? How has homosexuality become such a huge issue, and for what good reason? The ones who really lose in all of this are the American people. Remember, all of the expense to train a cadet is covered by taxpayers. Since recoupment is not an easily enforceable act on the part of the military, we are throwing away hard-earned money that belongs to the citizens of the United States. Sending one person through pilot training after the academy can cost additional hundreds of thousands of dollars. When that person is kicked out for homosexuality, the government is deciding to throw away all of that training that we pay for in taxes.

It is time for the American people to become outraged at all of this. Our government, which uses human rights abuses as a justification to invade other countries with military force, is committing human rights abuses right here in its own country and, even worse, on people who have volunteered to die for their country. At a time when we are realigning our national priorities to make sense of new problems, this should be one of the first things we address, both from a military spending standpoint and because of our need for a strong fighting force.

In addition to being fiscally responsible, as a society that seeks to evolve into something we can all be proud of, we need to eradicate the ridiculous ban on gay people in our nation's military to rid our society of one of its last few tolerated human rights abuses.

When I was a cadet, I heard stories of "fags" who were kicked out for being gay or for committing homosexual acts, or for even admitting that they had, once or twice in their lives, had a homosexual experience with someone. For anyone with homosexual feelings, fear was a huge part of their daily experience. I was now included in that group of people. Even more ridiculous was the fact that there were heterosexuals who had never even thought of being with someone of the same sex, but who had the same fear. Even heterosexual men had to behave in a more masculine way so that no one would ever accuse them of being a homosexual, which would cause a humiliating investigation for someone who was innocent of any of these perceived crimes.

The fear of being considered gay was rampant at the academy and it created a hateful antigay environment. While cadets had to make outward signs of their Christianity, they also had to be outwardly against homosexuality to protect themselves. My liberal-minded group of friends were already walking the line of disaster for our progressive mind-set. Other cadets, who followed the Academy's straight and narrow, were starting to take notice of my group's liberal thinking on many issues, which already made us suspects as possible "fags."

* * *

I knew that I would eventually tell my roommate Nathan about the adventure with Jodie and Allen Ladd because I would need him to cover for me if anyone asked him about the situation. I would wait to tell him until the time was right. The only other person I felt I could tell was Seth English, who was the most liberal-thinking person in the group. I think Seth was liberal minded because his military family's culture was very oppressive and he rebelliously took the time to explore ways of life that were different from his own.

That morning, I was in between classes and hanging out at the squadron. I knew that Seth had the hour off from class, too, so I knocked on his door. He opened it and, ironically, was acting stereotypically gay just to be funny. "Can I help you with thomthing, Mithter Lehmkuhl?" he asked with a comic look on his face. I wondered, for a second, if he knew what had happened the night before.

"Seth, I need to talk to you. Do you have a second?" I asked, in all seriousness.

"Yeah sure," he answered.

"Can we go down the hall?" I asked.

"Yeah," he said, though his tone suggested, *Uh oh, what's wrong now?* I wanted to go to a place where no one could possibly hear or see us without our seeing them. I took him down a hallway that was adjacent to Bull Ten and led to the C-store. There was a dark alcove about half way down where we could sit and talk. Three thick walls surrounded us and we could see anyone walk by and would know if they were listening. The hallway had barely any foot traffic so I felt pretty safe there. Seth and I sat down on the floor together in the corner and I told him the whole story of the night before. Toward the end of my story, I noticed that he had a smirk on his face.

"What?" I asked. He put his head down and then brought it back up. Then he put his hands on my shoulders and looked at me straight in the eyes.

"I think I'm gay," he blurted out all at once.

"Now don't go that far . . . " I stopped. I realized that he had just said that he thought *he* was gay and not that *I* was gay. I was stunned. For some reason, it hadn't occurred to me that someone else might be going through the same experiences that I was going through. I had seen Seth pretend to be gay and make fun of the way stereotypically gay people act, but I never thought he would do that if he were really gay himself.

"You really think you are?" I asked.

"Well, I'm almost sure that I am," he said, "but don't tell anyone."

"Jesus, Seth. I'm not going to tell anyone. Shit! Why didn't you tell me you've been thinking this?" I asked.

"Why didn't *you* tell *me?*" he asked. I thought about it for a second and realized that I wouldn't tell anyone because I still hadn't figured it out for myself.

"Have you told anyone else this?" I asked.

"No. No one. Other than the guy I've been messing around with," he said quickly and in a whisper.

I was fascinated. I had so many questions but I didn't know which one to start with. "OK. I won't ask you who it is, but is he a cadet?" I asked.

"Yes," he said with a smile on his face. He was very cocky—just as cocky as a straight guy would be telling me about a girl he was fooling around with. Just then an announcement came over the hallway loudspeaker that there were ten minutes until noon meal formation.

"Let's go," Seth said, "we can talk about this later. As we walked back to our squadron, we kept looking at each other with expressions of surprise and amusement on our faces. I hadn't even had a chance to ask Seth to cover for me or to give me an alibi if anyone asked if I had done what I had done. Somehow, I still felt safer knowing that he knew my story and that I, now, knew his. He could tell on me but, in an investigation, he would go down, too. It wouldn't be worth it. We both had something on each other.

On our way out to noon meal formation, Jodie stopped me on the Terrazzo. "Did you talk to Ladd?" she asked.

"No, not yet. I still think we should wait until after recognition," I replied in a reassuring way.

"Good," she said. "It's a choice you have to make, but I think it's the best one."

"I get it," I said.

"You're the one who has to talk to him because . . . " she started.

"Jodie, I know. Please. This is very stressful right now and I will take the responsibility and make sure that we're OK. I promise. I promise you are going to be OK. Do you trust me?"

"I trust you more than anyone. I love you," she said really fast. We heard the horns sounding across the Terrazzo, which meant we should have been in formation, so we ran toward the gaggle that was our squadron.

Noon meal formation felt different that day—as if I were in my own world, within another huge world, that no one knew anything about, even though *so much* was happening within it. As we marched by the chapel wall with all the tourists watching all four thousand of us march by, each looking exactly the same, I wondered if any of those tourists realized how different each one of us actually was. I wondered if any of those tourists had any idea of all that gay things were going on among all of us who looked, to them, like good little toy soldiers.

As I lay down to sleep that night, I thought about how amazing all of this was. How could I be so lucky to be able to exchange experiences and stories with Seth? Another possibly gay guy right there in my squadron? And if Seth thought he was gay, how many more cadets thought the same thing or, even better, *knew* they were gay?

chapter twenty-two

RECOGNITION 2

Recognition Week came for the freshman class and Cadet Ladd and I played the game. I was hard on him and he obeyed my commands and took my discipline and training, like he respected my authority more than he ever had. No one knew a thing about what was really going on in our heads as I trained him through Hell Week. We had moments together during that week when I knew what he was thinking and he knew what I was thinking. Sometimes we were both sweating and close to each other and having screaming matches in the hallway related to military knowledge and training. Our eyes were locked on each other's, and an attraction built between us that I had never experienced before. I didn't plan on having sex with him again, but deep in my heart—and through my adrenaline-lined veins—I *felt* that one day I would have to.

Just after recognition, I was able to talk to Cadet Ladd like a normal human being. We were now allowed to fraternize, like all recognized freshmen could with the upper classes. Freshmen were now considered upperclassmen too. There was no more superior-subordinate relationship between us. We were now equals.

About a week after the freshmen were recognized, Jodie and I had noticed that Cadet Ladd's roommate was gone again on a trip. We knew we could finally go to his room to talk to him about the embrace that had happened a couple of weeks before and Jodie wanted to take a moment to apologize to Cadet Ladd for scaring him. We pulled out the black rum again and had two shots each. We called it "liquid courage" to be able to talk to Cadet Ladd about the situation. We didn't have to call him "Cadet Ladd" anymore. We could simply call him, "Allen."

We walked into his room, late that night, probably around one A.M. As the door shut behind us, we let our eyes adjust and could see Allen sleeping soundly in his bed. Jodie climbed up the ladder and, again, startled him.

Adam sat up in his bed almost as if he had been expecting us to come in.

"Hi," he said. "I guess this time I don't have to call you Ma'am. Are you going to scare me again by telling me how much you love Cadet Lehmkuhl?"

"No," she said. "But Cadet Lehmkuhl is here. Oh, and you can call us 'Sir' and 'Ma'am' if you want to." She had a smile on her face. Allen turned around and saw me standing by the door.

"Wow," he said. "Both of you are here visiting me at once? To what do I owe this pleasure?" he asked in a playful way.

"This," Jodie said as she leaned over to give Allen a long and passionate kiss. Seeing this put me in shock since I thought we were going to his room to clear up what had happened and to have a discussion about it all. I couldn't figure out what Jodie was trying to do. All that had been accomplished, by this time, was that Jodie had just put herself in the same situation that I was in from weeks before. At least he was recognized now and this wouldn't be considered fraternization. I still found all of this to be odd considering the scare we had just been through over a mere embrace.

I walked over to Jodie and stood at the bottom of the ladder. I felt like I had more control there.

"And this . . ." she continued. With "and this," Jodie leaned off the ladder and put her lips up to my *lips*. For whatever screwed-up reason there was, I started French kissing her back. Maybe I was already so stunned by her kiss with Allen that I just let her kiss me as much as she wanted, without thinking about it.

As she backed away and pulled her lips away from mine, I looked up into the bed and saw Allen staring at us with a look on his face that was as shocked as the one on mine. Jodie looked at me and smiled.

"Are you okay baby?" she asked. Before I could answer, Allen spoke in a whisper.

"Do you two want to come up into my bed with me right now?" he asked. Now my brain was overloaded. I couldn't believe this was actually happening. Of course, *Jodie* was our spokesperson.

"Yes, we do," Jodie said before he even finished the question.

"Are you out of your mind?" I yelled at Jodie in a whisper. She didn't listen to me. She grabbed my hand and led me up the ladder after her.

"Oh my God," Allen whispered as we both got up onto the bed. From what I could tell, he was fascinated that he had us both in the bed. Jodie pulled off her T-shirt to reveal two perfect twenty-year-old perky breasts. "Oh my God," Allen whispered again as she pulled my shirt off me and grabbed my hand to place it on his chest.

I remember thinking to myself how incredibly hot this situation was despite my being scared to death. My brother used to make fun of me for being too conservative about sex and girlfriends and anything to do with dating. "If my brother could only see me now," I thought as I began to touch two perfectly-trained, worked-out, athletic bodies. Instantly, I was aroused and forgot about the risky situation we were in. I was officially caught up in the moment. I had gone from being scared to being fascinated by what was happening in front of me.

"Kiss him," I said to Jodie. The words came out of my mouth and I was as surprised as they were to hear them. Immediately, they stopped what they were doing and looked at me. They both gave up to my command and started kissing passionately. "Show me his body," I whispered just before Jodie, listening to me, pulled down his bed covers, revealing his totally naked and aroused body. By total instinct, and without being able to stop myself, I put my hand on him, and he let out a huge sigh along with a "yes."

"Yessss!" Jodie whispered. "Feel him! Touch him! Kiss him!" Just then Allen leaned forward over Jodie and started kissing my neck and grabbing me. Jodie pushed herself back against the wall and took herself out of the situation so she could watch us. I could hear her whispering as Allen and I made out with each other and explored each other's bodies. "This is the hottest thing I've ever seen. Don't stop," she whispered over and over again. "Keep going. Love on him."

"Love on" Allen is exactly what I did right there in front of Jodie. We touched and licked and kissed on each other until we had both taken one another to amazingly releasing orgasms.

This whole experience took about an hour from start to finish. It was the best hour of my life up to that point, sexually speaking. I had never felt the kind of rush, and passion, and love that I did with him, or the emotional fulfillment of having all of those feelings being reciprocated by another guy.

We were all lying down now and our breathing went from loud to soft, and then to an inaudible level. Out of the silence, I heard Jodie speak much louder than her previous whisper.

"I have to throw up . . . the rum . . . oh my God, the rum!" She jumped out of bed and headed toward the door so I yelled at her to put on her T-shirt before running out into the hall. I looked at Allen, who was lying down and looked like he was already sound asleep. I quickly went down the ladder and got dressed before running after Jodie.

"Wait. Where are you going?" Allen yelled to me just after waking back up and realizing that we had left him alone in his bed. I looked back at him and saw him, now, sitting up in the bed.

"I have to help her, I'm sorry, I'll talk to you tomorrow about all this, okay?" I asked.

"Goodnight," he said and then left a small pause. ". . . Sir."

He called me "sir" as if we had just finished another training session together.

"Goodnight," I said. "I'll talk to you in the morning. I promise." I closed his door and ran down the hall. I caught up to Jodie at the end of the hallway and pushed her into the girls' bathroom. It was four o'clock in the morning. As she vomited into the toilet, I got up on her and laid my chest on her back and put my face in her ear. The words that came out of my mouth were as uncontrollable as the situation that I had just created. I mumbled it at first and then I said it louder and louder, "We are so crazy. We are *so* crazy."

That next evening, Seth and Cadet Ladd were both playing water polo with me during intramurals. Since I had told Seth everything, he was giving me funny looks the whole time and I was avoiding looking at him because I didn't want Ladd seeing my showing any sort of crazy behavior, reacting to the night before. In the locker room, while we were all changing to go back up to our dorms, I told Seth to go ahead of me because I needed to talk to Ladd. He wanted to talk to me just as much as I wanted to talk to him.

On our walk up to the dorms, we fell behind the other cadets. I started the conversation. "How are you doing?"

"I'm okay. You?" he asked.

"Damn, that feels weird. You've never talked to me in such a relaxed way," I said.

"Well, what do you expect?" he asked. "You want me to call you 'sir' while we figure this out?"

"Yeah, I want you to call me 'sir' while we figure this out," I said in a sarcastic way. "No, what I want is for you to be able to handle this and be okay and to be able to not get us in trouble when someone asks you about it."

"Someone's going to *ask* me about it?" he blurted out.

"No! Or at least I hope not! Look, stop being so defensive and listen to me. What we all did was really risky and I just don't want us to get in trouble for it. For any of us to be kicked out for this would be a disaster. We would go through torture in front of our friends, our families, and in front of each other. I don't want to see anything happen to you or any of us. I need you to be able to handle holding up some sort of normalcy with me during the day. Can you do that?"

"Yes, I can do that. Don't worry. I'm not going to freak out. I'm not that freaked out about it. I was afraid that I hadn't heard from either you or Cadet Turner. I've been feeling pretty alone since this all happened. There was no one I could talk to and I spent the night worrying a little," he said.

"Well, talk to me now. Anything you want to talk about," I assured him.

"I guess I don't have anything to say really. I just want to know that it's all okay," he said.

"Yes, it's okay," I said. "I'm trying to figure out all kinds of things about myself. This experience has added to it. I've already met someone else who is having similar experiences." Allen stopped in his tracks and looked at me in disbelief.

"You told someone about this?" he almost yelled out loud.

"Shhh! Be quiet. Are you crazy? You want someone to hear you asking me *that* at the top of your lungs?" I warned. "Yes, I talked to someone about it but it was someone who has had an experience with another guy too."

"Now I'm going to say this once," he started to lecture, "I don't want anyone else to know about what we did and if they do know, I don't want them to know it was me that you were with." He was angry.

"Okay, I get it. Fine. I'm looking to figure out my life here and, like you, I don't want to get in trouble either. I won't do anything that's going to hurt either one of us, or anyone for that matter. The person I told, just so you know and because I respect you, is Seth English," I admitted.

"Jesus Christ! You told *English?*" he asked with anger on his face.

"Well, who else? I didn't know if you were going to freak out on me and I wanted him to give me an alibi so that I could deny the whole thing. Who better to tell? Jesus Christ is right! I can't believe we even have to go through this to cover something up that I found to be pretty fucking enjoyable!" I said with the same amount of anger and frustration.

"Alright, alright," he said.

"Look I don't have all the answers and I wish I did, but I don't."

"Have you done this with anyone before?" he asked.

"No, I haven't. Well, I've been with a guy before, but not like I was with you. I've never had mutual action like that," I said. I looked him in the eyes. He looked away. Then he looked back at me.

"I'm not gay, dude," he said.

"Then I'm not either, I guess." I thought for a second. "But what the fuck am I? I *liked* being with you. Fuck! Have you ever been with a guy before?" I asked.

"With one other guy, but we were little and we used to play with each other," he admitted, "but it wasn't anything like what you and I did."

"Do you feel like you want to do it again?" I asked.

"Well, Cadet Lehmkuhl," he took a deep breath as we continued walking, "I know that I've been thinking about it all day. I mean, thinking about what you and I did together. I can't get it out of my mind. I can't help thinking . . ." he stopped.

"What? You can't help thinking *what*?" I asked. There was a long pause.

"Nothing. Look, I thought about it and I've been excited a couple times thinking about it, but we can't ever do that again. We just can't. I'm not gay and we are two guys who shouldn't be doing that," he reasoned. I thought about what he said and put myself in his position and, as screwed-up as his reasoning was, he had a point that I needed to take. We should not have ever planned to do that again. He must have thought that I wanted to do it again. But he was trying to convince me that he didn't want to do it again. It was a game. I decided to play into it and just agree with him.

"Okay. Enough said. We'll *never* do that again. You're right. We can't," I said in a very satisfied way. Ladd looked at me to see if I was serious. I kept a poker face and he held his stare. He looked forward and continued walking. From this conversation, I realized that everything was going to be okay. I wasn't worried about his turning us in or making any trouble. I had the idea, from what he said, that he would be very quiet about the whole thing and also that he liked what we did together. I had the slightest hint that he would want to do it again.

Back at Bull Ten, I walked straight to Jodie's room and explained to her that everything was going to be okay. She made me recite, word for word, my conversation with Ladd.

"Thank God!" she said in total relief. "It's going to be okay."

"Yes," I said, "it's going to be okay as long as we keep our noses clean."

"Do you think you're going to try to do that again with him?" she asked.

"No, I'm not going to try anything with him. I told him we shouldn't do anything again," I explained.

"Did you have to tell him that? I mean, did he want to do it again?" she asked.

"I don't know. I really don't know. I know that he liked it. I could just tell," I said. Jodie felt better now and I was glad. I hated seeing her worried about everything and now I knew things would be fine.

I was thankful for the way things had turned out. I had experienced something mind-blowing and beautiful with a guy who I was really attracted to and cared about and, after, I had communicated my way out of trouble for all of us.

Now, everything had changed. A whole new world had opened up to me. I had a good friend who understood that I might be gay. I had experienced sex with a guy. A good friend of mine was proudly gay. Life was good. There was so much to explore and I intended to find out all I could. I was young and curious and ready to understand things. For now, at least, everything was under control so that I could make sense of it all. The challenge would be keeping my new secret under control throughout the journey, so that I wouldn't get into trouble with the military. "Is that possible?" I thought. As I drifted off to sleep with a million possibilities in my head, I couldn't wait to wake up again just to see what would happen next.

chapter twenty-three

DISCOVERIES

Kenny Bass, my first roommate at the academy, had been screwing around on his computer just before Recognition Week. In his last academy prank ever, he figured out a way to hack into the commandant's e-mail system and alter the message that told all cadets what the next day's uniform would be. Kenny, who loved to wear BDUs because of how comfortable they were, changed the following day's uniform from blues to BDUs. That morning, the entire cadet wing wore BDUs. Kenny came to tell our group of friends what he had done. We wore BDUs like everyone else. He thought it was the greatest thing in the world. What he didn't know was that the commandant, who was a one-star general, didn't think the prank was very funny, and assembled a team of twenty computer geeks to track down the person who had pulled it. Eventually, they tracked the computer traffic to the wall plate in Kenny's dorm room. He was brought in to the general, who personally told Kenny that he would be kicked out of the academy for a number of violations, including the biggest one—impersonating a general officer. Kenny was removed from the academy within forty-eight hours.

Our entire small group of friends was devastated. We had lost one of our core guys. Although Kenny could be eccentric and annoying, we loved him and he loved us. We were all depressed to see him go. Only the stress of the upcoming Hell Week would take our minds off our loss. The night that he was kicked out, we all sat around, taking swigs from a bottle of rum, in Nathan's and my dorm room. We talked about all the great times that we had with Kenny and agreed to never forget him or to lose touch with him.

Spring break happened just after recognition and I actually went home to the trailer park for the first time since I had left for the academy. I only spent a few days there. The plan was that I was going to buy my parents' car from them, drive it back to Colorado Springs, and keep it off-site until I was allowed to have it on the grounds. Juniors were allowed to have cars at the academy as long as their grades were good enough. Kory's sponsor, a woman by the name of Jackie, had agreed to let me keep my car in her yard until the summer came and I was officially a junior.

All cadets at the academy were given the chance to buy a car by being given a very low-interest loan and an infusion of $12,500 into their checking accounts at the start of their senior year. My parents knew I didn't have any money yet, but they were OK with my keeping the car for a year until my "firstie loan" came through. When that time came, I would send $10,000 to my parents to pay for the car they had given me. My parents drove a 1987 Mercedes 190E, which they had bought toward the end of my senior year in high school, mostly because I never did shut up about how cool I thought Mercedes were.

I drove the car from Norton to some far-off place in Massachusetts to meet Jodie, whose family was driving her down from Maine, where she had been vacationing over spring break. Jodie got in my car and she and I drove down to New Jersey to meet Kory, who was also driving his new, illegal car back to the academy. We were excited about going to New Jersey because I had bought the three of us tickets to the Grateful Dead show at Nassau Coliseum nearby on Long Island. I was eager to expose Jodie and Kory to the Dead and get their reactions to a band and a culture that I so loved.

We went to the show and all three of us had an amazing time. For them, their first experience in the preshow parking lot scene—or shake-down, as the Deadheads called it—was just as fun for them as it had been for me when I went for the first time. We ate veggie burritos made by some Deadheads in the back of their Volkswagen bus, and then we went into the show. They loved the scene and the crowd and really loved the music. After the show, we went back to Kory's and slept for the night.

In the morning, we started our road trip, in two cars, across the country and back to the academy. We had an uneventful trip, and once we arrived, I parked my car in Jackie's yard and covered it up.

After spring break, I took the Benz out a couple of times on the weekends but was careful not to park it anywhere on base for any extended period of time. A few people in my class knew that I had the car and one of them asked me for a ride to the airport on a Monday because he had to go home to a funeral. I had the car on base the Sunday before, so I told him that I would just leave it there for one night, against my better judgment, and take him to the airport the next morning before class.

The next morning, I ran him to the airport and drove the car back onto base so that I could make it to class on time. At the academy, missing class is a major offense, so that was not an option. I parked the car in the lower lots down by the field house and the athletic fields and walked to class, already dressed in my uniform. I went to three classes but had the fourth class period of the morning free, so I walked to the parking lot to drive the car back to Jackie's and then take a taxi back to the academy. But when I got to my car, there was a boot on the front wheel so that I couldn't move it. I went into a panic. *Had the base police booted it because it didn't have a military sticker on it yet?*

I called the number on the boot and reached the base police. They told me that there were orders on the citation for me to contact my AOC. *Oh man,* I thought, *I've just been busted as a sophomore with an illegal car.*

I walked up to my squadron with my tail between my legs and knocked on 's door. He told me to come in. "Mithter Lehmkuhl," he lisped. "It has been brought to my attention by a member of this squadron that you are in possession of a car before you are allowed that privilege. It has also been brought to my attention that the same goes for Mithter Kory Thtamp." I couldn't believe it. Someone had turned us in for having cars. I didn't say a word. "I have already written up your punishments." He handed me my Form 10, the punishment form used at the academy that lists the full hit for an offense. The punishment read "50/50/Y."

"Sir, fifty, fifty, and yes?" I asked in disbelief. This meant that was serving me a sentence of fifty tours, fifty confinements, and putting me on full restriction from all privileges until I served it.

"Mithter Lehmkuhl, I don't think that's a hard *enough* sentence for what you've done," he continued in his odd, feminine voice. "I'm also barring you from having a vehicle on base until your senior year," he added with a smirk on his face.

I pleaded. ", look, I brought the car out here over spring break because my parents were going to sell it. I have been keeping it off base and not using it, other than a few times. This morning, I used the car to run an errand and left it on base, like an idiot. I'm sorry. Please don't think I've had the car all year or that I'm in huge violation of the regulation."

"But you are, Mithter Lehmkuhl, and there are some people in the class just above you that have told me a different story. Are you saying that they're lying? Because if you are, then we need to have a full investigation by the Honor Thythtem Review Board."

I did *not* want to be investigated by an honor board. I knew right there that he had me. I did, in fact, have an illegal car on base before I was supposed to. "Sir, I don't want an honor investigation. I just think my punishment is a bit severe."

"Mithter Lehmkuhl, there are juniors in this squadron who don't have cars because I won't sign off on their right to have them—because they don't have high enough grades. They are being punished for not applying themselves in school. How can I expect them to follow their punishment and not have a car if I let sophomores drive around campus in Mercedes-Benzes?"

I tried really hard not to get angry at what he had just said. It was as if he was implying that I was rich or that my family was rich and that I was, somehow, a spoiled brat, which couldn't be further from the reality of my life. I was also fuming inside, knowing that some guy in the class above me was so jealous of me and of my Mercedes that he had taken it upon himself to turn me in. This asshole somehow also knew that I had left the car on base that night. It must have been an athlete who would have been at a late Sunday night practice. It was probably one of the juniors in Bull Ten who was on academic probation and who wasn't allowed to have a car. was getting angry with me, too.

I was in a world of hurt for so many reasons. *How was I going to handle marching fifty tours? How many weekends would I have to sit to serve all those confinements? What was I going to do with my car?* I would have to give it back to my parents. I couldn't have it for a whole year. There was nothing I could do.

I called my parents the next day and explained to them what I had done. My mom informed me that she had already received a call from . *Jesus Christ,* I thought. *This is like high school all over again—with the school calling my parents to tell them I'm in trouble.* I didn't know how I was going to survive another year there without a car, but I would have to. It was just going to make my experience suck that much more. I had done something I wasn't supposed to do and, in military tradition, was getting the harshest punishment available for doing it.

Summer break came, and I was conveniently given my first of three summer sessions as vacation time. I spent it, as usual, with my brother Bobby in California. Allen, as I was now allowed to call Cadet Ladd, went through survival training while I was, finally, a cadet cadre member working First Beast. I couldn't believe I was there already. I was that guy I had feared so much when I arrived at the academy on *my* first day. For as much hell as we were putting the new basics through, I was having a blast. I had begged Jodie to pick First Beast for one of her summer programs and she had agreed. We had separate rooms while we worked but, usually, we always crashed in my room because I didn't have a roommate during that program.

As usual, I was the most lenient cadre member for the basics and usually brought more humor and morale to them than anyone else. I realized early on that I wasn't much of a yeller, so I chose to let others yell at the basics. Every cadre member had a specific job, in addition to being part of the cadre. My particular job was flight specialist—the cadre member whom a basic could go to in order to discuss personal problems. If basic cadets decided to leave the academy before Beast was even over, they would come to the flight specialist first. Most basics steered clear of any cadre member at all, for any reason. When I was a basic, I would never have talked to the flight specialist. I was too afraid that what I would talk about would get around to the rest of the cadre and hurt me.

One particular basic didn't care about retribution and came to me all the time, asking me if he should leave the academy. Every day, he would come to me and tell me that he wasn't doing well in basic, but he couldn't back it up with any examples. "I think you're doing fine," I would tell him over and over again.

Finally, one day he came to me for his now-routine talk/counseling session and started crying. I asked him to please stop crying and to tell me what was wrong. He was shaking this time, and looked at me like he was a little mentally unstable.

"Cadet Lehmkuhl," he said in a broken voice, "I'm gay and this place isn't for me." I froze. This was the last thing I had expected him to say to me. I wondered if he was telling me this because he thought I was gay or if this was just a coincidence.

"Why do you think you're gay?" I asked.

"There is no *why*," he said. "I'm gay. I know that I'm gay." Here I was probing into this seventeen-year-old's life, not only to learn about him and his situation, but also to learn about myself.

He began to answer. "I know because I fell in love this summer. I fell in love with a guy. We had a summer romance and it killed me to have to leave him and come here. He didn't want me to come here. Neither did my mother. They're all against the military and my being in it. But I wanted to fly and I wanted to play soccer and have a full scholarship, so I took my appointment. It was just another college option for me. "

"Who made sure you were nominated by a congressman? Who did your application? How did you get in?" I asked.

"My father," he answered. "He did my whole application. He

pushed me to be here. I didn't really care. He's connected with some congressmen. He told me this would be the best for me."

This was typical for many at the academy. They were there because their parents got them in on a connection or by doing their applications for them. If there is one college in the United States at which a *desire* to be there is necessary for survival, it is the Air Force Academy.

After hearing his gay summer romance story and about his father's pressure, I knew that he should leave the academy. However, this guy had obviously had too many people in his life making decisions for him, so I wasn't about to tell him what to do. From our past counseling sessions, I could tell that he was not happy, and I had documented our conversations. I didn't know if I should counsel him about the boyfriend back home. At the time, the law was that I couldn't ask him if he was gay and he couldn't tell me. But he did tell me, and I had to make a decision.

Since we were one-on-one, I told him, "Look, you just told me that you're gay and that you had a summer romance with a guy. I don't know if this is true or if you're using this as a final excuse to get kicked out of here, but let me tell you something. If you want to get kicked out of here for being gay, it won't be easy. You'll get kicked out all right, but you won't go home right away. You're going to go through a complete investigation. During this investigation, they'll probably put you in the mental ward of the military hospital here and treat you like you're crazy. Then, because you have admitted to having sex with a guy, you could get thrown in front of a UCMJ judge who can decide your fate. Besides that, you'll end up with all of this on your military record for life, and it will be there in the archives for anyone to read. Now, let me ask you again. Are you really gay?"

"Sir, I had a summer romance with a guy. I swear that to you. Now, I realize that I should not have told you that. But I did. Now what are you going to do to me? Can I get out of here without saying that I'm gay?" he asked.

"Yes, you can," I said. "Look. I'm going to recommend that you be let go. All they need to hear is that you didn't come here for yourself and that your dad coerced you into this. If there is one thing they want from cadets here, it's that the cadet *wants* to be here. Obviously, this life is not for you—for many reasons. As for the gay thing, I am sitting here with only you so it's your word against mine. I happen to be sympathetic to the gay community and happen to be very against the current policies in place to handle homosexuality in the military. So, I'm going to tell you that I never heard you tell me that you're gay. If you tell anyone that you *did* tell me about it, I'm going to deny it. This way I'm not liable for *not* turning you over to the machine."

This well-built, five-foot-ten blond kid, who looked like he should be an model for Abercrombie & Fitch or Bruce Weber, looked at me with tears in his bright-green eyes and said, "I knew you would be OK with my story. I just somehow knew it, but I don't know why I knew it."

"It's OK," I said. "You're going to be OK. I'm glad that I'm your flight specialist."

"Cadet Lehmkuhl?" he asked.

"Yes, Basic Cadet Brenner?" I asked back with a smile on my face. We were finally having a normal moment.

"Can I just say that the first day I saw you in this squadron, that I was very attracted to you?" I didn't know what to say back to him. He went on but he looked at the floor. "I have fantasized about what it would be like to have you hold me." I sat up in my chair and became uncomfortable. He continued. "Every time you come up to me, I breathe heavier and my heart races and I . . . "

"Brenner!" I yelled.

"Yes, sir? Sir, I'm sorry," he said.

"It's OK. I get it. I'm going to help you get out of here. We're done for now. I'll make sure you're treated well until you leave the academy. I think you're making a good decision," I said.

"Thank you, sir." He got up and walked out the door. I sat there, again stunned by what I had just been through. This was a perfect example of the self-control that most people in the military have—gay or straight. Brenner was an attractive guy. I could have taken Brenner right there in my room. I could have locked the door, taken off his uniform—and mine—and messed around with him the way he wanted me to. But because I was in a military situation, with an obligation to remain professional, there was no way that I would cross the line and do exactly what was now, obviously, in my nature to do.

I had lacked this sort of self-control with Cadet Ladd, and I had beaten myself up for it a million times, knowing that I had broken rules that even heterosexuals had to follow in a military environment. I had heard enough stories from my roommate about guys at the academy having sex with seven or eight of the female freshmen in their squadrons. It happened all the time, because guys that age are not always the best at avoiding the heat of sexual temptation. Neither are girls able to avoid it in the same cases. I *had* avoided it, and that was a check mark on the good side of my personal report card.

Besides being somewhat aroused by this situation with Brenner, the whole concept of leaving the academy now invaded my mind. I knew that in just a few short weeks, I would be starting the first semester of my junior year. On that first day of class, I would, by association and by attending class, be committing myself to seven more years in the air force. I had a small anxiety attack thinking about it. I fantasized about being Brenner and getting to leave and be a civilian again. I wondered what it would have been like for me to leave during basic training. Back then I knew that I, personally, would never have been able to live with myself if I had quit. I wouldn't have been able to face my family at home.

Now, it was a different story altogether. Seven years is a long time to a twenty-year-old, and I was just figuring out that I might be a full-on gay guy. What would I do? I thought of the alternative to staying in. I would walk out after two years of school. But that wasn't the worst of it. I would be walking out after all of the blood, sweat, and tears that I had put into the academy. It would have all been in vain: basic training, freshman year, Hell Week, survival training, Soaring, my entire sophomore year of work, and all that I had learned about leadership as an upperclassman and as a cadre member for First Beast. No, I could *not* quit the academy.

Once I made the decision, right at that moment, I was proud of myself. The only reason I would leave was to avoid discovery as a gay man, but I knew in my head that I could survive if I really wanted to. I was savvy enough to live a double life, and that would be good enough. What I didn't realize, at that time, was how miserable and difficult a double life would be. Maybe I *should* have left and attended a civilian school. Maybe I would have been better off. I don't know. What I do know is that I had already learned a hell of a lot about myself at the academy, and I was set to learn a hell of a lot more.

First Beast ended and Brenner was freed into the civilian world, just as I told him he would be. I was sad to see him go and sad for the air force that it had lost such an intelligent individual. At the same time, I was happy for him and the freedom he was about to enjoy.

It was time for the First Beast cadre to brief the Second Beast Cadre on the basics they would now oversee. It was my job to brief the new Second Beast flight specialist, who happened to be Seth English. He didn't believe his ears when I told him about Brenner. Seth filled me in on the latest in his life and caught me up on where we left off at the end of sophomore year. I learned more about the other gay cadet in another squadron whom he was regularly sleeping with—a guy named Matt in Squadron Fifteen. Seth's parents' house in Colorado Springs was a convenient place for Seth and his guy to sneak off to and be together. He had told me the crazy stories of the sex they would have. It all fascinated me. I admired Seth because he always seemed to be so well adjusted with what he was doing. He was sure about himself and didn't second-guess his need to be with guys. "I'm gay for sure," he would tell me without flinching. And he wasn't worried about being caught.

"What if you get caught?" I would ask him.

"I'll deny it. I'll deny it all. Fuck 'em," was his answer. I loved that, too. Seth wasn't afraid, even though he was educated enough on the situation to know how seriously homosexuality was treated by the academy.

We talked for a while about the summer and the other basics coming into Bull Ten. We dished about which guys were hot and which ones were not. We talked about which guys might be gay and which ones were really straight. For the ones that we thought might be gay, we theorized about whether they were tops or bottoms. We kidded around and laughed about how we would compare notes when he was finished with them after Second Beast.

"Before I go," he said, "I have to tell you about some new 'family' that we have among us here at the academy." I liked how Seth referred to gay guys as "family." We could talk about it out loud and no one would really get the gist of what we were saying. Seth told me about two more guys in the Class of 1996 who he had found out were gay. One was a black guy named Douglas, who was on the intercollegiate track team, and the other was a guy named Thomas, who was a prior-enlisted guy in the same squadron as Douglas. They were both in Cadet Squadron Twenty.

"Wow," I said, "two more family members and both in the same squadron and both in our class. That's awesome! Gay cadets at the academy are like the stars in the galaxy. You can see a few but you never know how many are *really* out there somewhere."

"Ha ha ha! You're right! Listen, I haven't talked to those guys but I heard from Matt that they actually go out to gay clubs on weekends."

"Are you serious?" I asked excitedly. "I can't even imagine doing that! Do they wear disguises or a hat and glasses?" I asked in kind of a joking way.

"Why *would* they?" Seth answered. "If they see another cadet in a gay bar, then that cadet would be just as guilty, so it's no problem. And I heard they have a blast when they go out. They meet civilian guys who cream their pants when they find out that they're actual cadets from the academy."

"It's still kind risky though," I said in my paranoia, "because those civilians could just call the academy and turn them in."

"I know," Seth said with a grin on his face, "they have that covered, too. They always use fake names and never really tell a truthful story when the guys ask them about their lives. I asked Matt the same questions you're asking me. I think this is awesome. If we don't meet these guys and go out with them, then we should just go on our own. Me and you." I thought about it and felt adrenaline rush through my body.

"I can't imagine doing it . . . but we should. Just the two of us, so we get a feel for the place," I suggested.

"Yeah, that's a good idea."

"When will we go?" I asked"

"There's this place in Denver called Rodeo that they go to," Seth replied "We can go there when the school year starts back up."

"OK, I can't wait. I'll think about it for the rest of the summer," I said. "How many more gay guys do you think are here?" I asked.

Seth smiled. "I don't know, dude. But I bet we're going to find out." Seth walked out of my temporary summer room and, in typical Seth fashion, slapped his own butt before the door shut behind him. I laughed to myself and became very excited about the possibilities of the future. I was going to meet more gay cadets. I was going to go to a club for gay people for the first time in my life. I was discovering a world that I didn't even know existed.

chapter twenty-four

WHAT HAPPENS IN VEGAS

The third military block of my summer was set for Operation Air Force, or Ops, as we called it. Ops was an academy program that took all rising juniors, or second-degree cadets, and sent them to a real, functioning air force base for three weeks to learn about what is done on one. Once the cadets arrive at the assigned base, they are assigned to a duty officer, who looks out for their well-being and makes sure the cadets are seeing enough of the air force in action. Base assignments were random. Some cadets went to Minot Air Force Base in North Dakota and learned about missiles all summer, while others got Eglin Air Force Base in Pensacola, Florida, and were allowed to fly in F-15s. Finding out where you were going to spend a few weeks of your summer was a scary experience, and there were bragging rights to go along with getting a cool Ops base.

I ended up with Nellis Air Force Base in Las Vegas. I was *more* than happy. Nellis was not only a flying base; it was a flying base with almost every plane in the inventory present and taking off on training missions. Nellis was the home of Red Flag, the air force's equivalent of the navy's Top Gun program, at which the best pilots in the air force learn new fighting and evasion maneuvers in their particular air-crafts. Nellis was also the home of the Thunderbirds, which are the show planes of the air force. The Thunderbirds performed at special events to bring positive publicity to the air force and to awe civilians. On our graduation day, the Thunderbirds would perform for our class and the whole stadium.

I arrived at Nellis for Ops and met the other cadets assigned with me. There were five of us and I had never met any of them. Besides me, there were two girls and two other guys. The girls, Patty and Kelly, were very cool and roommates in Cadet Squadron Thirty-Five. The two other guys were Ron and Brian. Ron was a farm boy from Iowa who stood at a lanky six foot five; he didn't seem very athletic, although he was nice and soft spoken.

Brian was a practicing Mormon from Utah. He didn't smoke or drink—not even coffee. When we first all loaded into the van from the airport, we were talking about going to the casinos and staying out all night for the whole time we were there. In the same conversation, Brian told us that he was a Mormon and, although he wanted to see everything in Vegas, he couldn't drink so he said he would always be our designated driver. "Woo hoo!" we all yelled when he told us that. It was going to be a fun three weeks. I had never been to Las Vegas before and I was excited to see what it was all about—in addition to being excited about possible flights in different airplanes on the base.

The air force put us up in the visiting officers quarters, or VOQs, on the base. VOQs were great mini-apartments. They also set the five of us up with a white fifteen-passenger van. It looked dorky, but we were happy to have our own transportation. Patty was the coolest one of the group. She and I hit it off from the beginning. I could tell she was really liberal just by the civilian clothes that she brought with her. She dressed kind of earthy crunchy, with long, flowing skirts and old-style leather sandals that I called "Jerusalem cruisers" to make her laugh. She and I discussed how glad we were to be away from the academy and how much we couldn't stand the small-minded thinking there. I was tempted to tell her about my gay experiences, but I wasn't ready to just yet.

We had an amazing three weeks. We met the Thunderbird pilots and had lunch with them on several occasions. On other days, we were given Humvees, the military style of the Hummer, to drive on huge gun ranges, where we would shoot at far-off objects with M-60 machine guns that were attached to the roofs of the vehicles. The guns were actual rocket launchers. We each fired off a few rounds and watched in awe as the stove that we had aimed at in the distance was blown to bits by the impact-detonating shell. I learned, on that day, what a rush people get from the power of controlling a destructive weapon. Admittedly, in all the fun, it was a challenge to remember that those weapons have ruined, and will continue to ruin, people's lives.

We flew F-16s quite a few times that summer, and not just in leisure flights. We were put into two-seater F-16s for mock air-to-air dogfights against other fighters and bombers. Much of what I saw and did on those flights was, and still is, classified; I was blown away by it all.

Aside from the military excitement of Ops, we were in Las Vegas, so our nights were wild. The bars and casinos never close, and all of us were twenty-one years old and ready to party. We went out every single night and hit every major casino that Las Vegas had to offer. I tried gambling a couple of times and always came away a loser. While playing the slot machines, we were served free drinks the entire time. We would all get really drunk and Brian would drive us home. As with most college-age kids, drinking alcohol together had a bonding effect on us. I'll never forget our drunken rides home back to the VOQs. I caught glimpses of Brian in the rear view mirror of the van, and he would always have a smile on his face from hearing us say and do the craziest things. I really gained respect for Brian and the way he refrained from drinking while we appeared to be having so much booze-enhanced fun. I admired how he stuck to his morals.

The officer in charge of us for the three weeks at Nellis was a captain named Joe Morgan. We called him, naturally, Captain Morgan. We thought this was really funny, considering he was in charge of us during a time when we happened to be heavily involved in experimenting with alcohol. Captain Morgan would take us around the base showing us things. He made no secret of his attraction to girls, and he couldn't help but look at every one that walked or drove by. Captain Morgan may not have been gay but he would turn out to be very gay friendly.

On my third F-16 flight of the summer, I flew with a guy named Captain Jim Barbella. He was a six-foot-two, dark, handsome, Italian American who looked like a superhero in his flight suit. I remember getting fitted for our G suits just before the flight and seeing him in front of me with his flight helmet hanging from one hand, standing very casually, while two people were tightening the G suit around his legs. I was instantly attracted to him and had to actually look away when he looked me in the eyes.

We flew our F-16 for a few hours that day. It was definitely the most violent, fast-paced, and most skillfully maneuvered mock dogfight I had been in all summer. He was an incredible pilot with lightning-fast reflexes, and it all impressed me completely. By the time we got out of the plane and were walking back to the Red Flag Squadron, we were both soaked in sweat. The ride sapped our strength since we had been doing a lot of pushing and heavy breathing to keep from blacking out in our high G–pulling maneuvers. When he had let me take the plane over, I wasn't as hard on the controls as he was, but I still pushed it hard. As we walked across the 120-degree tarmac, he looked over at me with sweaty, matted, helmet hair and smiled as he said, "You did some good flying up there, partner. How long you been a pilot?" I looked at him and my imagination went wild with impure thoughts. I could have thrown him down right there to just to rub my face on his and maybe lick the sweat off his neck.

"Ever since I can remember," I said in the hopes of impressing him a little more. He just smiled at me and didn't say anything back. We got into the squadron and the air-conditioned air hit me like a ton of bricks. My whole body supercooled in the matter of a couple of seconds, and it felt great.

"Showers are down the hall and to the left," Captain Barbella told me. He placed his helmet back onto its storage rack as some of the techs started taking off his G suit. I didn't know what to do. If I had gone to the showers with him and the showers were open, there would have been no hiding my excitement toward this guy. As much as I wanted to see his body without the flight suit wrapped around it, I couldn't do it!

"I'll just take one back at my room," I said.

"Suit yourself, but I wouldn't want to be sitting next to you on that ride back to the VOQs. Ha!" he said playfully. I was still excited. I took a deep breath and then had to remember to laugh at his joke. He was still looking at me and could tell that I was deep in thought or, at the very least, distracted, which was preventing me from hearing what he was saying. I looked up at him and, this time, I couldn't take my eyes off his. His thick, dark eyebrows were canted downward at the sides, and he had a puppy dog look in his blue eyes. "You OK, partner?"

"Yeah. Yeah, I'm fine. Why?" I asked, pretending everything was normal.

"Oh, well sometimes I fly too hard and rough for my wizzo," he said. "I thought maybe your body was feeling a little weak, like my flying might be catching up to your head or, even worse, your stomach." The wizzo, or weapons systems officer, is usually a navigator who sits in the second seat of the fighter plane and handles the aiming, dropping, and shooting of munitions and weapons. He was referring to me as his wizzo, and I loved that.

"My body can handle more than that," I said, as I continued to look in his eyes with a smile on my face, while the techs took off my G suit. His face became serious and his eyes focused on me. The techs left with my equipment and now we were the only two people in the room.

"Well. That's really good to know in case we . . . " there was a pause in his sentence, " . . . *play* again in the future," he said before turning away and walking down the hallway to the showers. I stood there, speechless, adrenaline pumpin, and sexually aroused.

I called Patty on my cell phone and she came with our cadet van to pick me up from the squadron. I told her that I needed a shower and apologized if I smelled.

"Reichen, you smell good no matter what," she said. I didn't know what to make of her comment. We had had a buddy-buddy relationship during the previous week and half; this was the first time I felt that she was hitting on me.

"What?" I asked.

"Well, you know, guys have a smell to them. All guys do. Your smell is exceptionally good. Well, at least to *me*," she said. I was freaked out. I had just had this hot pilot hitting on me in the squadron and now Patty was hitting on me. The way she was talking instantly changed the way I felt about her. I couldn't trust her as much as I did before. I felt like there might have been an ulterior motive of a possible sexual interest to the friendship she had shown me since we had arrived at Nellis. I didn't say anything back.

"Reichen, we've been really friendly with each other since you got here. I know you like me as much as I like you," she said. I thought I knew where she was going with this conversation and I knew it wasn't a good place. She continued, "If there were some sort of attraction between the two of us, you would have just responded to my comment."

I decided to stop her train of thought. "Patty, why are you doing this all of the sudden? We've been friendly buddies up until now. You're changing everything by saying all this."

She quickly spoke to what I had just said. "Reichen, that's the whole point of what I'm saying. You *don't* want anything with me. Why not?"

"Patty, because I just *don't*, OK? Isn't is possible for a guy and a girl to be friends?" I asked.

"Well, sure it's possible, but usually there is *some* sort of spark to it all," she reasoned.

"What's your point, Patty?" I asked in a louder, annoyed voice.

She answered even more loudly, "My point is that I think you're a great guy but I think you have some issues that you need to discuss with somebody. And I think that I just might be that person."

"I have *issues* because I'm not trying to jump your bones, Patty?"

"OK, calm down. Maybe I went at this the wrong way," she admitted.

"Went at *what* the wrong way?" I asked, again, loudly.

"Went at the fact that I don't think you even *like* girls!" she yelled. There I was sitting in the passenger seat of this huge van with Patty driving. I had nowhere to go and no one to turn to. She had just called me out. I was silent for a good minute. Patty lowered her voice to a soft, caring tone. "I told you that you have a good smell because I wanted to see your reaction. I'm sorry. It was a mean thing to do," she said softly.

"Just drop me off at my VOQ. I can't even begin to have a conversation like this with you right now." I wanted to end with a statement that didn't confirm nor deny that I thought I was gay.

Patty was a smart girl and had picked up on who I really was. As I showered in my VOQ, I tried to calm myself by concentrating on the cool water hitting my head. This was all getting out of control for me. I felt scared at first, then angry. Then I started thinking of what lies I would tell Patty regarding any past situation during which she might have noticed my lack of attraction to women. I thought of every excuse in the book, such as *I have a girlfriend back home,* and *I recently had a bad breakup with a girl who cheated on me and girls just aren't on my mind,* and *I'm having fun out here and I don't want to think about girls.*

Wait. That last one wouldn't be a good enough lie, I thought. Every twenty-one-year-old straight guy thinks about girls all the time; I knew it from being around the horniest of them at the Air Force Academy. *I can't lie to her,* I thought to myself. *She's one of the people I can trust.*

I dried myself off and put on a pair of surf trunks, a T-shirt, and some sandals. I was tired from flying and wanted to lie out by the base swimming pool. I called Patty's VOQ and asked her if she wanted to lie by the pool with me. Shortly afterward, she came to my room and we walked to the pool together. Temperatures that day had reached 105 degrees in Las Vegas. The wind blowing across the lawns and streets felt like it was hot enough to burn our skin.

At the pool, while we were lying on our towels, the lifeguard walked over to us and said, "One of the little air force brats crapped in the pool so you can't go in there. We are disinfecting it and it takes twenty-four hours."

"Shit!" I yelled. "It's a hundred five degrees out! We have to be able to go in the pool."

The lifeguard said, "Look we haven't even had the chance to go in and get it out. We saw it float into the filter intake over there." He pointed.

Patty got up from her towel and dove into the pool right in front of the lifeguard. "Wait!" he yelled at her. Patty stayed underwater until she reached the filter intake. "Get out of there! I'm going to get in trouble and so are you."

Patty peeked into the filter intake. "Yep. I thought so," she yelled back. "I've been swimming all my life and we used to play this trick at public pools when we were kids." She reached in and pulled out what looked like a tiny brown log and held it up in the air. "It's a Baby Ruth bar!"

I could hear parents and other people around the pool laughing and making comments like, "Well for *heaven's* sake!" I stood there with my mouth wide open. Patty had intrigued me since I'd met her, and now she had done it again.

I looked at the lifeguard and asked, "Well, is it safe to swim amongst the germs of a Baby Ruth bar?" He looked at me, shook his head, and walked away. Slowly people made their way back into the pool, and thank God, because it was unbearably hot out.

Patty and I went for a swim together and agreed that we would talk in a few minutes when we were cooled off and ready to lie out in the sun. When we were both ready, I started the conversation. "So about what you asked me before. Yeah. You can't say a *word* to anyone."

"I won't, don't worry," she said with a gleam in her eye. She was waiting for me to say something more, like a little kid waits for a lollipop when she visits the bank with her mother.

"Yeah Patty, I think I'm gay," I said. I had done it. I had actually admitted it to another person.

"Who knows about you? Besides me?" she asked.

"Well, I've pretty much told my roommate, Nathan. I've told my friend Jodie. I've told Seth English, also in my squadron. The guy I've actually messed around with knows. He's now a sophomore, thank God."

"Did you mess around with him before he was recognized?" she asked, as if elated to hear of such a scandal.

"No, but I wanted to," I admitted to her with a smile.

"Oh my God! I love this!" she said while clapping her hands together. "So wait. You've told all these people but no one has turned you in?"

"No. It's not like that. I've had a reason for telling each one of those people. They're all kind of involved somehow."

"Involved *how?*" she asked.

"OK, you're getting too personal. I don't really want to talk about all of their situations. But I'll tell you about my own."

"I understand your fear, believe me," she said. "The academy is one fucked-up place when it comes to all the different kinds of *real* people there are in the world. They just aren't accepted at the academy."

"How do you understand, though? I don't get it. You've actually thought about gay stuff before?" I asked.

"Well, yeah," she admitted.

I whispered, "Are you gay? Are you a le . . . lesb . . . lesbian?" I could barely get the word *lesbian* out of my mouth.

"Well, I wouldn't call myself a *lesbian* per se, but you know."

"No, I don't know. What?" I asked eagerly, waiting for a confession.

"Well, I've been known to dabble on that side of the tracks," she said with a huge smile on her face. "But I just play a little. I've already hooked up with a couple of hot male officers on this base since we've been here this summer, so I can't consider myself a total lesbian." It was once again confirmed to me how many illegal *heterosexual* hookups actually took place in the military.

"Holy shit! Patty, I *love* you!" I was lying on my towel with my chest on the ground and my arms in front of me. I buried my face in my arms and laughed. "This is so awesome," I said with my face still buried.

"And I'm not the only one at the academy," she said in a serious tone.

"Well, I *know* that. I've already been informed of several other 'family members' in other squadrons. Tell me, who do you know who's gay? Is one named Douglas and the other one Thomas?" I asked.

"No. There's a Douglas and a Thomas?"

"Oh, yeah." I felt like a high school kid gossiping with his friend about who slept with whom on the football team and the cheerleading squad.

"Well, I know a hell of a lot more than just *two* guys," she said as if she were a magician with tricks up her sleeve.

"Patty, tell me. Help me. Make me feel like I'm not a freak. Help me to feel more comfortable," I pleaded.

"OK. But you can't say I told you so."

"I won't!" I assured her.

"OK, well I know of about ten guys and about two chicks." I was listening with the widest eyes and an open mouth. "Cadet Engle."

"What?" I asked in a yelling whisper. "Not the senator's son, Chris Engle? Not *hot* Chris Engle!"

"Yes, dear," Patty said as she saw the excitement running across my face.

"Who else?" I asked.

"Jake Lester." Patty was naming these people and I was amazed at how *easily* I was getting this information and how awesome I felt as each name was called off. Jake Lester was a fairly hot guy from San Diego who had, in the first semester of our freshman year, developed testicular cancer. The whole cadet wing knew of his struggle and he ended up losing one of his testicles in surgery and undergoing chemotherapy while *continuing* to attend classes at the academy. I had always thought of him as a strong guy, but now I liked him even more because I knew he was gay.

"Steven Rider," she said. I was blown away. Steven Rider was the guy Jodie had been fooling around with and had actually lost her virginity to. I was confused.

"How could Steven be gay? I know a girl he has sex with."

"Well," Patty said, "that one isn't totally confirmed, but I have pretty good evidence."

Steven was gorgeous. He was an athlete on the academy water polo team. He was from Hawaii and stood at six feet three inches, and had brown hair, brown eyes, and the most chiseled face I had ever seen. Besides this, he was funny. He had nicknames for everything. He had nicknames for different sexual positions. He had twenty nicknames for a penis, and nicknames for hard-ons. His humor was a little perverted, but in a campy way that made it palatable. The idea of his being gay fascinated me.

Patty continued with names and I was blown away by every one, even though I didn't know them. I made her describe each person in detail, including what squadron they were in. I made her tell me a story about each one. Patty's squadron was in Sijan Hall, across the Terrazzo from Vandenberg Hall, which was my dormitory building. Interestingly, all of the people she pointed out were in Sijan Hall, and I barely knew anyone over there. Even more interesting was that all of the people she and I had named, except for one, Thomas, were in the class of 1996, *our* class. Thomas was in the class of 1997. Together, we added up the names and counted *nineteen* cadets who we knew were gay.

These were just the ones we *knew* about. We lay there, burning in the sun, pondering how many more there were at the academy. How many more were self-admitted gay people? How many were gay but hadn't yet realized it? We estimated that since we knew about twenty in our class, there might be twenty more whom we didn't know about, and about forty or fifty more who were repressing it or who hadn't figured out their own sexuality yet. We cited a few names of guys we *knew* had to be gay although they continued to try to date girls or to go out of their way to prove to everyone that they were straight. We reasoned that the repression factor would be greater at the academy than at other places because cadets usually came from more conservative backgrounds. They would be more afraid to admit being gay for fear of tarnishing the image of their very political families or losing the respect of their conservative families. Others were repressed due to their strong sense of "Christianity," which told them that they would go to hell for being gay. And some, believe it or not, wouldn't come out for fear of losing a hell of a lot of family money.

That was *ninety* possible gay people in our class, we decided. "If there are about nine hundred people in our class, after all the attrition since basic training, then that works out right," Patty said.

"What do you mean?" I asked.

"Well, there is a widespread belief that ten percent of the population is actually gay. This supposedly includes those that aren't out of the closet or those that won't admit that they're gay."

"Wow, ten percent. I had no idea. So maybe I'm not a freak," I said with a smile.

"Oh, Reichen, you're no freak, honey. Have you looked in the mirror lately?" she asked.

"No, not really," I answered. I was telling the truth. I really hadn't looked in a mirror in a very long time. I'm not talking about looking in a mirror to try to fix my hair or to wash my face, but really taking time to look at myself. In fact, I hated looking in the mirror because I hated what I saw. I would hardly ever look into my own eyes in a mirror because I continued to be ashamed of my looks and saw the very thing that everyone had made fun of for so many years of my life. I avoided mirrors like I would avoid the plague. I was still like this, even at twenty-one years old. "I hate looking in the mirror and seeing myself. That's the thing. Some of these gay guys have looks going for them. I think I'm going to have a hard time because I don't have that," I confessed to Patty.

Patty coughed as she looked at me and said, "What? You don't have *looks* going for you? Reichen, you're known by a lot of chicks at the academy as one of the hotties."

"What?" I asked in disbelief. "You're putting me on."

"Uh, no, I'm not. Are you really serious? You don't think you're good-looking, if not completely hot?"

"No, Patty. I'm not good-looking, but thank you for trying."

"Oh, I get it," she said. "You're one of these guys who knows he's good-looking but doesn't want to let on to anyone that he knows it so that he seems more likable and humble."

I looked at her completely seriously. "Patty, I have always thought I was the ugliest person around. That's why I talk to people so much. I'm always trying so hard to be nice because I know I have to get by on personality. But people *still* shy away from me." I continued and told her of my childhood where I was made fun of for being skinny and ugly.

"Reichen, you need help. You need me to explain some things to you. Guys and girls alike are actually intimidated by how you look. Don't you know that? They don't know what to do when they see you. That's why they shy away from you," she tried to explain.

"Whatever. Again, Patty, thanks for trying. I appreciate it."

"Whatever, Reichen. But do me a favor and look in a mirror. And I mean look at the whole package. Have you checked your body out lately? Uh, yeah, look at that, too." I could have been flattered by what Patty was saying, but I knew deep down that she just didn't see what I saw—and knew—was there.

I actually did go back to my room and look in the mirror. Just as I thought, I saw the same thing that I always saw. I was skinny. My ears stuck out way too far. My legs were too thin for my body. My rib cage stuck out, and my neck was too long. These were all the things that other kids reminded me of when I was growing up.

Before I left Las Vegas, I was lucky enough to get a personal visit to my VOQ from our very cool buddy, Captain Morgan. Midmorning on a Saturday, after we had all partied it up the night before at some casino, Captain Morgan knocked on my door. I was still sleeping. I opened the door to find him in jeans and a T-shirt. "Can I come in?" he asked.

"Uh, yeah. Of course. Come on in," I said, very groggy and somewhat hungover.

"Hey, man," Captain Morgan said, "this is going to sound crazy but you can take it however you want to." I perked up, wondering what he was going to say next. He continued. "I just have a message to pass along from somebody."

"OK," I said, sort of in a questioning way. Captain Morgan laughed.

"Calm down, Lehmkuhl. It's not a big deal. Sorry for scaring you. Seriously, it's cool. God, you cadets are so damn high-*strung*!" he said and laughed again. "OK, it's, uh, from Captain Barbella. Do you remember him?"

"Yeah," I said. "The bad-ass pilot I flew with. We were in his F-16 together. That guy's got some amazing reflexes."

"Yes, he does, yes, he does," Captain Morgan said. "He also has a big crush on one of you cadets. And he wanted me to make sure you had his number." He handed me a piece of paper with a number written down in a guy's chicken-scratch writing. I was kind of disappointed. Here I was, having to set up one of my female Ops mates with a man whom I found incredibly attractive. I was envious.

"OK. So which one is it? Patty or Kelly? I'll make sure she gets it," I said.

Captain Morgan turned away from me and walked toward my door. I followed him to the door. He turned around with one hand on the door knob and one hand reaching toward me. I shook his hand. As he backed out the door, he said, "Yeah, I don't believe he's ever met Patty or Kelly." The door shut and Captain Morgan was gone.

As I processed what had just happened, I began to wake up. My heart was racing. Captain Barbella had just sent his buddy Captain Morgan to give me his phone number. I reviewed the conversation we had just had over and over in my mind, fascinated by the *language* that Captain Morgan used in order to cover his tracks and those of Captain Barbella.

I didn't know what to do with his number. I thought about calling him right away, but then decided against it. Maybe that was too eager. Or maybe that would show him that I really liked him. I put the number down and took a shower. By the time I was done showering, so many thoughts about this guy were running through my head that I couldn't resist. I picked up the phone. Every ring felt like an eternity and every ring sent more and more of that sex-adrenaline feeling through my body. He picked up.

"Hello?"

"Captain Barbella. It's Cadet Lehmkuhl," I said as if I were making a business call. I didn't know what to expect.

"Hey there buddy, what's going on?"

"Not much, I just have your phone number here . . . " I said in an open-ended way.

"Cool, well uh, what are you up to today?" *That* was the question I was waiting for. That confirmed it. I was the one he wanted to see.

"Well, I'm hanging out in my VOQ trying to recover from a hang-over," I said and then laughed.

He laughed with me. "Yeah? Well, I'm in the same situation, recovering from a wild night myself," he said.

I took the bull by the horns. "Well I'm glad we're talking then, because misery loves company."

"Yeah?" he asked. "Well this misery would *love* some company." I couldn't believe this was happening. "Why don't you get ready and I'll drop by and pick you up," he suggested.

"I'm already showered," I said.

"Me too," he said. His voice got deeper and more focused. "I'll be there in less than five minutes."

"OK," I said. He hung up the phone and so did I. I was so excited I couldn't stand it.

Minutes later he pulled up in a black BMW 5 Series. I was standing outside the VOQs. He rolled down his passenger window so I didn't have to see him through the tint, and he waved at me. Even though I wanted to run, I walked toward him and got into the car.

"Where do you want to go?" he asked. I was stunned by how hot he looked.

"Uh, maybe to a hotel casino?"

"Good idea. I'm up for that," he said. "How about Caesars Palace? We'll get a room there and have some fun. Gambling. We'll have some fun gambling," he said with a smile on his face.

We drove to Caesars Palace hotel and casino and got a beautiful room with a view of the Strip. As soon as the door to our room was closed, we went at each other like two dogs that hadn't been fed in weeks. He stripped off my shorts and T-shirt and threw me on the bed, kissing and licking my entire body. He had some stubble on his face and I remember it feeling amazing wherever he was kissing me. He was on top of me on the bed with one of his hands pinning my two hands together. It was a game of strength and will. As I would playfully get one hand unpinned, he would stop kissing me until he pinned both of my hands on the bed again. Eventually, I broke loose from his hand and pulled his shirt off. He had a perfect body, just as I had pictured, with a dusting of hair on his pecs and down the middle of his whole torso leading to a thicker treasure trail going into his shorts.

The whole idea that I was doing this with a pilot I had flown with was driving me just as crazy as his physical beauty and the feel of his body. "I *love* your body," he would say to me over and over again. "You taste *so* good." I absolutely loved that he was telling me that as he rubbed his chest hair on me. I was in complete heaven and doing whatever I could not to explode into orgasm. I wanted this to last forever.

He took his shorts off in one quick swoop. He wasn't wearing any underwear. I looked down and saw his huge erection. I didn't know what to do. I felt inadequate for a moment because he was larger than me. When I had messed around with Allen, we were almost the same size so it wasn't an issue. But this was ridiculous.

I must have had a concerned look on my face because he told me not to worry, that he wouldn't hurt me with it. He knew how big he was and I found that to be sexy. We messed around for a good two hours, just about bringing each other to orgasm and then slowing down to keep it going a little longer. Finally, we both finished at the same time. He collapsed and lay down on me. We were covered in each other's wetness and sweat and lay there sleeping this way for about another two hours. I fell fast asleep, loving the feeling of this beautiful man on top of me. I felt safe and secure and, after such a verbal session, I felt better-looking and more physically desirable than I had ever felt before.

He took me back to my VOQ. On the way, he asked me not to say anything to anyone and I asked him to do the same. He said that we probably shouldn't do it again, because we would get attached to each other and that there would be no way for us to see each other again. It sort of crushed me but, being clueless as to how this all worked, I just agreed not to call him again. I asked him how old he was and he said he was twenty-nine—eight years older than me. Ever since then, I have checked out guys who are older than I am. I have always remembered that hot pilot, Captain Barbella.

We did, in the end, have one more time together. On the night before I left for the academy, Captain Barbella knocked on my VOQ door at about eleven. He came in dressed in his flight suit and combat boots. We had each other again but not as intensely, and I got the impression that he just wanted to be held, even more than have sex. As we held each other in bed, I wondered what it was like for him to live such a private and secret double life. I thought about how lonely he seemed to be. I wished I could stay in Vegas and have a relationship with him, but I knew it couldn't happen. I did know, just from that experience, that I would never want to live my life as a lie as he was living his. I wouldn't ever be able to handle it.

After he left, I lay down in my bed and thought about going back to the academy in less than a day's time. I had so much to look forward to on the social front. Even though I didn't have a car to use, most of my friends would have wheels, including Seth, and we had plans to visit a gay bar in Denver. I wondered who I would meet. *Would I see other cadets there? What would they be like?* That would be the coolest thing I could have imagined in my ongoing quest to understand my sexuality.

It had been an incredible summer in Las Vegas. I flew some of the most amazing and advanced jets in the world. My friends and I had gambled and drunk at every casino we could find. I had learned from Patty that I wasn't alone and that I wasn't a freak for having these new feelings and experiences.

Now that I was beginning to accept myself, the stakes grew higher for my survival at the academy. I was setting myself up for disappointment and hard times because, even though I was evolving in my own beliefs about gay people, the rest of the academy was not. I would have to handle it all to the best of my ability; now I had enough knowledge of life as a gay man to do just that.

chapter twenty-five

CAKE: HAVE IT AND EAT IT

I couldn't believe it. I was going back to the academy as a junior. I was finally feeling like a legitimate member of the cadet wing. Nathan and I made sure that we were roommates again. The two of us had gotten along so well in the past couple of years that we wouldn't have it any other way. Nathan listened to me often and gave me his best advice on how I should survive at the academy as I developed into a whole new person. Nathan stayed silent about all that he had heard and all that he had seen. He was a loyal roommate and a loyal friend.

The first room I visited was Allen Ladd's. He was a full-fledged sophomore now so there was nothing taboo about our hanging out in public. I knocked on his door and he opened it and got a big grin on his face.

"How was your summer?" I asked him.

"Oh, lots of fun, like everything else here at the good ol' Air Force Academy," he said in a sarcastic way. He looked *good*. He had had third-block vacation, or "leave," as we called it, and spent the entire time in the sun, surfing off the shore of southern California. The tired look from the stress of freshman year had faded from his face. He looked healthier, stronger, and manlier than I had ever seen him. I realized, as I watched him while he was talking to me, how much I had missed him while we were away all summer.

By this time, Seth and Nathan knew about my relations with Allen and, because of the way he handled them, they didn't like him. They told me that they just didn't want anyone treating me the way that he had. They would have preferred him to continue having a relationship with me rather than protesting the situation and making a broad statement about how he was not gay. "What a pussy," Nathan would say about him. "If you're gay, you're gay. Don't pretend like you're not. And he's got *you* Reichen and won't even step up to the plate. He's such a pussy." I was in awe when I heard Nathan talking this way. He had gone from a straight guy who hated all gay people to someone who was mad because a man that I was fond of was giving me the brush-off. Seth, on the other hand, didn't like Allen because he thought Allen was likely to get us caught for doing what we had.

"He'll turn on you in a second," Seth would warn me. "Anyone in that much denial doesn't care about you. He'll *always* look out for himself. Mark my words." Ironically, Seth feared Allen and his ability to get us all in trouble, while Allen feared Seth because he thought Seth was too loose with his "gayness," and thought that this would get everyone in trouble. The academy and its environment were both to blame for all of this fear among its members.

I would tell both Seth and Nathan that they needed to relax. I would explain to them that I brought this whole gay idea into Allen's life and, because it was new to him, he just didn't know how to handle it yet. I promised them that Allen would come around. They would both grumble under their breath at my excuses for Allen's behavior. I did, however, very much appreciate how concerned they were with my well-being.

My conversation with Allen was wrapping up and, before I left the room, I had to ask him the inevitable. "Did you miss me?"

"What?" he asked, stunned that I would ask him that question.

"Did you miss me at all? Did you think of me? You know." I said, inferring that he might have missed me in some intimate way. His voice moved to a whisper.

"Look, none of that this year. OK? Let's turn over a new leaf," he said looking at me with a very serious look on his face. I stood there feeling like I had just been punched in the stomach. I felt my hands shaking a little, like I had just realized I lost something important to me. I whispered too, out of respect.

"Turn over a new leaf of *what?* Lying to ourselves? Dude, I missed you. I thought about being with you many times," I explained. He put his hand on my shoulder and got in front of me.

"Yes, yes, yes!" he said, still whispering, looking into my eyes, trying to console me. "Of course I thought about you and *it,* and what we did. But we can't do that again. We already agreed to that. Don't mess up our friendship by pulling this stuff on me this year. Let's be friends. Let's be *normal!* Just a couple of buddies hanging out." When he finished those words, I was choked up and couldn't say anything. I realized that I had bigger feelings for Allen than I ever thought I did.

"OK," I nodded. I couldn't swallow. I couldn't look him in the eyes. I turned around and walked out.

Just before the door shut behind me, he yelled, "Later, bro!" just in case someone in the hallway might hear. The whole situation sickened me. Not only was he planning on pretending that he wasn't gay and had never done anything gay, he was going to pretend that he didn't have feelings for me. Dismissing my affection for him and his for me was part of the lie he was OK with living. Seeing him think this way made him much less attractive to me.

Maybe I was raised differently than Allen, but even then, like now, I can't imagine giving up true love for anything. Maybe what I couldn't accept back then was that he didn't truly love me like I truly loved him.

I went back to my room and Nathan was in there. I had teary eyes and a lost look on my face. "Hey, you!" Nathan yelled out. "Uh oh. What's wrong? Jesus, it's the first day back and someone's already pissing you off?" I laughed as much as I could, considering the state I was in.

"Hey, Nathan," I said as I cleared my throat.

"Alright, shut the door and sit down. You're going to tell me, right now, exactly what's going on. You need to. I can tell."

I told Nathan about the conversation I had just had with Allen. Nathan wasn't so supportive.

"Good! Don't be friends with him. That'll show his pussy little ass! He doesn't want you. So walk away. It'll be the best thing for you. There are other swordfish on the Terrazzo. We know that, right?" he asked, smiling.

"Yeah, I suppose you're right," I said.

Over the next few days, we fixed up our room and started the routine of the next school year. My grades were holding steady at around a 2.5 GPA and I was happy with that. It was as well as I could do, and I knew it. I had too much in my head to apply myself any more to school or anything else. Again, I wish I had found someone to talk to at the academy who was a professional, but that was a pipe dream for me.

About a week into the semester, Seth came into our room to show me a new feature he had found on our computers. He took me to the C prompt on the computer and typed in some crazy, long address that included the University of Missouri in it. Suddenly, a chat room popped up on the screen with about fifty other chatters in it. I watched in awe as I saw a conversation rolling up the screen. I found the need to join in and, as I did, was even more fascinated that people began answering me. "Who *are* these people?" I asked Seth.

"All random people, just like you! Isn't this cool? Hold on, I'm going into my room to log on and we can *chat*." Seth laughed as he ran out of the room. Suddenly he and I were talking back and forth, too. I stayed in the chat room long after Seth logged off and made a couple of online friends. They were fascinated that they were talking to a cadet at the Air Force Academy and I was fascinated by their stories of normal civilian college life.

I visited this chat room every day for about two weeks. In 1994, chat rooms were a cutting-edge communication system. Large numbers of people from almost every college across the country were logging onto the chat room set up by the University of Missouri.

One night, I was in the chat room corresponding with a guy who said that he wanted to talk to me because he had heard from another chatter that I was a cadet at the Air Force Academy. As we chatted, I learned that he had been kicked out of the academy after his sophomore year, for an honor violation. He had lied about being somewhere that he hadn't, and the honor system crucified him for it until he was dismissed. He asked me all about what the place was like now. I told him it was pretty much the same. He had been a sophomore when I was a freshman, so he hadn't been away from the academy for much more than a year.

With no warning, "Well, I'm glad I'm out now because I actually like guys and can be with them now," came running across my chat screen.

"What? You like guys? Like how?" I typed.

"I like to cuddle with them and, well, I'm gay," he typed.

"WHAT'S YOUR NAME?" I typed.

"Brian Virgo," he typed back. I *ran* over to my yearbook and looked him up. He was handsome.

"Wow," I typed. "You're a good-looking guy."

"Surprised I'm gay?" he typed.

"Not really," I wrote. "Many of the gay guys here are pretty hot."

"WHAT??" he typed. I paused and didn't write anything back. "WILL YOU CALL ME?" he wrote.

"Yes. What is your number?" I wrote. He gave me his number and I logged off. I went into the squadron payphone room and called him with my calling card. His voice was deeper and manlier than I had expected; he didn't sound like the stereotypical version of a gay guy that the media and my peers had presented me with all my life.

"Hey, it's me," I said.

"Hey "me." It's good to talk to you. So, what's up? Have you ever been with a guy?" he asked.

"Well, yeah. One here and one officer when I was on Ops Air Force." I loved that I didn't have to explain to him what *Ops* was.

"Yeah, well what did you guys do together?" he asked.

"Well, I can't really talk about it right now, but maybe sometime when I see you. I will say, though, that every time I've done something with a guy, it's like they don't want to do it again and they pretend like it never happened.

"What's your name? I want to see you in the yearbook," he asked. I told him my name and he looked me up.

"Sweet. Just a little blond boy," he said.

"Well, I'm bigger now. You're looking at the freshman yearbook picture." Our conversation went on for three hours. By the end of the conversation, he had convinced me to come out to Los Angeles to meet him.

As soon as we got off the phone, I went to my AOC, who was now a major. I explained to Major Pacer that I had a friend in need in Los Angeles whom I was worried about and that it was a private matter. I told him that this was all I could tell him. I had learned never to lie directly to someone's face, and that it was better to be vague than to make something up. After all, this was, indeed, a friend in need. He was my friend now and he was in need of seeing me. Major Pacer was cool enough to grant me a weekend pass to Los Angeles.

I ran back to the phone room and called Brian to let him know that I could come. He couldn't believe it. I put a plane ticket on my credit card and called my brother's girlfriend, because I knew I couldn't explain this to my brother. I told her that I had to come to LA but that I didn't want my brother to know I was coming and that I couldn't really talk about it. I asked her to pick me up at the airport and take me to the Disneyland Hotel, where Brian had booked us a room.

"Of course, honey. You can explain this all to me some other time. Whatever you're doing, I'm sure you'll handle it fine," Jill said.

"Great! Thank you so much. You have no idea," I said.

That Friday, after class, I was packing my bag when there was a knock on my dormitory door. I opened it—it was Allen. He walked in and saw me packing. "Where are you going?" he asked. I didn't want to tell him.

"I'm going to visit a friend," I said quickly.

"Where is your friend?" he asked.

"LA," I said.

"You're going to LA for the *weekend* to visit a *friend?*" he asked incredulously.

"Yeah," I said nonchalantly.

"And you have permission to do this?"

"Yes, Allen. Jesus!" I said.

"OK, well do you care to tell me what it's about? I know you're up to something. I can just tell," he said.

"Allen, you haven't come around me for two *weeks*."

"Yeah, I've been taking my space and I actually wanted to talk to you about some things," he said as I continued to pack.

"Well, we're going to have to talk when I come back, because I have to get in a taxi and get to the airport."

"Reichen, *who* are you going to see? Just tell me and I'll go."

"I'm going to see a guy I met. He used to be a cadet here. *He* wants to see me," I said, even though I was choked up inside and just wanted Allen to tell me that *he* wanted me.

"Wait. Like, you're going to see, like, a guy? Like a *gay* guy?" he asked with this disgusted look on his face. I saw his face and grew instantly mad. I walked up to him and faced him so I could speak to him in whisper.

"Oh, don't you judge me. I've been trying to figure out all these crazy feelings I've been having because of what *we* did and you've done nothing but pretend like it never happened. I'm trying to figure out who the hell I am!"

"By going and visiting some random freak in LA?" he yelled too loudly.

"Shut up!" I yelled in a whisper. "Who are *you* to make a comment about it? Why do you even care?"

"Well," he said, "I didn't think you were the type to hook up with some random guy. That's what he is, isn't he, a random guy?"

"You're jealous!" I said in a loud whisper.

"I am *not* jealous! You wanna know what I am?" I turned away and he grabbed the back of my shirt. I turned around, ripping my shirt from his hand.

"Let me go," I said in a loud whisper. "This whole conversation is ridiculous. You're the whole reason I'm doing this. I'm confused. I'm desperate. I missed you this summer and you act like it doesn't mean a thing. I need to be around people who care enough to want to see me."

"So you go see some *freak?*" he asked as his face became red.

"Well it's better than hanging around here with you and all of these other posers who pretend like gay sex isn't happening all over the place! This mentality is everywhere. Oh, and I'm getting better at figuring out who's guilty of it, too." I had to remember to lower my voice to a yelling whisper again. "I can smell it on people now and it makes me *sick*. And, well, you . . . *reek* of it! And I've had the misfortune of having an experience with someone who I *thought* had more character than you actually do. So yes, I'm going. I'll let you know how it goes, because I know how much you get off on it."

"Fuck you!" he yelled in a whisper while pointing his finger in my face. I grabbed his finger so hard I almost broke it off his hand. He pulled his hand away from mine, recoiled, and pushed me backwards. I fell to the floor on my butt. I got up and moved toward him with everything I had. I shoved him up against the door of my room. I held him with one hand and slammed the other against his chest as I spoke, fast and direct, in a harsh, spitting whisper.

"Don't *ever* point at me or push me, you little pussy! I will FUCK you up and don't you forget it!" I let go and walked back to the bag I was packing. He moved off the door and stood at my sink, looking at himself and fixing his hair and uniform in the mirror.

"Well, this wasn't the conversation I wanted to have, but OK," he said.

"What conversation did you have in mind?" I asked.

"Don't worry about it," he said and walked out. He left me there feeling very confused and wondering what he might have said.

Eventually, Nathan came into the room as I packed. I explained the situation to him and he offered me a ride to the airport. On the way he made me promise to call him if I were in trouble. "I understand that you need to do this, but I'm going to worry about you," he said.

"I promise I'll call if I need you," I said.

On my way out to Los Angeles, I thought about how proud I was of myself for at least getting out and figuring out who I was, rather than letting my feelings fester inside of me. Even though what I was doing was well outside the norm of the academy experience, I knew deep down that what I was doing was the right thing from a total-life perspective.

At the airport, I called my parents. I had always been so open with them that it was time for them to know, somewhat, that I was involved with a guy. I used a pay phone that was in a more private alcove in the airport. The conversation went pretty easily and satisfied my desperate need to feel love from someone.

"Mom and Allen?" I asked, after they picked up different extensions. "Hey, I'm at the airport and I don't have much time, but I just want to tell you both something."

"OK?" they said and asked together. They knew something was up.

"I'm not in trouble or anything like that so you can both relax," I said.

"OK, good," my mom said.

"Listen, I don't know how to say this other than to just say it."

"Go ahead," my mom said, "just say it honey."

"I want you guys to know that I've actually been sleeping in the same bed with this guy. Another cadet," I said. My heart was beating hard.

"What do you mean, *sleeping* with him?" Allen asked.

"Well, I mean we're in, sort of a, uh, relationship? Like we're messing around with each other at night," I said. There was silence for a good thirty seconds.

"Hello?" I asked.

"Yeah." Allen said.

"Yes, honey, we're still here," my mother said.

"Well, is this something you're experimenting with? Or is this something that you like and you're telling us that you're going to continue doing this?" Allen asked.

"Well, I like it. I like it a lot. And yes, I'm going to keep doing it," I said with reservation, nervous about how they would react.

"OK, well, aren't you worried about getting in trouble?" my mom asked.

"Well, of course I am," I said to my mom. "That's why I'm telling you this."

"Honey, well then we're worried about you. I don't want to see anything happen to you. You better not let anyone know that you're doing that!" my mom said.

"I won't, Mom," I assured her.

"Well, if this is something that you're doing on a regular basis . . . then, well, uh, you're probably, um . . . gay," Allen said.

"I know that, Allen. I think I might be gay," I said. I started shaking. "Is that OK?" I asked in a humble voice. There was silence again.

"Of *course* it is, sweetie!" my mom said, abruptly, as if to answer for the both of them. "We're just worried about you."

"Well, listen, thank you, guys. I just wanted you to know," I said. "I have to catch my flight now." There was silence again.

"Call us soon, honey. We love you," my mom said.

"I will. Love you," I said. There was silence. I hung up the phone.

I knew that I had just dropped a bomb on my parents, but I had been thinking about it for a while and I knew that it had to be done at some point. I would have preferred not to hide my sexuality at the academy; there was no way I would hide it from my parents. I was somewhat confused by the way they took the news. Instead of reacting to the fact that their son just came out of the closet, they were more concerned with my safety. I was relieved that I had told them, but I knew that we would have hours of future conversation about my being gay. Although my parents were understanding people, there was no way that they were happy with what they had just heard. For the next few days, I worried about what they were going through in reaction to my coming out to them.

* * *

I arrived at LAX when it was dark outside. Jill picked me up in a Mazda Miata. We had the top down and had fun catching up the whole way to Disneyland. On the way, she pulled out two tickets to a Janet Jackson concert and said, "Here, I got these for you and your friend." She had a huge smile on her face. They were for the following night, Saturday night, at Angels Stadium in Anaheim. I couldn't believe how thoughtful she was to do that.

"I told your brother you're here. I'm sorry, but I just had to. He doesn't know why you're here but he said to stay safe," she said.

She dropped me off at the hotel and we said good-bye. I went to the front desk and asked to be connected to Brian's room. He picked up and told me his room number. I went upstairs and he opened the door to the room. There was a very good-looking guy, about twenty-two years old, with dark hair and blue eyes. He was shorter than me, and much more stocky. I shook his hand and he pulled me into the room and hugged me. We hugged for a good five minutes and then he kissed me.

Brian was my first actual guy-to-guy make-out kiss, and I remember it feeling so foreign to me. I felt the stubble on his face next to mine. His lips were stronger than a girl's lips, but his tongue was just as soft. It felt incredibly nice and natural to me. Now it was obvious to me that I was supposed to be with a guy rather than with a girl. I had never felt the same kinds of instant connections any girl I had ever been with that I had with guys.

We left the hotel and he took me out to dinner. On the way there, in his car, he reached over and held my hand. That was another crazy feeling. I hadn't had a guy just hold my hand in a normal situation. The feeling made me instantly aroused and feeling a guy's big hand on mine made me feel safe.

After dinner we went back to the hotel. Brian could tell I was a little nervous so he didn't try to push sex on me. We did, however, take off our clothes and get into bed together. He pushed his strong body up against mine and held me really tight. I remember feeling really secure with him holding me and somewhat validated by a guy's embrace and his accepting me enough to lie naked with me. Thinking about all of this relaxed me and I fell fast asleep.

The next day, Brian showed me around Anaheim, where he had grown up. He pointed out old haunts and different areas of interest. We had a nice time but, as the day went on, I realized that he was a very stubborn kind of guy and liked to have things his way. I knew that, from a relationship standpoint, we would not be compatible and that I would probably never see him again after this trip.

That night we went to the Janet Jackson concert and had a great time. We sat next to each other, our elbows, hands, and feet touching all night. Although I knew I could never live with him in a relationship, I still found him physically attractive. I had flown to California to experiment, not to find a boyfriend. Seeing all the straight people around us who had no idea that we were two gay guys who had slept together the night before fascinated me. This made it more fun for me because I knew that our business was ours and no one else's. Only he and I were privileged to know what we were capable of doing.

We had to leave the show early because, frankly speaking, we kept giving each other hard-ons and couldn't wait to get back to our room to have sex. In the room, we had a session much like the one I had with the pilot out at Nellis Air Force Base in Las Vegas. We slept in each other's arms again and, when the morning came, it was already time to take me back to the airport. We both agreed that we had a nice time but neither of us said anything to the effect of "keep in touch."

I arrived back at the academy to find a note in my room from Allen that read, "R, please come see me when you get back. Allen." I had just been through a big ordeal over the weekend by meeting Brian, and I was too drained to deal with Allen and his questions about the weekend. I decided to avoid going to his room. In fact, I avoided it all week long.

The next weekend came and I spent most of it marching tours and sitting confinements from my car offense. I finished up my final punishment tour by Saturday night since I had served some of my punishment over the summer, monitored by my summer AOC. I was relieved to be done. That night, Seth came to me and said, "We have to celebrate the completion of your punishment and the lifting of your restriction. Let's go to Rodeo!" Rodeo was the gay bar in Denver that we had talked about before. I felt a burst of energy through my body at the idea of going there.

As we walked out of the squadron, dressed in jeans and polo shirts, or the "going-out" uniform, as we called it, I passed Allen in the hallway. He saw that I was leaving to go out and that I was with Seth and looked at me like he really wanted to talk to me.

"Seth, hold on," I said.

"OK, I'm going to make a call from the CQ desk. Just meet me back here," he said. "But we're running late, so don't be long!"

I walked down the hall toward Allen. He led me into his room and said, "Where have you been? Why didn't you come to see me?"

"Because I've been overwhelmed with school and everything, I don't know. I didn't want you to question me about that guy, and I've been marching a million tours," I said.

"Where are you going now," he asked.

"I'm going to Denver with Seth. We're going to a gay bar," I whispered in his ear.

"What? Why!" he yelled. "Jesus! This is the shit that's going to get you in trouble! *Why* would you do that?"

"Because I *want* to, Allen," I said in a very calm and mellow voice. "I guess I'm still searching. But listen, I'm not going to let you scare me out of this so I'm leaving now. I'll talk to you when I get back or maybe later in the week?"

"Fine," he said with a brooding look on his face.

Seth and I took off in his car for Denver, feeling more excited every minute. We parked in a public lot and walked a ways to the bar. We got to the entrance and there were a group of guys who looked like they might be bar regulars gathered just inside the door checking out who was coming in. When they saw us, all talking stopped and, for the first time ever, I knew what an attractive young girl felt like when she walked into a straight bar. These men stared at us from the moment we went through the door, while we finally received the drinks we ordered, and until we found a good hiding place in the back corner of the bar. We were finally there, at a gay bar, just as we had planned months ago.

We scoped out the guys and decided which ones we wanted to talk to. Our problem was that we had high standards because we were so used to being around guys who were athletic, clean-cut, and intelligent. Those attributes were a turn-on for both of us. The civilian world was not coming across so athletic, clean-cut, and intelligent, so we had a hard time. The music was good and we ended up dancing with the crowd as the night moved on. Overall, we had a great time. We sobered up and drove back to the academy. Seth drove because I didn't stop drinking as early as he did, so I was still a little buzzed when we completed the hour-and-fifteen-minute drive from Denver.

I went into my room and, knowing that Nathan was gone on a weekend pass, I locked the door, stripped off my clothes, and climbed into bed. Only my small desk light was on, so I couldn't see much in the room. As I climbed up the ladder, I was startled to find someone lying in my bed. I froze, standing there buck naked, on the ladder to my bunk. As my eyes adjusted, I saw that it was Allen. He had his eyes open and was pushed up against the wall, leaving enough room for me in the bunk. We looked at each other for a minute but didn't say a word. I continued to climb up the ladder and pulled the covers back to find him under them, naked also. "Come here," he said in a whisper and put his arm out for me to get under. He spooned me like I used to spoon Anne when we would take naps together. I felt safe and Allen gave off an amazing energy as he held me with his entire body.

As I lay there falling asleep in his arms, somewhat buzzed from the alcohol, I guessed why Allen was in my bed. He was tired of hearing that I was going out on the town and looking for other guys. Well, that was at least half of it. I had hope, somewhere within the many crazy thoughts in my head, that the other half was because he actually cared about me and didn't want to see me hurt by some other guy. We didn't say anything that night, but we were definitely communicating as he held on to me more tightly than ever.

chapter twenty-six

DOPPELGÄNGER

The rest of my first semester of junior year went fairly smoothly. Allen and I saw each other often enough to keep us both happy and I continued to go to Rodeo on weekends with Seth. Allen never really acted like my boyfriend or wanted to commit to me so I continued to search. I wanted someone who gave me all that I needed, including some sort of intimacy beyond sexual experiences. I wanted someone who might want to be with me for the rest of our lives.

I chatted with a few guys when I went to Denver with Seth, but I would always lose interest after I had talked with them for five minutes and found out that we weren't compatible for some reason or another.

Just before Christmas break, I received an e-mail, through the cadet e-mail system, from one of the gay guys in another squadron whom I had heard about. I was actually surprised that it took this long for me to make contact with one of the other gay cadets. I had been so wrapped up in my personal problems with Allen and my search for a good guy that I was uninterested in getting involved with the other gay cadets at the academy. When I received the e-mail, I couldn't believe my eyes. This guy said, blatantly, that he was gay and had heard about me and thought we should hang out. This was sent across an e-mail system that flashed the following words when we would log on to it:

*THIS E-MAIL SYSTEM IS THE PROPERTY OF THE FED-
ERAL GOVERNMENT AND ALL E-MAILS ARE MONI-
TORED AT ALL TIMES.*

I lost my temper when I saw what this guy had written. I deleted the
e-mail and then quickly deleted it from my "deleted items" box. *What
if someone who was monitoring this system saw his e-mail?* I thought in a
panic. "Who is this asshole?" I said out loud. "Jesus Christ!" I got up
and walked as quickly as I could to Seth's room. I told him to come
back to my room. When he finally arrived, I told him what Jake Lester
had just done.

"Oh, God," Seth said. "I actually met that guy. He's a little strange—
it's a little too obvious that he's gay. He strikes me as someone who
would do this."

"Well, I don't even want to write him back!" I said. "What if I get
monitored? And it's not like I want to go to his *room*. This guy is
freaking me out."

"Listen," Seth said, "if you get questioned about it, just say that you
have no idea who the e-mail was from so you deleted it. They can't
make you say something. You don't know who he is. It's as simple as
that. If he wants to out himself, then let him. He doesn't have to out
you. It's not like he knows anything about you."

"Well, if I'm questioned, would you back me up that I don't know
him?" I asked. "For some reason, I feel like I need backup."

"Yes, I'll cover for you. You're fine." Seth put his hand on my
shoulder to reassure me.

"Jesus, why are people so stupid? God, I thought *we* were dumb and
risky, but this is ridiculous!" I yelled.

Nathan chimed in with his deep voice. "If I see this guy, I'm gonna
kick his ass." Seth and I looked at Nathan's back as he sat there doing
his homework. Then we looked at each other. We tried to hold back
our laughter and then broke out in a stifled but obvious laugh. Nathan
turned around and looked at us laughing at him.

"What?" he asked. Seth and I laughed even harder.

I tried to explain why we were laughing. "Nathan, here we are all pissed off at this guy and you blurt out in your deep, Texas accent that you're going to kick his ass. We didn't even know you were listening." Seth and I laughed a little more before he had to go back to his room to study.

Finals week came and went and Christmas break was upon us. As usual, I went home to my brother's house in California. On the first night I arrived, his girlfriend Jill and I had a long talk while my brother was at work. I told her about the past two years and that I thought I was gay. She took it well and was very accepting of me. "Your brother would flip out if you told him that," she warned me, "but I have a girl that I want you to meet, before you think you're sure that you're gay, OK?" she asked.

The thought of meeting a nice girl actually appealed to me at that point—the gay thing had become so challenging, secretive, and complicated.

Since I was in Los Angeles, I had the chance to visit Allen's family. I stayed at their house for two days. His parents had no idea I was anything other than merely a friend of his. I sat through a few meals with his family and realized how political they really were. They didn't talk about anything other than politics and their con-servative view of the world. I developed a better understanding of Allen by meeting his family. I felt sorry for him and realized the pressure that he was under to be a certain way. He and I didn't sleep in the same bed or even the same room while we were at his house. Anything close to intimacy between the two of us would have freaked Allen out.

On the last day I was in LA, Allen came back to my brother's with me to spend the night. He and my brother's girlfriend, Jill, got along really well together. They hit it off so well that it became obvious to me and to my brother that Jill had a small crush on Allen. The situa-tion worsened as the night moved on—to the point that my brother asked me to remove Allen from his house. Although Jill had the crush, Allen found it necessary to reciprocate her flirtations. I think he did this to prove his ability to be "straight." He needed to show off to me, Jill, *and* my brother, even at the cost of being thrown out.

The next night, after Allen's drama had settled, my brother and Jill brought Mara Howard to my brother's house. We all hung out for a while and I realized that I really liked her. She had a bubbly personality and was as immature and playful as I could be. She also knew how to class it up and mix in to a situation with good manners. She was about five foot six, with beautiful long brown hair and green eyes. She had double-D size breasts and was all-around gorgeous.

Later that night, Mara and I broke off from the group and went to the mall together to see a movie. We were already interested in each other and she was holding my hand in the mall. I couldn't get over how we were received by people. It was so different from what I was experiencing in the gay world, where I had to hide everything and do everything in secret. Everyone in the mall was staring at us and smiling at us as we walked by. I couldn't help but feel proud to have her next to me. It was so *easy*. We didn't have to hide our affection. We didn't have to discuss how our relationship might work. It was just happening and all I had to do was go through the motions I had learned by living in American society since I was a little kid.

We drove back to my brother's house and sat together in the hot tub, making out for a few hours. "Where did you come from?" she asked. I enjoyed making out with her, fantasizing about having a "normal" relationship. Mara represented the idea of leaving the difficulties of the gay world behind—at least in terms of what everyone would see of me on the outside.

We spent about six days together and took lots of time to sit in the hot tub or on the couch in front of the television, holding each other. As I lay with Mara on the couch, I thought about how I felt. I liked being the guy. I liked being the person who was holding her. I liked making her feel good. But I couldn't deny one thing. I didn't feel the passion and the adrenaline rush that I felt when I was with a guy. Speaking from the raw part of my mind, I also didn't get sexually aroused from holding Mara.

However, because I liked all of the other things that were making my life easier, I denied to myself, once again, that this was the case. *Maybe I'll develop a liking for her and be able to get aroused after a while,* I thought, even though the only time I could get aroused enough to play with Mara sexually was when I would daydream about a gay experience I had had. *Ah . . . so* this *is how gay guys have girl-friends and are able to pretend,* I thought to myself. It's actually not that tough to do. If you put your mind to it, you can go through the motions and, I imagine, go through them for a very long time; but deep down inside, a big hole in your heart will remain. I believe this goes for all of the supposed converts who say they used to be gay but now are straight. That's a big lie. They're lying to everyone else and lying to themselves. There is absolutely no way to deny what it is in one's nature to be and do.

God, or the universe, or whatever higher power is out there, *made* gay people gay. There is no denying what one actually is. People can fool everyone else, and they can even fool themselves. However, they will never fool whatever it is that made them, and that which made us is that which can grant us happiness. Trying to fight *that* only leads to pain, discomfort, and unhappiness. Unfortunately, I put myself through yet another time in my life during which I would discover this truth— after a great deal of pain and confusion for myself, the girl I tried to pretend with, and other people around me.

Mara and I continued to talk and have a relationship, with growing expectations, throughout the remainder of my junior year and through my senior year. She came to visit me at the academy and I went to visit her at the University of Arizona. She became involved with my friends and I became involved with hers. My friends found it odd that I would move backward to exploring a heterosexual rela-tionship, but they communicated with me every step of the way and, ironically, accepted my choices. They figured this was yet another step in discovering my true self.

I became involved with Mara's family and she became involved with mine. Everyone absolutely *loved* us as a couple and, truthfully, so did I. I wanted nothing more than for us to be the hot, wonderful couple that everyone thought we were. I wanted nothing more than to be completely in love with Mara. She was a wonderful person in all ways, but there was something missing, and that was the spiritual connection that two people who are in love share. I know now that I was created to be truly intimate and spiritually connected with a man, not a woman, but I denied it for as long as I could.

I went back to the academy to start the second semester of my junior year. Coming back from winter break was a tough time. Many of the cadets were depressed after leaving their families and loved ones, and we all knew there was no break in sight until spring break, which wouldn't come until April, so we called the days between winter break and spring break "the dark days."

Because I had been an avid skier since childhood, I was always been eager to ski the many incredible resorts Colorado had to offer. Part of my excitement of getting into the academy was attributable to its being in Colorado, at the base of the Rocky Mountains. This was the semester when I had my ducks in a neat enough row that I could take some time to ski.

The academy offered unbelievable discounts on skiing and chairlift passes at all of the ski resorts in the West. They not only had deals with all the resorts, but military discounts as well. Skiing for a day cost a cadet about a quarter of a regularly priced lift ticket. Added to this, the academy's Morale, Welfare and Recreation Department would set up weekend ski trips. It rented a block of condominiums for cadets at a reduced rate and added on a lift-ticket package. An entire weekend of skiing, complete with transportation to the resort on academy buses, lodging, ski rental equipment, and food, would cost about $100. We knew what an incredible deal this was, so many of us took advantage of every trip offered, when our budgets and school workloads allowed it. The condominiums we would stay in were not too shabby, either. They were really nice, usually with views of the resort and the mountains. They had big bedrooms with their own bathrooms, fireplaces, big kitchens, and sometimes hot tubs. We felt that we lived like kings on these trips.

Fortunately, Allen skied. We went on these trips together as much as we could. On our first trip, we had a weekend ski deal at Vail resort. Luckily, we weren't forced to use the academy buses to get there because our friends had cars by then. Allen grumbled about it but Seth drove us to Vail that time. When we arrived at the condo, we found that it was beautifully set on a hill with a view of Vail. It had big bedrooms with king-size beds, each with its own bathroom. We had secured one whole condo for our own group. Jodie, Seth, Kory, Allen, Nathan, and I all shared the three-bedroom condo. I secured one of the rooms just for Allen and me. We skied two awesome days and, at night, Allen and I were able to be alone in our own private bedroom.

Other trips were not so safe because Allen and I would share the condo with a group of people who didn't know us. We would always, however, get our own room in the house, so that after we were all done hanging out and drinking with the others, Allen and I would eventually both end up in our bed with the door locked. If any of the other guys sharing the condo with us knew what was actually going on in that room they would most likely have been mortified.

One weekend, one of the upperclassmen in Bull Ten let Allen and me borrow his jeep. We drove it to Aspen and spent another awesome couple of days together. We appeared to be best friends during the day, tearing up the mountain on skis, drinking with the guys in the lodge, making fun of each other, and even wrestling in the snow, but at night, we were lovers. This particular trip to Aspen was more memorable than the others because the jeep gave us the freedom to explore the area. On Saturday night, after skiing, we got in the jeep and drove into downtown Aspen to have a few drinks at a bar. After just one beer, we agreed to get out of there and go somewhere else where we could be alone.

We drove the jeep along an old country road that took us miles away from any sort of civilization. Allen and I were looking at each other with *that* look. "Pull over here," I said. The road we were on seemed abandoned and it hadn't been plowed in a while. Just as we were pulling over, a light snowfall began. The moon was as bright as could be and made the night look like daytime. We could see for a good mile in any direction and the only thing around us were white fields of snow. Allen stopped the jeep. We still had our ski pants and jackets on, along with our warm Sorrel boots. We started making out in the car.

"Can we go outside?" Allen asked softly. I nodded. We got out of the jeep and Allen picked me up, and in one swoop put me on the hood of the jeep, on my back. He climbed up on top of me and undid the buttons on my ski pants. Before I knew it, were both lying on a warmed hood, looking up at a moonlit sky, with snow falling on us, after having had amazing sex. It felt like there was no one in the world but the two of us. I remember the sensations during sex—feeling that everything in the world was beautiful to me from every sense that my body, mind, heart, and soul had to offer. I will never, ever, forget that moment and that beautiful night.

Allen was satisfying me often at this point in our relationship and I wasn't really looking for much else in the world. I was concentrating better on my schoolwork and getting along with people better in general. Military formations weren't as annoying to me and military rules were things I was learning to accept, rather than things that I wanted to rebel against.

But when I wasn't looking for love, some sort of love seemed to find *me*. On one night at the beginning of February, Brian Bowman, the blond guy who used to lead my flight in basic training, came into my room to chat with me.

"What's up, man?" he asked.

"Not much. Just finishing up a paper here," I said. My room was dark and Nathan was in someone else's room studying. It was around midnight and we had school the next day. Brian was wearing his issue academy robe. He always wore it kind of as a joke because, as upper-classmen, we were not required to wear it anymore on the way to the shower: we could have our own robes.

"Feel like a drink?" he asked as he pulled a bottle of tequila out from under his robe.

"Oh, man. Why did you have to come in here tonight of all nights, Brian? I would love to have a drink with you but I can't with this paper due tomorrow," I explained. I really liked Brian Bowman. He wasn't afraid to break the rules and that was enough to make me trust him more than others at the academy. I knew that if it ever came down to it, Brian would defend me or even lie for me to keep me out of trouble.

"Are you afraid?" he asked, with a huge smile on his face. He walked over to my sink and opened the medicine chest mirror that was above it. He pulled out the military-issue rinse cup that I used after brushing my teeth. This was a pretty big cup. Brian proceeded to fill it to the very top with tequila—about four shots' worth. He pulled Nathan's desk chair over to me and sat down in front of me. He handed me the cup.

"No way," I whispered. "Are you crazy?" He smiled, brought the cup back to his lips, and downed it. I couldn't believe that anyone could drink that much tequila at once. Still sitting there with the cup and bottle of tequila, he began to fill the cup again. "That's enough!" I said. He stopped pouring and handed me the cup. I took what was probably the equivalent of two shots. I had always been a lightweight when it came to alcohol, so I knew I shouldn't drink any more than that.

"So how have you been," he asked in a wistful and calming way. "I've lost touch with you." I was already feeling the effects of the tequila.

"You know. I'm doing fine. I just keep rolling along with everyone else."

"I think you're one of these people in the squadron I don't keep in touch with anymore but I really should. I think we have a lot in common," he said, again in a wistful way. His voice was turning me on, but I was doing my best to think of *anything* else.

"Yeah, I think so. I like you, Brian. You're different from everyone here. You're open-minded, like all my friends. I like that."

"I know that about you, too, and that's why I like you. You know, I always have your back," he said with a smile.

"And I have yours," I said, as I really started feeling warm and buzzed.

Since basic training, I had always just wanted to stare at Brian. He was so beautiful that I always wished I could find a way to just look at him for a while and admire his beauty as a man. Since I was getting drunk, I did just that. I just kept looking at him. I looked at his eyes, his hair, his nose, his lips, his teeth, and his skin. I looked down to see his very athletic, blond, hairy legs coming out from the slit in his academy robe. He watched my eyes the whole time, with a gentle smile on his face, appreciating the way I was admiring him.

"I know what you're looking at," he said.

With a pretty strong alcohol buzz coming on, I just nodded at him, as if to say we were on the same page. He looked at me for another minute or so and then he put down the bottle of tequila. He was still holding the cup in his left hand. As he lowered the bottle to the floor and sat back up, I watched the way my desk light reflected off his skin and the side of his head. He nodded at me. Then he reached down with his right hand and pulled his legs apart to reveal that he was naked under the robe. I looked up at him in bewilderment and took a deep breath. I couldn't believe he was doing this.

"Are you afraid?" he asked.

"No, I'm not afraid. But what are you doing?" I asked, shaking my head.

"I don't really know," he said, wistfully, while he continued to study my face as I studied his. He put the cup on the desk and reached for my wrist with his left hand. He pulled my hand toward his body so that it would rest on his inner thigh. He leaned in and kissed me on my lips.

Click, click, click. Someone was trying to turn my doorknob.

Damn it, I thought to myself, *is there* no *privacy in this Godforsaken place?* Brian must have locked the door when he came into my room, thank God. I pulled away quickly but Brian didn't. He stayed calm and collected and backed away from my lips, gently opening his eyes and smiling at me. He pulled his robe over to cover himself to a point of decency and nodded for me to get the door. I walked over and opened it. No one was there. I looked down the hallway to see Nathan walking away from the door.

"Nathan!" I called. He stopped and turned around. He had a smile on his face.

"Are you *busy?*" he asked playfully. I knew I couldn't answer "yes" because I didn't want to get Brian in trouble. I wanted all to appear normal.

"No, it's cool," I said. "Brian is in here and we're just talking." Nathan came back and locked the door once he was inside.

"What are you boys talking about?" he asked. Just then, Brian pulled out the tequila and the cup.

"This," he said with a smile. Brian must have been toasted on the tequila by then, so I was afraid of what he might say. He gave Nathan a shot and asked if he wanted more.

"I'm fine, I need to get to bed. Big day tomorrow," Nathan said.

"OK guys, I'm outta here. On to the next room with my bottle of joy," Brian said. He walked out and Nathan gave me a strange look.

"I don't even want to know," he said with a smile and giggle.

"No worries," I said, with the same smile and giggle. Once again, I had found another person who had *something* going on his head that involved needing to be with a guy.

My eyes were being opened more and more every single day. I kept a list in my head of people at the academy whom I was slowly finding had some sort of proclivity toward being intimate with people of the same sex. It continued to fascinate me. The more I found out about people, the bigger our group became. By now, I knew that many people knew about me. I was hopeful that it was only gay cadets who knew I was gay, but I wasn't sure. I wondered how Brian knew about me. He didn't hang around with any other gay guys I knew of and most of his friends were definitely outwardly straight. I worried about who knew about me and who knew about other people. After thinking about it, I realized that I was sitting in the middle of what could be a huge scandal. What if someone like Jake Lester sent an e-mail to someone and was caught? Who would he name as possible gay people if he were questioned and threatened with losing his academy appointment?

Ironically, during this time in my academic career, I was taking an English class in which we were studying *Frankenstein* by Mary Shelley. In the story, Dr. Frankenstein had a double life: one as a mad scientist, and one as a respected physician. After reading the book, the instructor had us all discuss and write papers on the many forms of doppelgängers, the German word for *exact double* or *double life*. As we continued our discussions in class, I related in a huge way. I was living my own doppelgänger every single day. I had my secret gay life and I had my open, "normal" life, with a beautiful girlfriend and a pressed uniform.

This English class had really put my whole life into perspective. Our study of the phenomenon of doppelgängers included two lessons: that there is always an element of dishonesty to people who live this way, and also that living this sort of life *always* ends in tragedy.

chapter twenty-seven

DENVER FIRE

After Brian Bowman came into my room to mess around with me, I thought about the need to communicate with all of the other gay people at the academy. We needed to have some sort of enforceable code of secrecy. I went on a mission over the next week, visiting rooms of guys who I knew were gay and having talks with them. I even explained to them how we could write e-mails to each other without being identified as gay. Rodeo, the gay bar, would be referred to as "getting a bite to eat."

"Do you want to get a bite to eat together this weekend?" meant something entirely different now. If we absolutely had to say that someone was gay, we would refer to someone as having "family." We wouldn't say that they *were* family because that would be too obvious. We would say something like, "I think that Cadet Engle in Squadron Twenty-five has some family in town." I was a firm believer that, in our situation, we needed a system of rules and coded communication if we were to stay out of trouble. Now that we were always organizing our outings and get-togethers, the need for this had become even greater.

A cadet can seldom leave the Air Force Academy's huge Colorado Springs base; it's still not big enough for the cadets who want to escape it. Sometimes, being at the academy is like being in a small high school where everyone knows everyone else's business.

It often seemed like everything that I did at the academy was documented somewhere in the name of accountability. Going out on a weekend pass or even a day pass required filling out a form saying exactly where I was going.

Since the Air Force Academy's honor code included, "We will not lie, steal or cheat, nor tolerate among us anyone who does," this sometimes called for some creative reporting when it came to writing down where I was going to be. The most common entry on the sign-out logs was COS, meaning Colorado Springs. That seemed to satisfy the AOC because he just figured I would be out at some restaurant or maybe even a bar close to the academy. If I were to write "Denver," the AOC would become a little more suspicious when he reviewed the sign-out log. An additional explanation would be necessary, so I had to be very careful. If I said I were going to be in COS and ended up getting a speeding ticket in Denver, the academy would surely find out about it and disaster would ensue.

Policemen around Colorado Springs and Denver could spot a cadet from a mile away and whenever a cadet had any contact with the police, that policeman would put in an extra call to our Air Officer Commanding back at the Hill to get us into some extra trouble. Colorado Springs was proud of its cadets and the positive, conservative image that the academy brought to the city. In uniform, cadets would get all sorts of sympathy and extra help from people when we were outside the academy. We had blanket respect.

But the police saw things differently than the general population. They waited for us to do something wrong. They knew the truth, which was that many of us were merely kids who were simply dressed up to look nice, with all kinds of bad ideas about how to have a good time. The odds of not getting in trouble while we were outside of academy grounds were stacked against us by the police, so lying on a sign-out sheet was risky and stupid, because being caught doing so was considered an honor violation and grounds for immediate dismissal. But now that we had about six gay cadets who would go out on weekends, we almost always *had* to lie about where we would be.

We were three weeks into my second semester of junior year when I began receiving coded e-mail messages from the other gay cadets regarding our going out to Denver on a pass on the upcoming weekend. Shortly after the e-mails were sent, Seth came to my room at about five P.M. Friday and said that he had actually found out that one of our instructors, a captain from the Chemistry Department, was gay, and that he had a house in Denver where we could all stay for the weekend.

Hearing that there was a gay officer who would put up some gay cadets wasn't even mind-blowing to me. I had seen so much at that point that nothing was really surprising. The news actually made sense to me—but I didn't understand how someone gay could make it to the rank of captain, having to hide and lie for that long. Even though I was gay, breaking all the rules of academy tradition, I still had a lingering respect for air force officers. After all, the reason I was even at the academy was to become an officer. Graduating meant getting through all of the bullshit of the academy in its entirety and becoming a second lieutenant. Getting through the four years already seemed as if it was taking forever, so to me, a captain was someone who was eons ahead of me in life and accomplishments.

After some thought about this gay air force captain, I became more nervous than happy. Terrifying thoughts ran through my mind. *How did this gay captain find Seth? Was Seth being too out to people? Was this a trap by the Office of Special Investigation? Why would a captain want to risk his job by befriending a bunch of cadets? Was it a good idea to reveal to yet another person who we all were?*

I asked Seth all of these questions. I told him that if we let this guy into our circle, we would have to explain everything to him—who we were, to whom he would not be allowed to talk about us, and our way of doing things so that we were assured of never being caught. Against my better judgment, and with Seth's agreement that I would get to talk with this captain, I agreed that I, too, would stay at his house after we hit Rodeo that night in Denver.

I had never asked to be the leader of the pack or to be the one who would watch over our growing group. I sort of made myself that person without realizing it. We had never had any formal meetings with all of us together but as our group grew, I knew that we would eventually need some structure to preserve ourselves, or else we would be sitting ducks. I had set and communicated to the others all the rules I thought we needed to follow. If someone didn't want to play by my rules, I found them to be a threat. Our environment was so harsh that I considered it OK to excommunicate someone for inappropriate behavior. Besides avoiding Jake Lester for sending that stupid e-mail to me the previous semester, I had never actually tried to excommunicate someone, but the thought of it was well within my mind as our group of gay cadets and sympathizers continued to develop.

Shutting someone out completely would not come without consequences and I knew that. All involved would have to agree to ignore them, and fear of that person would have to be instilled, as a safety mechanism, in all of us. If that person tried to come after us, we would all have to have the exact same response, if questioned separately. Our allied story would be set up, in turn, to take down the person trying to hurt the group. We would have to do anything to keep ourselves safe and undetected.

That night, we drove to Denver, as planned, in a few different cars. Making me even more nervous than meeting a gay captain was Chris's guest, a newbie sophomore from Thirty-first Squadron. It quickly became apparent, as we approached the front door of Rodeo, that this guy was not twenty-one years old when he asked Chris if his fake ID would work at the door. "Goddamn it, Chris!" I said. They both looked up at me. The newbie looked like he was afraid of me. Chris had a guilty look on his face. "Why would you risk getting us nailed by bringing a guy who needs to use a fake ID?"

"It's a good ID. I checked it before we left. He'll have no problem at the door," Chris said. As we walked closer, I noticed there was a policeman standing next to the bouncer at the door of the club.

Many gay clubs had a policeman at the entrance because gay people were often targets of violence in Colorado. Just three years before, Matthew Shepard had been beaten and left to die on a cold night in neighboring Wyoming. Sometimes we went to Poor Richard's Corner in Colorado Springs, where there was a gay-run coffee shop. This was terribly risky because it was so close to the academy. We wore our baseball caps pulled way down, enjoying ourselves, even though as we sat outside of the coffee shop, cars would go by and about every minute, and someone would yell "faggot!" or similar vitriol from his car window. Some would throw things at the gay people who were sitting outside, peacefully enjoying coffee. Garbage from their cars, coins, and glass bottles were all fair game for the bigots who wanted to hurt gay people.

I blamed all of this hateful behavior on the huge presence of the right-wing Christian organizations that are based in Colorado and, particularly, Colorado Springs. The Family Research Council, the Promise Keepers, and Focus on the Family are a few of the highly intolerant groups there that instill fear and anxiety in their members regarding issues of homosexuality.

I was nervous as hell. If the policeman noticed the fake ID, he would ask us if we were cadets—because we were so obviously cadets—and then the real trouble would begin. At nine P.M., we entered the club. But the fake ID worked. The plan was that we would stay at the club until around one A.M. and then head to the gay captain's house to meet him and sleep there. All of us would leave the club together and if one of us wanted to hook up with someone in the club, then that person would "trick out," or do their thing *away* from where we were staying. ("Tricking in" meant bringing a boy home.)

At about midnight, I was talking to a nice guy who was a probably around twenty-seven years old. He was interested in me and asked all kinds of questions. He guessed that I was a cadet, but I completely denied any association with the military. I think I probably lied to him about everything in my life in order to put up what I felt was a necessary wall of protection.

One of the big problems with the military's Don't Ask, Don't Tell policy is that people are not only lying at work, they are lying to their own kind just to protect themselves. Don't Ask, Don't Tell should be called by its true name and purpose, "Permission to Lie." Any policy that inherently tells someone to lie lacks any integrity, and will eventually break a person down as he continues to follow the philosophy. The policy will also, eventually, break down the organization that sanctions it. Don't Ask, Don't Tell will eventually put a wedge between not only gay people and straight people serving side-by-side in the military because of the lies that it fosters, it will eventually place gay people themselves against one another. Gay military members become too afraid to come out, even to each other, for support.

Seth ran up to me and whispered in my ear, interrupting my conversation with the hot guy, "Holy shit, Reichen, the bartender just took Jason's fake ID." I went into panic mode. I told my new acquaintance that I had his number and would call him later. I gathered up everyone I could and told them we had to leave the club right away. On our way out, the policeman, of course, stopped us.

"You boys with the guy that was using *this?*" asked this very overweight policeman with a southern drawl.

This was one of those moments when one decision might affect the rest of our lives. Lying to a police officer and getting caught would mean instant dismissal from the Air Force Academy for all of us. Admitting that he was with us would mean that the policeman would want to ask further questions. Then he would find out that we were cadets, and probably send our names to the academy anyway. Tolerating Jason's fake ID would surely get us kicked out, too.

I reasoned that the biggest risk would be to say we *weren't* with Jason. Then the cop would question Jason, which could lead to all of us being in trouble, since this newbie had no experience in the lies that had to be told to keep us all safe. Our offenses would include lying about not knowing him, lying about where we were, lying to a police officer, being gay, tolerating a fake ID, and, to top it all off, encouraging and tolerating underage drinking.

I stepped up to the plate. "He's with us, officer," I announced. After thinking about it for a few seconds, the police officer told us to stand there and demanded a valid ID from Jason. The only one he had with him was his military ID card that proudly stated "Cadet" underneath "RANK."

Once the cop saw Jason's ID, he asked for all of our military IDs. He wrote all of our names on a pad of paper and told us he was going to report us to the academy. I stood there, calm, already thinking of what lies we would have to tell to get out of this one. *Who was going to be the sacrificial lamb? Who were we going to have to frame to get the rest of us out of this? Could we come up with a set of lies that would free us all?*

He took our names and, surprisingly, let us go without giving Jason a citation. I guess he figured the academy would deal with us harshly enough, and that was fine with him

Our usual way of dealing with the vulnerability of our situation as a group was no longer going to work. It was time to organize militarily. We needed to have a serious meeting. There would be no introducing ourselves to the captain tonight. There would be no sleeping in Denver. It was time to get back to the academy before any police business made its way there first. I needed to round up every gay person I knew at the academy before the morning. They needed to hear what I had been thinking for months. I drove Seth's car toward the academy, with the radio turned off. I listened to the wind hitting the windshield as we sped down Route 25, gathering my thoughts.

Seth lay in his passenger seat, passed out from drinking and from all the excitement. I spoke to him, even though he was probably too out of it to hear me. I recited different lies that might possibly save us. I would come up with something that sounded right, but then I would find a hole in the lie. Then I would start with a new one. "OK. Here's what we'll say," I said over and over again, trying to figure a way out of our dismal situation.

chapter twenty-eight

TOWN MEETING

We pulled into the academy at about one thirty A.M., driving through the north gate off I-25. When you know you're doing something wrong, every authority figure looks like the enemy. The security policemen at the gates of the academy, who usually appeared to be protecting us from intruders, looked like evil gunmen who wanted nothing but to get us in trouble. I showed my ID as I passed the guard and he waved all three of our cars through one by one.

We parked and walked up the long concrete path from the parking lots to the academy campus. On the way up, I listed, out loud, people I wanted us all to find. Seth and Chris made suggestions of people I had forgotten. "Where are we meeting?" Seth asked.

"Go to the Bull Ten Squadron northwest stairwell and go down," I said. "But keep going down until the stairwell ends, below the lowest floor of dorms. I was just down there the other day. The lock was popped open on the door and the lock code was clearly visible. Someone must have left it that way, so now I know the code. I'll have the door cracked. Tell everyone that they have to come alone. Don't come in couples or groups. No one can be seen entering the lower stairwell. When you get in the door, turn right and follow the hallway until you see a ladder and chute on your right-hand side. Climb down that ladder and meet in that room. It's a main control room with lots of chairs and a large monitoring station."

I was proud of my decision to meet in the academy tunnels. As freshmen, a few of us had found that same unlocked door in the middle of the night and let ourselves in. From that first time underground, I thought of how amazing that place would be for all kinds of things, including secret meetings, hiding out, or even sex.

"Are you fucking crazy?" Chris asked quickly. "You want to meet in the academy tunnels?"

"Yes. That's where we're meeting," I said. I had already scoped it out. It was the perfect place, and I knew it.

The academy's tunnel system is a vast array of multidirectional and multilevel tunnels that were built, along with the academy, in the Cold War era of the 1950s. When you're in them, you realize that these were built as a safe haven for academy cadets and personnel in the event of a nuclear attack. The rumors were that the tunnels connected to the tunnels of NORAD, the huge military situation monitoring complex built inside a mountain in Colorado Springs.

There were golf cart–like vehicles down there that hadn't been used in ages. There were signs telling you where you were in relation to the rest of the tunnel system. There were signs pointing in the direction of certain key destinations, such as a main command-post control room, where communications would originate in the event of an attack. There were storage barrels filled with MREs and drinking water that could probably support the cadet wing for six months or more. The tunnels had a lighting system that didn't miss a hallway or crevice. There were switches everywhere that, with one flick, would light a hallway that looked like it was a mile long.

The most attractive part about the tunnels, to cadets, was that they were off-limits to us. Being caught roaming their halls would be a huge regulation violation. However, the chances of being caught there at night were slim to none. Although no one worked in the tunnels at night, there were signs of activity that *someone* worked in them during the day. We found rooms full of tools, and electrical and phone panels on the upper levels of the tunnels that were obviously maintained by workers each day while we were all at class, playing sports, and just being cadets. But at night, those sheds, bays, and offices were empty. There was no sign of human beings, until we arrived.

At three A.M., we had exactly twenty cadets, including myself, all gay, in the "control room." It baffled me that all of them made it. Each one of them was a good enough friend of a good enough friend of mine to be convinced that they absolutely had to be at this meeting. Here, I had gained control of a situation that might have spun out of control and created one of the biggest U.S. service academy scandals in history. I realized how powerful we, as a group, really were.

I had been in the control room for about an hour jotting down notes in an Air Force Academy notebook I had bought at the campus bookstore as a potential gift for someone. Ironically, this notebook had a big picture of the Air Force Academy chapel on the front, along with a picture of the academy's Honor Wall, which read, "We will not lie, steal or cheat, nor tolerate among us anyone who does." The contents of this notebook would now be dedicated to beating the academy's honor system.

I started the meeting by introducing myself. I never said I was the leader, but what I did say was all based on the notes I had written down in that notebook:

"My name is Reichen. A lot of you are my friends. A lot of you are friends of my friends. If you can listen to what I have to say and understand why I'm saying it, we can provide for each other the safest environment possible. Tonight, it came to my attention that we, as a group—and we are a group whether you like it or not—can no longer go without some sort of structure and code to follow to prevent disaster. The day we all swore the Oath of Office to our country and said we would die for the United States was the same day that we swore to be severely punished if we were caught being gay or for having 'homosexual relations,' as they like to call them.

"Today, thousands of service members have been discharged from their duties and from the military, across all of the Department of Defense branches. Each discharge comes with it a thorough investigation.

"Some of you have looks of total fear on your faces right now. I have probably struck a chord with most of you. You don't consider yourself gay. You can't believe that you're even here. Why? Because you're not gay, you tell yourself. Well, let me tell you something. I've heard about and had confirmation on each and every person in here that you've been with a member of the same sex in some sort of compromising way, and if I or anyone in here who has heard the same thing reported you to the OSI, then an investigation would get you in trouble.

"I'm not here to *out* any of you or even to make you admit that you're gay, to me or anyone else. Some of you might be straight, or not know what you are. The fact is that you were remembered tonight by a handful of us to be at this meeting. You can leave right now if you don't want to hear any more. If you leave and try to tell on the people who stayed, *you will not win,* and that's my promise to you. In turn, your confession to the OSI or your AOC will force you to look like the only gay person at the Air Force Academy, and you will be kicked out before anyone who stays here is kicked out. I will *personally* make sure of that."

At that moment, I was calling everyone's bluff. I had no idea how I would keep the guys who stayed safe. It was just a grand idea in my head that I could execute such a plan if I wanted to. It was the only way I knew to make sure that no one would get scared and try to turn someone else in for "committing homosexual acts," which happened often at the academy.

The stories were revolting. A friend of mine would mess around with his roommate in a moment of passion. The next day, the roommate would turn my friend in to the AOC, saying that my friend had come on to him in the night. It was the only way for the scared and guilty to protect his own hide—by making someone else look like the villain. The knee-jerk reactions of air force officers successfully enabled this system of betrayal and made it easy for hypocritical cadets to save themselves. Within twenty-four hours, my friend would disappear from the academy, in the middle of the night, with no explanation. I had just started a group that would be no less brutal in its self-preservation, and I wanted everyone to know how serious I was. I felt vindictive for what I had just said to the group, but at the same time, I felt justified.

I continued very proudly and sternly, "Who wants to leave?" I looked at the twenty faces and they looked at each other. Some looked straight at me and obviously had no intention of leaving. Some looked at me with anger for bringing them into this meeting. I could tell that they did not want to associate with a bunch of gay guys and girls. "Last chance," I said. "Remember, I'm here saying these things because I believe that no one in here has done anything wrong. If you want protection, I'm setting it up for you." I waited about ten more seconds. No one left.

"Now," I said, "welcome to our, uh . . . control room." I smiled and felt a surge of energy through my body. In front of me were two women cadets. One was a cheerleader and the other a gymnast. Behind them were two football players, a lacrosse player, two swimmers, a water polo player, a senator's son, a senator's grandson, two members of the academy honor guard, the son of an instructor at the Air Force Academy Prep School, a black guy who was a track star at the Academy, a wrestler, and five guys with GPAs over 3.8. This was not a group of underachievers by any stretch of the imagination. They were quick, dedicated, and smart. Convincing them of what I had to say had to be done perfectly. It had to make sense. Communicating my point had never been so important to me.

I continued with the story of what had happened that very night in Denver. I explained whose names would be given to the academy, including my own. I told them that our last order of business would be to discuss a way of getting out of trouble. If enough people had the same story, then we would be in the clear. Before that, I wanted to establish some rules for a code that I had jotted in my notebook.

"The first rule that we must establish is that *no one* in this room can ever mention these meetings to any person not here tonight. If you want to talk about this meeting with another person who *was* at this meeting, then you make sure that you're alone and that no one can hear you." Some of the cadets were taking notes as I spoke. "We will have a meeting once every two weeks. If you don't come to the meetings, don't expect the maximum amount of protection that you can have from the rest of the group.

"Rule number two: if you want someone to join us, then you must first propose to the group the possibility of their joining us at a biweekly meeting. *Never* tell a new person about this group or that they can join before discussing that person among us *first*. If we approve of that person, then that person can meet with me. I will fill them in on the rules that we're establishing now. If they run off and try to turn us in, we will already be holding their balls in our hands because we will have discussed their risk to us before they even came to the first meeting. We will make them look like a crazy person and they will go down and be kicked out before we ever will. Do not doubt that they will deserve it for trying to turn you in for being what you are."

As a couple of people laughed at me, I could see the look of relief on some of the faces of the guys who had been angry with me before. They even nodded their heads at me in agreement, and were happy that I was being so strict. They seemed to like me more when I went over the consequences of screwing over anyone in the group.

"If you break any of the rules that we make up tonight, then consider yourself not part of *us* anymore. This is not child's play. These are our lives, our futures, and our careers that we are holding in each other's hands. No one in this room will be able to take the group down. The group *will* be too strong.

"Rule number three: we decide what to do about situations as a group. There is no dictator. If at any time you feel that what the group is doing may unnecessarily harm an innocent person, then *please* speak up. We're here to protect ourselves, not to retaliate. However, if the only way to protect a person in our group is to make an attacker look bad, then that *is* what we will do.

"Rule number four: loyalty to the group is a must. We will no longer tolerate getting in trouble for things that straight people can do right out in the open. Any person at the academy—or anywhere else for that matter—trying to hurt one of us for doing something such as having consensual sexual relations, will *not* be tolerated. The person trying to take one of us down will end up going down themselves. We will band together to make sure that no one here gets in trouble for things that are inherently good—things that would be OK to do with an opposite-sex partner.

"Rule number five: we are not a gang. Using this group to get someone out of trouble in any other area, such as for an honor violation or a regulation violation is a last resort and must be discussed with the group. We must aim to be just as ethical as other cadets. Again, we are simply protecting our right to our sexuality. We are not here to circumvent the rules that other cadets must follow. We must follow this rule to uphold the integrity we promised to keep when we became cadets.

"Rule number six: if you know of someone who is in trouble for a homosexual act, *please* contact me or another member of the group immediately. I or one of you may call a meeting of those of you who can help them with a confession or a letter, and we will help that person.

"Rule number seven: if you mess up a story or cause someone in our group to be in danger when faced with a situation of harassment of a gay person by the military, then you will have no protection from us.

"Rule number eight: we have one mission. We're here to protect each other against a ban on gay people in the military by all having the same story in case we are ever questioned. The rule is to keep that in mind.

"We can add more rules as we go along. These eight rules are the most important for now."

I moved to a new topic and looked for a show of hands of people who knew of others whom we should consider for our group. Hands flew up, including my own. I passed around a sheet of paper. Sixteen new names were written down. Even I was surprised at some of the people I would be approaching. We all discussed each person in detail. This took about an hour to do. I reminded the group that if any of these new people turned on us when I went to speak to them about our group, I now had nineteen people behind me, ready to vouch for me during any sort of questioning. They would all say that I would never approach a person about any sort of gay subject at all. In two and a half hours, I had created a society that I knew, at that moment, would not let me down.

From that night, I learned something that I still carry with me today. When I spoke like a leader and acted as a leader, I was one. If the majority eventually fell away from me, it would be because I had not done my best or given it my all. I vowed to myself to make sure this would never happen.

As we discussed the last topic of the night—the fake ID—I was amazed at the creativity of some of my attendees for getting us out of trouble. I had invited Jason, the newbie with the fake ID problem, so that everyone could see what a group like ours could do in action. Jason was a water polo player and had never considered himself to be gay before. He had messed around with Chris a couple of times and found himself in a serious situation.

Our final story was that we met Chris's cousin in Denver. There had been no fake ID at all. It was Chris's cousin's ID that ignited the confusion. With the help of the other fourteen members of the group, the six cadets whose names had actually been recorded by the police officer now knew to all say the same thing, and it went like this:

We met Chris's cousin at this place called Rodeo. Chris's cousin dropped his ID at the front when entering the club. Thirty minutes later, a woman picked up his ID and handed it to Jason, asking if it belonged to one of his friends. Several of us saw the woman pick up the ID and hand it to Jason. Jason put the ID in his wallet. He looked for Chris's cousin, but by that time, Chris's cousin had left the club, or at least we couldn't find him. Jason held on to the ID to give back to his cousin later. At the bar, while talking to me, Jason looked young to the bartender, who thought he might have been drinking, but was not. Jason was asked to show ID. Even though Jason was not ordering a drink, he pulled out Chris's cousin's driver's license, mistaking it for his own, and had it confiscated. No one had asked for ID to enter the club, which is how Jason got in. After the cop took our names and gave us our IDs back, we found Chris's cousin outside talking to a girl around the corner from the club. We gave him his ID, and we all came home. We did not know that Rodeo was a gay place because there were some hot girls there. If we had known, we wouldn't have been there long.

That was our story and it was flawless, as long as more than two people had the same exact story. I repeated the story one more time beginning with, "Here's what we'll say. Everyone listen closely." We agreed that the story was great. Everyone believed that avoiding the punishment for being caught in a gay bar was worth the lies we would have to tell. Everyone also agreed to learn something from this lesson.

"One last thing," I said. "If anyone mentions this meeting to an authority and tries to get us in trouble, here is what you will be met with. The story, if any of us are questioned, is that it was that traitor who asked us to come to the meeting, and that we refused to go to such a crazy thing."

"Agreed!" everyone said in near unison. I finished with, "This meeting is done. I'll see you in two weeks and two days, Sunday night, with our new members." It was 5:45 A.M. and time for bed.

I fell asleep and woke up at about eleven. the next morning. It was a weekend free from any cadet football games, SAMIs, or parades. I felt safer than ever and in control of my alternative life.

By midnight that Saturday, five of our original twenty from last night's meeting had stopped by to give me new names to discuss at the next meeting. There were over twenty more names to discuss. I couldn't believe it.

Just days after our Denver scare, Seth and I were awaiting our inevitable call into our AOC's office. Every time we saw a note on the clipboard on our door or a message at the CQ desk for one of us, we assumed that it was about our being in trouble.

Finally, that day came at the end of February. Seth and I were called into our AOC's office together. Beforehand, we met with each other went over the story again. We agreed that we would act *very* nonchalant about the whole thing.

We went into Major Pacer's office. He had been given a list of questions to ask us about the Denver incident. We were surprised that he didn't separate us. As he asked questions, we unfolded the story for him exactly as we had discussed it in our group.

"Why, thank you, gentlemen," he lisped. "It doesn't sound like there's going to be any problem. You're telling me the same thing that the third-class cadet in Thirty-one is telling his AOC," Major Pacer said.

"Sir, thank you," I said politely. "It was a crazy mix-up and the policeman didn't realize that we were simply trying to help someone out, not trying to use a fake ID."

"Yes. I realize that," he said.

"Sir, is that all?" I asked.

"Yes, boys, that's all," he said and let us go. Seth and I walked down the hall to my room. We shut the door, locked it, and jumped up and down while slapping each other's hands, chests, shoulders, and faces. We were doing it quietly but we were getting our excitement across. We were in the clear.

chapter twenty-nine

AFRAID OF NOT LIVING

One day at the end of February, I was on my way out to morning meal formation, and I saw Brian Bowman sitting at the CQ desk. He was in his flight suit, going over flash cards for his T-3 check ride that day. T-3 was the program for those cadets slated to fly for the air force after graduation—I had just started the program myself. Before leaving the academy, we had to complete primary flight training. The T-3 was a brand-new airplane that the academy and cadets alike were very excited about. The airplane was fully maneuverable and fully aerobatic, so we could do more with it than with the older-style planes that had been provided to cadets in the past for primary flight training.

I grabbed Brian's flash cards to quiz him on the aircraft knowledge that he needed to know. "How's it going?" he asked and winked at me with a smile. Every time I saw him, I would think about the time in my room with the tequila. I worked with him and his flash cards for a few minutes and wished him good luck. He didn't have to go to formation that morning because he had to catch a bus to the academy's airfield.

I went to breakfast and to four classes that morning and happened to have my afternoon free that day. I got back to the squadron just in time to change into the updated uniform of the day. As I ran down the hallway to my room, I saw a few people sitting down in the hallway, blocking my door and Brian's door, which was across the hall from mine. "What's going on?" I asked. No one answered me. I got a sick feeling in my stomach. Seth came running down the hall toward me in his flight suit. He had been at T-3 that morning as well.

"Reichen," he said.

"Seth," I said. I instantly got tears in my eyes and no one had even told me anything yet. I could just tell by the way Seth grabbed my shoulders that something was really wrong.

"OK. Just stop for a second. Let's stay calm," he said. I felt more tears forming in my eyes.

"Seth, I'm calm. Look at me. OK. I'm calm. Tell me what happened," I demanded.

"OK," Seth began to speak but his eyes were turning red as well. "OK. There was an accident out in the T-3 practice area today. A plane went down and made a black hole in the ground. It burned on impact." Tears fell from his eyes. "The fleet was immediately called back and grounded. The only plane that hasn't come back yet is Brian's." I stood there in shock.

"What do you *mean* not back yet? You mean they don't know if it's *his*? How could they *not know*, Seth? Are they fucking *idiots*?" I asked with tears pouring down my face.

"Calm down. Don't get upset just yet. That's why we're all sitting here. We're waiting to hear for sure what happened," he told me.

"Oh, that's what we're waiting for," I said in a trance as I looked at everyone around me sitting on the floor with their heads down.

There was no question in my mind. Brian was gone. I could feel it. I went into my room and Nathan was in there on his bed lying down in his flight suit.

"Were you down at T-3 too?" I asked.

"Yes," he answered sadly. "Brian was in that plane. It was him and his instructor, who is married to a woman with twins on the way."

"Jesus Christ!" I yelled. "What the hell happened? We don't have cadet planes that can come back safely? Jesus!"

"We don't know what happened yet. Just try . . ."

"Try what! To be calm when this guy . . . this guy . . . who I fucking *love to death* . . . who I went through *basic training* with . . . this guy who told me he had my back . . . and I told him I had his . . . God, Nathan!" I lowered my body to the floor and sat with my legs crossed, holding my abdomen. "Not Brian. Why Brian? Seriously! Of all the people here! Oh, God. Jesus! Why Brian? He's not the one they should have taken. Nathan, why Brian?" I stayed on the floor and cried my eyes out. I had the cry that I had waited to have for two and a half years of the academy. Nothing seemed to matter at that moment because someone that I really knew and cared for was dead. None of the rules that we lived under mattered. Noon meal formation was cancelled for our squadron. That didn't matter. Good grades didn't matter. Antigay policies didn't matter. A guy whom I considered to be part of my family was dead.

Later that day, we found out that Brian and his instructor were practicing spins and ended up in an inverted flat spin that they couldn't get out of. Spins are a state that an aircraft can enter when it gets too slow. It loses lift and falls out of the sky in a swirling motion. Most planes have procedures to exit a spinning state. Brian's plane lost all lift and plummeted to the ground. Apparently, the design of the new T-3 wasn't good enough, or the procedures didn't allow it to recover.

Months passed as we slowly, and only partially, recovered from losing one of our own. I was able to go into Brian's room with his family. They let me take some of his USAFA T-shirts, which we wore for athletics and with certain uniforms. I still have one that says "Bowman" on the front. The last time I left his room, I saw a small piece of paper he had written on that was taped above his desk. It read:

I'm not afraid of dying. I'm afraid of not living. —Janis Joplin

This was the perfect quote to describe Brian. He *was* afraid of not living. On that crazy night that he and I spent together, he asked me, "Are you afraid?" twice. I will never forget Brian and his free spirit, or his lack of fear. He was a beautiful person, inside and out.

chapter thirty

WINEFEST TO SUMMER REST

Another academy milestone was upon me. It was time to order our class rings, which would arrive in time for a special end-of-the-year dinner and be presented to the junior class to wear for the remainder of our time at the academy. Besides picking the color of the stone and the number of diamonds we wanted, we also had to pick the words for a personal engraving on the inside of the band. At one of our biweekly underground meetings, we all proposed writing the same thing on the inside of our rings. Many different ideas were suggested, some good and some bad. One suggestion was to write what we *always* had to say before we discussed how we'd deal with any authority figure at the academy. Those words were, *Here's what we'll say*. Once that was suggested, we had unanimous agreement among our group. These words would be printed on the inside of the rings of many, if not all, of the people in our group. Doing this really increased my morale and made me feel like I was a part of something.

Another way that Seth and I decided to boost our morale was to put together the next WineFest. He and I spent a few weeks scoping out the big dinners at Mitchell Hall, and after each one, we went in to recover the leftover bottles of wine that were left on the tables for the trash. When we were done collecting, we had about forty bottles of wine stored at his house in Colorado Springs.

This time, we would put WineFest together by inviting our new underground group and all of their sympathizers. The friends of gay cadets knew nothing of the Underground, as we now called it, because our rule was never to tell anyone about the group until he or she actually came to a meeting. Another rule was that we could never talk about the group unless we were alone with another member of the group—so we couldn't even mention it at WineFest. The beauty of the Underground was that no one knew of us but *us*. Our activities were the only ones at the academy that weren't public knowledge for the whole academy system. The Underground had become strong. Toward the end of my last semester of junior year, we had no fewer than forty-five members attending our meetings. And we had successfully pulled at least twenty of us out of various bouts of trouble for "alleged homosexual acts" with strategies that began with "Here's what we'll say."

Now it was time to party. Seth and I rented a huge house in Vail for a three-day weekend. The house had about eight bedrooms and slept more than thirty people. We had more than that—there were about sixty attendees for WineFest that year. The rule was that everyone had to bring some sort of alcohol for everyone else to enjoy.

When we all had finally arrived at the house, it was a sight to see. There were sixty academy cadets, some of whom were gay and some of whom were gay-friendly although heterosexual. The group was special in that many of them happened to be artists or musicians who had always hoped to perform more but couldn't because they were cadets. People brought guitars, harmonicas, bongo drums, and violins. It was a neat group of people. Some people were drawing pictures of the amazing views we had out of the house's windows. I was so proud to be in that house that weekend. I loved the people around me and I felt that, in all the time I had now spent at the academy, I knew that there really *was* a great group of people that related to me and that I could relate to.

WineFest turned into a drunk-fest. We drank and yelled and screamed, and ate, and made fun of people, and had sex. We released all of the tension that the academy had built up in us over the past year. Every single person there needed it. To this day, I have seen people in

various cities who remember me from WineFest, and we always remi-
nisce about that wonderful weekend.

Finals week came and kicked our butts and we found ourselves in
the very last summer of our academy careers. We were now rising seniors, or firsties, and it felt *so* good to be there. I spent my first summer
block of the three on vacation.

Nathan and I spent the first week of vacation together. The Grateful
Dead happened to be playing at Sam Boyd Stadium at the University of
Nevada in Las Vegas. I was finally allowed to have a car again, and my
firstie loan had hit my cadet bank account. I bought a used red Saab con-
vertible just before summer break. In celebration, Nathan and I decided
to take the car on a road trip to see the Dead in Vegas. I had already introduced Jodie and Kory to the Dead, and Nathan was jealous. He wanted
to see them, too, especially after listening to their music so often: I had
played the Dead in our room every day for the past two years to calm me
down. By the time Nathan was going to his first show, he already knew
all the songs and would regularly sing them with me in our room.

He was excited. We played the Dead and sang along in the car all
the way to Vegas. We spent a few days in Vegas and saw three Dead
shows. We hung out in the parking lot for hours each day, talking to
Deadheads and getting a kick out of their stories. Nathan was loving
life and I was so happy to have him there. During the shows, the air in
the stadium was so hot that the fire department came in with huge fire
trucks and shot huge amounts of cold water down on the crowd. It felt
amazing. On the road trip back to the academy, Nathan and I were
dirty, muddy—and ripe. We needed showers more than ever.

Allen Ladd had talked me into going to Europe with him for the last
two weeks of the three-week block. We flew there and stayed with his
mother, who lived in a flat along one of the most popular roads in
London. Allen and I went to every pub we could find that had a pint-
for-a-pound deal on Guinness lager. We drank a ton and got together
on our guest bed when his mother would fall asleep. We traveled to
Amsterdam and Scotland and went sightseeing. We stayed in hostels
together and held on to each other at night. No one who saw us
showing affection toward each other seemed to care, and I loved that.

The only bothersome thing about our trip to Europe was Allen's need to hit on girls right in front of me. I knew him well and I could see that deep down he was chasing girls in order to make *them* feel good, rather than himself. He couldn't let go of that side of his life. I could have gone the entire trip without talking to a single girl, but that was just me.

I went to a few places on that trip that I had been to when I was in high school and first met Anne, before starting the romance that we had together. I thought about how far I had come as a person and how different I was, compared to when I'd met her five years before.

The second block of my summer was filled by my being a cadre member for survival training. I had signed up to be a partisan—the people who lived in strategically located camps that survival students would happen upon during their navigation sequence through the woods. The partisan's job was to give students of the program food and water and to help them figure out their next stop on their way to safety.

Playing a partisan was awesome. I was assigned to a camp where I would meet my two new best friends for the entire next year. When I met them, I was sorry that I had gone three years without knowing them. Juliette Ford was a senior in Third Squadron. She had lived two floors above me for three years. Donny Coleman was another senior, in Thirty-second Squadron, who loved the Grateful Dead—among lots of other music that I liked. The three of us hit it off in training, before we actually went out to live in the tent-villages. We decided that we would all have a tent together for the two weeks that we lived in the mountains.

Working as a partisan was one of those wonderful times of my cadet career. We lived out in the woods of Colorado, and cooked our own food. Being away from the academy in a camping environment was a refreshing change. We were told to be as bohemian as we could be, so all of us brought out the most hippie-type of clothes we could find. We gave each other fake names that we used when the students were present, and figured out all of these screwed-up foreign accents to speak in. Juliette was Natasha, Donny was Jacko, and I was Sven. When the students weren't around, we would still get into character and call each other by these names, talking in foreign accents until we cracked up laughing, rolling on the ground.

"Natasha," I would yell in some, Eastern European accent, "get me some firewood from the forest."

"Sven," she would yell back. "I'll get right on that. And you can be biting me, too," she would reply in an Indian accent.

Over the two weeks we were there, we seldom dealt with the students. They would come through and be there for only a couple of hours. We would yell at them to hide outside our camp, so that in case we were interrogated by the enemy, we could say that we didn't know they were there. The three of us stayed up late each night talking with a flashlight on. We smoked packs and packs of cigarettes together and ate Cheetos, which we dipped in ranch dressing. This was our favorite food while working the program. We set up a hammock in a little nook in the woods, and during the day, all three of us climbed into the hammock and read to one another.

Before Brian died, he had given me his favorite book, *The Celestine Prophecy*, to read. I never read it until I was out in the woods working as a partisan. Every day, one of us would take a chapter of the book and read it out loud to the other two. It became, and remains now, my favorite book. In the story, there is a lot of talk about nature and trees and the world coming together in a spiritual way. It was easy to imagine while we were away from the academy. The book also talked about the presence of energy in human beings and in all living things and how to recognize, use, and celebrate that energy for the best living situation possible.

The three of us looked as if we were related. Juliette was tall, at about five foot eleven, with beautiful blonde hair. Donny was six foot two, also with blond hair. They both had blue eyes, and we all had great tans because we lay out in the sun on big mountain rocks for a few minutes every day when we weren't meeting about incoming students. When the program was over, the three of us vowed to hang out during our senior year and forever after.

During the third block of my last summer of the academy, I worked Second Beast. I learned that the Second Beast cadre actually lived in the dorms back at the Hill and simply drove out to Jack's Valley early in the morning. The only time we had to stay overnight at Jack's was when it was our turn to "sit flight CQ." Each flight of basics had a CQ tent assigned to it that only upperclassmen could enter and sit in. Every night, one or two cadets had to sit flight CQ.

Allen was working with me that summer at Second Beast. We had a good time, but I could tell, over those three weeks, that his feelings for me were growing more distant. He had gone home during one of his summer break weeks and had rekindled a relationship with one of his high school sweethearts. He had voiced his opinion about the Underground and my involvement with it a couple of times. He refused to have anything to do with it and didn't want me to go to any more meetings. I would tell him that he didn't understand how important the Underground was to me, but he wouldn't listen. He was tired of messing around with me and living in fear while hiding it. Living that way would wear on anyone.

The only time Allen and I connected while working Second Beast was when he and I arrived late to a morning formation. We were staying together in our temporary summer room back at the Hill and had woken up late. Our punishment was to sit flight CQ for three nights in a row. The toughest part about our punishment was that we had to stay awake. It would get very cold out at Jack's Valley at night, so we would bundle up in serious BDU winter jackets, long johns, and stocking caps. On the second night of our sentence, we broke down and had one of our riskiest sessions ever. We stripped off our BDUs and quickly had each other for a few minutes on the hard floor made up of the wooden slabs that had been laid down for all the tents of the tent city. On the third night, we did it again. Other than this, Allen showed me no intimacy whatsoever over those three weeks.

I didn't put much effort into training the basics of Second Beast. Frankly, I was burned out on anything academy, military, or training related. None of the other cadre really ever saw me and neither did the rising basic cadets. I had fun with a few of them and they loved me for it but, in general, they all saw me as the most laid-back, easy-going firstie in the whole squadron. I liked that they saw me that way. I was proud of it, in my now-rebellious mind.

chapter thirty-one

DELMONICO'S

Three school years and four summers had gone by. I was really a firstie at the U.S. Air Force Academy. If, on that first day of improcessing, someone had asked me to guess what I would be like by my senior year, I would never have said that I would be where I was or that I would be the person I had become.

These last two semesters were going to be very different in Bull Ten. We were given a new AOC: Major Pacer had been reassigned. I missed him, strangely enough. He annoyed me when he was around, but I had grown used to him and knew how to deal with him. Our new AOC was Major Green. He had come from the aviation world of the air force and was completely clueless about running a cadet squadron, and we sensed that immediately. Luckily for us seniors, he asked our class to guide him into making good decisions for the squadron. We figured that, by the time we graduated, he would catch on to our complete knowledge of how to *work* the system, but by then, we would be long gone.

The academy had also decided that the class of 1997, Allen's class, would not stay in the same squadron all four years, as our class was allowed to do. Now that 1997 had completed two years, the authorities decided to shuffle the class into new squadrons. The reasoning was to get the cadets used to the actual air force experience of doing a job for a few years and then being moved and stationed elsewhere. If it had done this to our class, I would have been very upset. The bonds that I formed in Bull Ten were, to me, the most sacred of any I had experienced in my life. This shuffle devastated me because it took Allen out of Bull Ten. He was moved to another squadron in Vandenberg Hall. It was not too far away, but it was still different. We were no longer just a few doors down from each other and would no longer see each other on a day-to-day basis. Our already dysfunctional relationship would become even more difficult to hold together. I spoke to Allen about the switch and I had an eerie feeling that he was glad to be leaving, ready to move on to a new life and away from the drama surrounding us.

Just a couple of weeks into the year, I followed my end-of-partisan-cadre-promise and contacted Juliette again. We started doing everything together—going on long runs, tanning, and going out on the town almost every day to talk and smoke cigarettes. As firsties, we were now allowed to leave the academy every day, as long as our academic and military duties were fulfilled. Juliette and I made it a point to be gone as much as possible. We figured that the less people saw us, the better.

We had been hanging out for about a month when she told me that her roommate, on the swim team, was looking at renting a condo off base to go to on weekends. She and others on the team were looking for others to join them in paying for the condo. I was immediately excited by this idea. First of all, possessing apartments or houses off base was grounds for being kicked out of the academy. It was completely illegal—precisely because there was so *much* incentive for cadets to have a place off base. Having a private, secret space meant that there would be times when no one would know where we were. An academy committed to accountability did not like this idea.

After years of having our lives documented, the idea of privacy was enticing. Having our own kitchen and place to cook food was also fascinating to us. Having our own bedrooms and bathrooms after having showered in front of people for so long and having used public toilets several times a day would be wonderful. We were treated like children in so many ways at the academy; as seniors, we were itching to feel grown up.

I told Allen about the condo idea and he was equally interested. There were so many people involved in this operation that my monthly rent, including utilities, was only $32. Seniors were paid $500 per month at that time, so I could afford it. Allen and I agreed to pay and got our own room in the condo. The place was pretty nice. It had three stories and five bedrooms, with bathrooms off almost every bedroom. Everyone there knew that getting caught would mean *not* graduating, so we were very strict about the place. We had to make up rules about whom we could bring there and whom we could tell. We never referred to the place as "the apartment," or anything close to that. The condo was on Delmonico Drive in Colorado Springs, so we called it "Delmonico's." We had fun yelling across a room that we would meet someone else at Delmonico's. No one knew what we were talking about.

Needless to say, I experienced great times at Delmonico's. I got along well with the other paying members. Juliette brought in her friend, Abbey, who was supercool, and she got along well with Allen and me. The condo was a safe haven to us all on so many fronts. We would march onto the football field on football game Saturdays, and then jump in our cars and drive to Delmonico's to watch the game on a big television. We'd sit there, drinking beer, laughing at all the cadets who were stuck at the game. We threw a couple of parties there, only inviting cadets whom we deemed cool enough to keep our secret. We made full-course meals and ate together like normal human beings. I was thankful to have our own place.

Another highlight of Delmonico's was my meeting a girl named Carrie Dell. She was on the diving team from the class of 1998, two years junior to me, and was absolutely beautiful. I confided in her about so many things and we became amazing friends throughout the year. She helped me through many issues with Allen and she remains one of my best friends today.

Allen and I were able to be together there often. Some nights, we would have the place to ourselves. Unfortunately, he was losing interest in continuing our relationship. We had long and heated discussions at Delmonico's during which he would tell me he couldn't be gay anymore. He would talk about how his family would disown him and how he was a Christian and knew that what we were doing was wrong. He told me that he wanted to be with girls and not guys, and that he wanted to be "normal." I would thank him for giving me the heads-up and promised him that I would continue in my quest to emotionally separate myself from him. My efforts would be blown on a regular basis. Often, Allen and I would have a couple of beers together and play cards. It would take a matter of an hour for us to feel an undeniable need to be together and we would break down, go to our room, and have each other.

The longer this pattern continued, the more frustrated I became, and the angrier Allen was at himself, and at me for tempting him into all that he was trying to get away from. Finally, on a weekend just before Christmas, Allen and I had our very last argument and discussion. He couldn't do it anymore and neither could I. I was sick and tired of feeling used for sex when he got drunk, followed by days of his ignoring me in an effort to "cleanse himself" of the gay life that he was living with me. I realized that I wanted someone who cared about me, and Allen wasn't filling that slot. I was also tired of feeling like I was pushing myself on someone who didn't want me anymore.

Our fight started at the condo. It almost ended there when I told him that he should never come back to Delmonico's again. He agreed that would be best, since most everyone there was a friend of mine and the only reason he knew them was through me. I drove him back to the academy that night and, on the way, I told him that this was *it*. For the first time ever, I told him how much I loved him and how I would do anything for him. But then I explained that I would never again be able to talk to him because it would hurt too much.

We both cried profusely on the way back. We parked the car and finished our conversation, both grudgingly agreeing that we could *not* be friends. It just wouldn't work. Allen got out of my car and slammed the door. I'll never forget the details of that night. It was raining and Allen walked over to my door and looked at me crying through the window. I sat in the driver's seat and I looked up and yelled, "Just go!" to him. He turned around and walked away after looking up into the sky and yelling, "Fuck!" as loud and as long as he could. Believe it or not, we never talked to each other or contacted each other again. Many people have asked me to contact him, but I think I would be saddened at what I would find, so I've left him alone. I have never forgotten the times I spent with Allen and I never will. My hope is that, someday, he will realize that I truly loved him and that it will put a smile on his face.

After that night, I went into a severe depression. I couldn't concentrate on schoolwork and all I wanted to do was sleep. I went home to my brother's house for Christmas and buried my sorrows by accepting Mara's love and attention and letting her spoil me. But during that break, I told her that I thought I was gay and that I had been in love with a guy. Being the cool, California-raised girl that she was, she didn't care. She told me that it was "all good" and that she still wanted to be with me for as long as we would last. I thought that was great of her and it made me want to continue our relationship. I would go through the motions until it was clear to me what I should do next.

chapter thirty-two

TROUBLE IN PARADISE

Meetings of the Underground were still held often and our group was alive and well, with about fifty cadets at every meeting. Some of the Underground cadets had figured out the tunnel system and could get to our meeting point from all the way across the Terrazzo by their own hallway stairwells. We continued to get cadets out of trouble by making sure we all had the same story and we remained a tight group, following the eight key rules of our organization in order to keep us safe.

The Underground wasn't just good for getting people out of trouble; it was also good for preventing it. We developed a whole way of life. When we went out, it had become instinctual to have our alibis perfectly memorized before we came back to the academy. "Here's what we'll say," would start every story proposal to keep us safe and away from trouble.

One weekend, just before spring break of senior year, I was at Seth's house in Colorado Springs because his parents were away for the weekend. He had hosted a couple of gay cadets from the Underground for a night or two. One of them, Thomas, had brought his boyfriend with him. The boyfriend was a security policeman named Mitchell from the Air Force Academy base, although he was not assigned to be anywhere near cadets. I don't know how they met, but I thought it was cool that they had found each other.

I stayed with the whole group that weekend and witnessed a great deal of drama between Thomas and his boyfriend. I remember thinking that they probably weren't so happy after all. The argument ended with Thomas storming out of the house, leaving his security policeman boyfriend there with us. I ended up talking to Mitchell for quite a while and he filled me in on their whole relationship. I can't remember what the problems of the relationship were, but I remember sympathizing with Mitchell. He gave me his number and we kept in touch over the next few weeks.

Thomas had completely stopped talking to Mitchell. He wouldn't return Mitchell's phone calls or answer his e-mails. Finally, after weeks of this, Mitchell and I were talking on the phone and decided to hang out. I met him at Delmonico's and we were alone. Mitchell was a short, stocky guy and was twenty-four years old. I was very attracted to him even though he was different from the guys I had previously been attracted to. He was quiet and soft-spoken and let me take control in almost all situations.

As soon as we got to Delmonico's and realized we were alone, Mitchell and I got it on together. We had good chemistry. I also used his affection to heal myself from the emotional trauma I had experienced after breaking it off with Allen. After that night, I wanted to see Mitchell again and again, on a daily basis.

I don't know how Thomas found out about us, but it was inevitable that he would. At a regular Sunday night Underground meeting, I realized that Thomas wasn't there and neither was Jake Lester. Usually, both of these guys would write an e-mail if they couldn't make it, and I could think of no reason why they wouldn't show up. I asked Seth if he could find out where they were and he said he would go to their rooms during the meeting to figure things out. I still kept a watchful eye on Jake, since our first encounter had been his sending me that careless e-mail.

We were finishing up our meeting in the tunnels at about two A.M. when Seth came back down to wait for me.

"I need to talk to you," he said in a very concerned voice. "Ask everyone to stay for a few extra minutes." When Seth asked me that, I knew there was trouble. "Thomas and Jake are out to get you," he said in a whisper.

"What? What did I do to them?" I asked.

"Jake just hates you from the beginning, and Thomas knows that you're sleeping with his ex-boyfriend. They told me that they thought you had gone too far in abusing your power over the Underground, and that they were going to turn you in."

"Turn me in? Are they out of their minds? Do they know that it will be the end for them, too, and that they'll be investigated?" I asked.

"Thomas doesn't care. He wants out of the academy. Jake is convinced that they'll both get away with it."

I freaked out. Seth called the meeting back together.

"OK everyone," he said. "One last issue and we can all go to bed. Get ready for this one." Seth explained the entire situation to the group of about fifty guys and girls, including the graphic detail that I was now sleeping with Mitchell, who was Thomas's ex. Lots of oohs, aahs, and laughter arose from the explanation. I was embarrassed and cringing, but this group knew *everything* about me—and I knew everything about them. It didn't matter. It was for my own safety. "There is a good possibility that these guys are going to blow the whistle on all of us. On our whole group." I went over and stood next to Seth. As I did, guys were joking and yelling out words out like "player" and "boyfriend stealer." I felt the need to speak to everyone briefly.

"We've done this before and we're going to have to do it again. It's time, in my judgment, to excommunicate two of our members tonight," I pleaded.

"Yeah! Knock 'em off," one of the guys yelled.

"No, seriously," I said. "It's time. These two guys must not ever be allowed to come down to one of our meetings. They are armed with *your* information and they are dangerous, as indicated by the words that they used to express their anger at me. Is it agreed that everyone in here will grab a buddy and have an alibi for where they were tonight?

All of you must have an alibi made up and have your story straight before you go to bed. Here's what we'll say if someone asks: 'No, I wasn't at any meeting. You can ask so-and-so, too. I was with him and we were up late doing homework in his room.' We will always deny the existence of this group and will laugh at anyone who claims that it does exist. Does everyone here agree?" I asked. Every person in the room raised his or her hand.

"I'm noticing that Chris Engle isn't here tonight. Can someone please fill him in on all of this?" I asked. A few people nodded their heads and we left it at that. I should have pointed at someone and assigned him to speak to Chris but, in the confusion of the current situation, I forgot.

The next twenty-four hours were nerve-racking. All day long I had been thinking about these two guys who had now turned on me and, as far as I was concerned, the entire group. I had never fully trusted Jake Lester, and I had always known that he sensed my desire to keep him at arm's-length distance. Now, I had asked our entire Underground to turn against him and I knew they all would. The safety that they had found in our group brought them to a level of loyalty that would be unmatched by even the largest threats of a scandal, which this was sure to be. We had trained ourselves, over and over again, on what to do in a situation like this. We would deny, deny, deny, and make Jake and Thomas look like they were making up stories. If either of them had come to me and admitted to being angry with me, as everyone in the group had learned to do, I would have compromised to make them happy, taking care of my family. But this was not the route they were taking to solve their issues with me.

Nothing happened the next day. I wondered if these two guys had been bluffing just to scare us. Maybe they had figured they would be foolish to try to turn me in. I started feeling confident that they had rethought everything and were going to back down. I felt the same way until the next morning at 2:30 when Cadet Chris Engle knocked on my door, waking Nathan and me. I let him in and locked the door. I told Nathan to go back to bed. Chris was crying and shaking. We had to whisper because it was so early in the morning. He started speaking at me frantically.

"Why didn't anyone *tell* me?" he yelled in a whisper.

"About two nights ago? No one came to you?" I asked.

"No! No one fucking came to me! I didn't have a chance to get to him either!" he said.

"Get to *who?*" I asked, while grabbing onto his shoulders.

"To Jason! My *boy!* My little Jason, oh, Jesus Christ, Reichen! He disappeared. They took him in the middle of the night. I went to see him just a couple of hours ago, like I always do, you know, to check on him. I love him, oh, God I love him so much!" he was crying hysterically but trying to keep it low.

"Calm down for one second. What did you find in his room?" I asked, trying to stay calm myself.

"There was *nothing* in there. All of his belongings were all missing like he was never here! They took him!"

"Do you know about Jake and Thomas threatening to turn me in?" I asked.

"Yes! Why do you think I'm here right now?" he yelled.

"Shh! Shut up! You're going to make this worse unless you *continue* to whisper with me, do you understand me? You have to calm down and explain this to me. I'm confused!" I had to say in an angry tone. He broke down crying again.

"Yes, yes. Oh, God, yes," he said. "I understand. What am I going to do?"

"OK," I said calmly. I turned on a light under my desk so I could somewhat see him. He looked awful. His beautiful face was red and wet and his eyes were swollen. "Where did you go after you left Jason's room?"

"I went to see Patty. I woke her up. She told me about the meeting that both Jason and I missed. I *told* him that we were stupid for missing it! I don't know, maybe it wouldn't have mattered. I know him. I'm sure he panicked as soon as they started asking him questions. I could have been there with him if I had known. I'm sure he said one wrong thing and they decided to *keep* him! Where do you think he *is*, Reichen? Jesus Christ!"

"Don't worry about that, Chris. We're going to find out. I promise you. Let me think for a second, OK? Why in the hell would they take *Jason* of all people?" I asked him and myself and God.

"Because! I already talked about this with Patty. We figured it out. Those assholes wouldn't turn you in. That would be too hard, and you have too much protection from everyone. They went after the weakest link so that he would be arrested and *you* would get to see our group failing in front of everyone in it. I was angry after I talked to Patty. She tried to stop me but I went to Jake Lester's room. I barged in and . . . gone! He's gone, too! They took him! I went to Thomas's room. Same thing. They've all been taken! Those assholes made a decision to go down and took *Jason* with them. He's so innocent. The only guy he's ever been with is *me!* This is all my fault, goddamn it!" He was angry, almost to the point of being uncontrollable.

"OK, listen to me very closely. You are going to be nothing if they take you, too, so you have to be strong right now and you have to help me round everyone up for a meeting." I pulled out a list and handed it to him. "I want you to go back to Sijan Hall and find everyone on this list and get them to the tunnels immediately. We're doing this for Jason and you and all of us. We need to talk. All of us together need to talk. OK? Can you do this for me, Chris?"

He pulled himself together and wiped his eyes. "Yes, I can," he said, looking down at the floor. I grabbed his chin and moved his head up so that he looked me in the eye.

"OK," I said, "then go. Now." He left my room and I put on some clothes. I stopped and decided to put on my uniform because I might have needed to be dressed if the meeting lasted into the duty morning. I went through Vandenberg Hall and woke up twenty-two people before heading down to the tunnels. If there is anything about cadets that's a sure thing, it's that they know how to move—and move fast. Within just twenty minutes, we had over fifty cadets sitting on the concrete floor of our underground control room. I looked across and admired how quiet and ready to listen and work everyone seemed to be.

I explained the situation. I had Chris stand up in front of everyone to tell him what he had seen. Chris asked if anyone else knew of any other person who had been taken in the middle of the night. No one raised their hand. Knowing that Jason was the only one brought Chris to tears.

"I warned everyone two nights ago that something like this might happen with these guys. Was anyone here questioned about them?"

"Yes!" about four people yelled out.

"You were questioned yesterday?" I asked in a panic.

"Yes, we both were," said one water polo player, pointing at his teammate. "They were very upfront with us and said that we had been named in a 'misconduct investigation' involving Jason, who's on the water polo team with us. Taking us both in separate rooms, they asked if we knew Thomas, Jake, or Jason. When we heard the names, we knew it was time to deny everything. We both gave the same story. We said that we had no idea who Jake or Thomas were, and that we had only talked to Jason a couple of times, since he was new to the team, and that we didn't know anything about him. They asked if we had gone to any meetings on Sunday night organized by Jason. Luckily, we are each other's alibi buddies, so we both had the same story. We were up late studying in my room. That was our story. They let us go."

"OK," I said, "so these two have named only Jason, saying that he was the one planning our meetings. There will be no further meetings in this location from here on out. Does anyone not understand this? OK, good." At that moment I felt a rush of anxiety come over me. I realized that these two had broken up a system that had been working for so long. Our group was being destroyed. I couldn't speak as I looked out over all the familiar faces that I had been so proud of. I knew that people could see the look of complete despair on my face.

Seth, who had arrived slightly late, was by my side. He stood in front of me to save me and continued with the meeting, "OK. There is a chance that everyone in this room has been named by Jake or Thomas. Here's what we'll say, if we are asked about them at all. We'll say that we don't really know them but that at some point in our cadet careers—and we can all make up our own individual times for the incident—they *hit* on us. We were freaked out by the situation and, although we don't have anything against gay people, we told them never to come near us again. They wanted us, but we didn't want them near us. It was an unwanted sexual advance. Does everyone understand that?"

In unison, as if we were in Beast again, in a crisis situation, they all yelled, "Yes, sir!"

When I heard the roar of *yes, sir!* I lifted my head up and felt a little stronger. I couldn't believe my ears. The group was on automatic mode at this point, and the spirit of what we were doing was being driven forward without my help. I was proud of our group.

Seth continued, "The problem is that we don't want to hurt Jason. I don't know what he said that would make them take him away but he's probably going to be gone for a while. They're going to put him through hell before they release him. There's a chance that he has been taken to the mental ward at the academy hospital. Some of us may want to discreetly check on that. If he is there, we'll find a way to visit him. Any visitor to his room will be documented, so be careful of what you do. This is a person who is now obviously under investigation for homosexuality."

I moved next to Seth and looked out over everyone. Seth could tell I wanted to speak so he moved aside. I was coming out of my state of shock. "I just want everyone to know how much you mean to me. I don't know why these guys turned on me like this and if I could explain it, I would. I have a feeling that it was a power issue. Jake and Thomas always seemed to me like they were two friends who were not very happy with the leadership that Seth or I have shown all of you. I want you to know that I never wanted to be a dictator, and if *any* one of you had ever come to me and said that you thought it would be best if I stepped down from a position of making decisions, I would have stepped down in a *second*. That's how much I respect and care for everyone in this room. I would even have gone to bat for Jake or Thomas if they had needed me to, and I hope you all know that.

"On an administrative note, I want you all to notice that this is Don't Ask, Don't Tell in action. The policy does not work! The policy says not to ask a military member if he or she is gay and tells individual military members not to say that they are gay, but it does not cover when someone *else* reports *you* as being gay. Then, a full investigation can happen. That is the tragedy that is happening right now. Do not trust a system that has been set up to harm gay people. It's a system that tells us to lie, and that is a system that will always fail."

Seth spoke again. "That's it. Deny meetings. Deny knowing those guys other than being harassed by them. Deny anything gay about yourself. Get with your alibi-buddy and create alibis for every time you can think of in the past two months that you were in a homosexual situation. This meeting is done. Look for an e-mail or a visit to your room stating where and when we'll meet again." Everyone got up and left quickly.

"I'm going to bed," Seth said to me. I nodded, gave him a long hug, and he left. The only two people left in the tunnel were me and Chris. I hugged him and he began crying on my shoulder.

"They took my boy," he said over and over again as he hugged me tight. "I'm so scared for him. He's so sweet and innocent and beautiful. His parents are going to freak out when they get a phone call." Just then he looked up at me and his eyes became wider. "What if he turns me in? What if Jason names me?"

"Jason is *not* going to turn you in," I said to reassure him that all would be OK now.

"What if he has no choice? Reichen, do you know who my *mother* is?" he asked. I put my head down and looked at the floor before I answered him.

"Yes, she's a U.S. senator, I know," I said quietly.

"Yep! A U.S. fucking senator, Reichen!" He had more tears in his eyes and it was killing me. "Do you know what they'll do to me if this gets out? Do you know what kind of media attention they will focus on this whole goddamn place and on my *family*? Oh, God, they would *never* forgive me. My mom and dad . . . they would testify in court to put me in jail just to preserve their fucking Republican moneygivers! They would *have* to abandon me in a very public way just to save face and their political careers!" He broke down crying again. He walked away from me and yelled out loud so that it echoed through the miles of tunnels that were around us. "I hate this goddamn, fucking,

horrible, ridiculous, fucked-up, crazy, conservative, bigoted place!
You took my boy, you fucking assholes! You took him away from
me!" He turned to me.

"Reichen, Jason is my *life*. Do you understand what it's like to be in
love with someone who is just as in love with you?"

I stood there, almost losing my composure, but I wanted to be
strong. He walked over to me and hugged me. I spoke into his
shoulder. "I've tried so hard, Chris. I've tried every fucking day to
figure this out. I know what it's like to *love* someone with more of me
than I ever knew I had. But I don't know what it's like to have it given
back to me by that person. You are truly lucky. Even if you never see
Jason again, do you know how *lucky* you are? Do you know how *lucky*
you are just to have experienced that? Most people in this world will
never know what you know. So think of that, OK? Please? For me?" I
begged in only the crackle of the voice I had left.

"OK," he said, "for you." He let go of me and turned to start
walking away.

"Where are you going, Chris? I want to stay with you. Do you want
that? I think you need someone around you," I said.

"No, no. I'm fine. I just want to be alone." I looked at him with a
face that let him know I disagreed with him. "No, Reichen. Just . . .
please. I need to be alone."

"OK," I said. "Come and see me later." He didn't answer and
walked down the hall and around a corner until I was the only person
in the control room.

I spoke to the walls. "Well, thank you. This is it. This is good-bye,
I guess. Thanks for letting us stay here. Thanks for giving us protection." I laughed out loud, wiping the tears from my face. "You were
supposed to be built for the fucking Cold War. You were supposed to
be here to protect people from a big bomb. And you probably could
have. Ha! Isn't it ironic that you could protect people from a nuclear
bomb, but you couldn't fully protect a bunch of . . . " my voice went
to a whisper, " . . . gay guys? How sad, eh? It's OK. I forgive you. We
all forgive you."

I walked down the long hallway and climbed the ladder. As I

emerged into the cadet stairwell, I saw the sun rising from the east. It was already light outside. We had been down there for hours. I continued to walk up the staircase until I was on the top floor. I stumbled, emotionally drained, but in uniform, past a bunch of cadets who were walking out to morning meal formation. I knocked on Juliette's door. Just as I was knocking, her roommate walked out and kissed me on the cheek. "Hey, Reichen. Juliette is running late. She's still in there getting ready. Are you OK? You look so tired, sweetheart." I nodded and walked past her, not saying a word. I shut the door. Juliette turned around and was buttoning up her blue uniform shirt, getting ready for another day at the Hill.

"Hey, baby doll!" she said with a smile, as always. She quickly noticed that I was not well. Her face dropped. "What's wrong, baby? Come here." I walked toward her and put my head on her shoulder. She was confused and asked me to talk but I just kept my head down as she ran her fingers through my hair. "Shh. Whatever it is, it will be OK. It will be *OK*. Shh."

She took me back to my room. I got there and Seth was waiting in there with Nathan. "Have you seen Chris?" he asked.

"Not since the meeting this morning," I said. "He went back to his room."

"No, he didn't. After leaving the meeting, I decided to go to his room to wait for him. I thought about it and decided that he needed someone there. He never showed up," Seth said in sort of a panic. I thought for a second.

"Shit. Where could he have gone? His car? Let's go to his car!" The four of us—Nathan, Juliette, Seth, and I—all ran out of the squadron and toward the senior parking lot. We all knew that we were missing formation and would get in trouble. We might even miss class, but we didn't care at that point.

We ran across the Terrazzo, down the ramps toward the athletic fields, and through the parking lot. Juliette spotted his car. "Here it is!" She ran toward it. "Oh, God!" she screamed. "Oh, God! No, no, no!" Chris had a Range Rover that his parents had bought him for getting into the academy. The car was running and Chris was slumped over the steering wheel. He had taken a hose, probably from the pool cleaning room in the cadet field house, and attached it to his tailpipe. He had fed it into his back window and rolled it up so it would hold the hose. Then he had started the car.

Juliette opened the door and pulled his body off the steering wheel. I moved in next to her to help her. We were crying and screaming at him. His face was blue and his body was cold. We tried shaking him as we yelled to him to wake up. I pulled him out of the passenger seat as Juliette opened the back door. I laid him in the back seat. "I'm taking him to the hospital!" Juliette yelled as she cried.

"I'm going with you!" I yelled.

"No, you're not," she said and pointed at me. "That is worst thing you can do right now. I'll say that I found him like this and jumped into his car. The last thing you all need is to be involved in something like this. Now get back up there and I'll call you from the hospital!"

Juliette pulled the hose off the tailpipe and sped off with Chris. We stood there stunned. I sat down on the ground. "What the fuck?" I looked up at Seth and Nathan. "What the fuck, you guys? Why?" I yelled, "Why?" Together, they picked me up.

"Come here," Seth said.

"You're going to get your uniform dirty," Nathan said. "Let's go. We have to get to breakfast. It sounds ridiculous, but we have to. We'll have answers in a couple of hours. Just pretend. Pretend everything is OK, like we always do." I looked at Nathan in disbelief. "Do you know how strong you are?" he asked. "Well if you don't know, I'm going to tell you. Now you're going to come to breakfast with us and you're going to go through this day. You're going to be OK. If you need anything, Seth and I are here to help you."

I did just that. I went to breakfast. I went to class. I went to intramurals. I went through the motions, just as I did every day. All day, I thought about how I couldn't wait to graduate. The academy had given me all that I could handle.

chapter thirty-three

PEACE AT LAST

Chris Engle lived through his suicide attempt, but for a long time, he wished that he hadn't. For months, he worked to regain motion in his arms and legs and had trouble forming complete sentences. The academy admitted him to the mental ward of its hospital and evaluated him for months. The authorities never determined why he had tried to kill himself. He wouldn't give up any information as to what happened that night. He was discharged from the air force for medical reasons and his family made no secret of their shame over his behavior.

For the rest of us survivors, the big day had finally come: May 29, 1996. It was my Air Force Academy graduation day. Virtually everyone in my family came to see my special moment. My grandmother, the pilot, was invited as one of the Air Force Academy's VIP guests of honor. She was asked to sit in the press box with all of the current military generals and where the president of the United States sits through most of the ceremony. As only my grandmother would have it, she opted to sit in the stands with her family instead.

Mara was there and, believe it or not, she still wanted to continue a relationship with me after graduation. Donny Coleman and I had already packed his truck for a full United States road trip for the sixty days of leave that every cadet is awarded on graduation day.

Sitting in my assigned chair, along with about nine hundred of my classmates, I could not believe I was there, nor did I understand just how I had made it to that day. I thought about the person I had been when I entered the academy, compared with who I was then. I thought about my upcoming obligation to serve in the Air Force for the next five years. I thought about how I, someday, would be a captain—a decision maker in our U.S. Armed Forces. *What would happen to me? Would I make it?* I wondered.

I looked to my right, and sitting with me in my row were Nathan, Seth, Jodie, and Kory. They looked so proper and stiff in their parade dress uniforms and their bright-white wheel caps. One by one, they all winked at me, as if to say "I love you." I winked back at them to say the same.

I removed my class ring from my finger and, when he saw me do it, Seth did the same thing. We both looked inside our rings and read *Here's What We'll Say* written into the white gold. We looked at each other with smiles and tears in our eyes.

After receiving our bachelor's degree diplomas, we came to the point in the ceremony when the Thunderbirds flew overhead and we all jumped up to throw our hats into the air. As I heard the Thunderbirds roar past, preparing to throw my hat harder than I had ever thrown anything in my life, I looked up at the sky, past the planes, and I smiled at God, who was clearly looking down on me. "Good job," I mumbled under my breath, "and a great sense of humor, too." He smiled back at me as I threw my hat into the hundreds of others that were already in the sky.

I lost track of where mine went. Maybe it never came back down because God had caught it himself to keep as a souvenir of one of the toughest tests he had ever assigned anyone. My hope is that he keeps it somewhere close to him, and that it reminds him to keep me safe from hatred and bigotry, forever.

AFTERWORD

The day after graduation, I left on a sixty-day cross-country road trip with Donny Coleman. We hit all the most popular destinations, among them the national parks and almost all of the major coastal cities. I was also fortunate to spend a good amount of time in Maine with my family.

Finally, I reported for duty at Los Angeles Air Force Base. Like all the other gay former cadets, I hid my sexuality for fear of losing my career and substantial officer's commission. As part of my cover, I even lived with Mara Howard, but that didn't last long. I eventually had to tell her that I could no longer live a double life and that a separation was in order.

I moved in with two friends, who happened to be heterosexual but who knew about my sexuality. I had fun there and even dated a couple of guys in spite of having to see them in complete secrecy.

After three years at Los Angeles Air Force Base working in Satellite Systems, I was transferred to the Air Science Department of the University of Virginia, where I recruited new officer candidates for the Air Force ROTC program and the Air Force Academy. What a supreme irony—a gay man recruiting cadets into an institution that outlawed homosexuality.

Having completed my five-year Active Duty Service Commitment two years later, I left the Air Force. I moved back to Los Angeles to train as civilian pilot, earning my FAA Commercial Pilot Certificate along with my Flight Instructor certificates. I also found personal happiness with Chip, whom I'd met before I was transferred to West Virginia. We were married in front of our friends and family at the Hotel Bel Air on February 2, 2002.

I started a private air charter brokerage, Tribe Airways, and ran this business until the day I was approached by a casting director for TV's *The Amazing Race*. I had never seen this reality show, but competing for the million-dollar prize seemed like a fun thing to do. However, if I was going to be out to the entire county via national television, I wanted to do so as part of an openly gay couple. I thought it was important for America to see two men in a committed, loving relationship, so I asked Chip to join me as my teammate. We were cast, competed against eleven other teams over a five-week period, and actually won the prize.

As the show's winners, Chip and I appeared on the cover of a handful of magazines, including *Us, The Advocate*, and others. Unfortunately, the relationship began to unravel. Shortly thereafter, Chip and I separated. I stayed out of long-term relationships for about a year. I chose instead to concentrate on the increasing requests I received to work in television, film, and modeling. Additionally, I spent a great deal of time working with charitable organizations such as The Servicemembers Legal Defense Network (SLDN), the Gay Lesbian Straight Education Network (GLSEN), the National Gay and Lesbian Task Force (NGLTF), and the Gay and Lesbian Alliance Against Defamation (GLAAD).

Over the past few years I've appeared on the TV shows *Frasier, The Drew Carey Show, The Young and The Restless*, and *Days of Our Lives*, as well as in the films *The Most Unfabulous Social Life of Ethan Green, Partners*, and *The Scorned*. I also created an Internet radio show called *Coming Out With Reichen*, where I helped people of all ages came out of the closet in a safe and supportive environment.

My dream came true when the Q Television Network invited me to host a daily talk show, *The Reichen Show*, on their cable TV network. After seven months, however, the network suffered a loss of funding and closed down.

I'm a true believer in the notion that our lives are constantly unfolding for us exactly as God and the Universe have planned. We may not always see the path clearly, but everything happens as it should. Certainly, I could never have predicted where my life would take me after the Air Force. I count myself today as being incredibly blessed. Like so many others, I've learned to keep an open mind, relax, and seek out happiness along the journey.

ACKNOWLEDGMENTS

I'd like to thank the following people for making this project happen:

The thousands of U.S. Armed Forces servicemen and servicewomen who happen to be homosexual and who have sacrificed their lives, as well as their freedom, to be who God made them, honorably and humbly serving their nation and our people.

Lance, for being the first to read the rough draft of this book and for pushing me to the finish line with all of his encouragement.

Jon Malysiak, for contacting me and pushing me to start this project after I had given up thinking that anyone would help me tell this story.

Don Weise at Carroll & Graf, for aiding me in the editing process, and for taking on my book and embracing the project, me, and my story.

My mother, Ann Tetreault, and my stepfather, Ray Tetreault, for asking me, every day for a year, if my book was done, because they couldn't wait to read it.

My brother, Bobby Lehmkuhl, for always accepting me and supporting me as the person that I am and for hearing me every day as I describe to him the ride that is my life.

My father, Robert Lehmkuhl, and the rest of my family, for making me a person who is strong enough to endure those challenges that I've described in this book.

The Air Force Academy graduates who lost it all to a vicious system of abuse and intolerance simply because God created them as homosexuals.

Those of my friends from my Air Force Academy days, my air force active-duty days, and my civilian days, who encouraged me to tell this story.

My grandmother, Betty Stagg Turner, who, from above, watched over me as I wrote and who gave me good instincts and advice from the first to the last sentence.

The God who made me homosexual and who continues to be proud of me for meeting the various challenges of this world.